On the Scene with
Migration and Dictatorship

ON THE SCENE WITH MIGRATION AND DICTATORSHIP:

An Interdisciplinary Approach to the Work of Uruguayan Playwright Dino Armas

Gabriela Christie Toletti, Ph.D.

New Dominion Press • Norfolk • Virginia

On the Scene with Migration and Dictatorship:
An Interdisciplinary Approach to the Work of Uruguayan Playwright Dino Armas

Published by:

New Dominion Press
New Dominion Media/New Dominion Press
1217 Godfrey Avenue, Norfolk, Virginia 23504-3218
www.NewDominionPress.com

First Printing: August 2018

Cover Design, Graphic Design, and Typography by New Dominion Press
Illustrations by Gabriela Christie Toletti

Publisher's Cataloging-in-Publication Data
provided by Five Rainbows Cataloging Services

Names: Christie Toletti, Gabriela, author, illustrator. | Christie, Charles C., Jr.,
    photographer.
Title: On the scene with migration and dictatorship : an interdisciplinary approach to
    the work of Uruguayan playwright Dino Armas / Gabriela Christie Toletti.
Description: Norfolk, VA : New Dominion Press, 2018. | Includes bibliographical
    references.
Identifiers: LCCN 2018951291 | ISBN 978-1-548-97731-3 (pbk.) |
    ISBN 978-0-692-16158-6 (Kindle ebook)
Subjects: LCSH: Armas, Dino. | Uruguayan drama. | Literature--History and criticism.
    | Dictatorship in literature. | Uruguay--Emigration and immigration. | Latin
    America--Social conditions. | BISAC: DRAMA / General. | LITERARY CRITICISM
    / Caribbean & Latin American. | POLITICAL SCIENCE / Political Ideologies /
    Fascism & Totalitarianism.
Classification: LCC PQ8520.1.R33 O58 2018 (print) | LCC PQ8520.1.R33 (ebook) |
    DDC 809.89/89--dc23.

First Edition

Printed by:
CreateSpace Independent Publishing Platform, North Charleston, SC

Dedication

To our dear friend and *maestro* Dino Armas

and

to my beloved husband Charles "Chuck" Cody Christie Jr.

List of Photographs and Illustrations

- Dino Armas and Gabriela Christie Toletti in Montevideo (June 17, 2014)

- El Cerro Forever

- Departing from the Old Airport

- The Magic of Doña Mercedes

- Memories of Playa Ramírez

- Susana is our Perla

- The Media's Clutches

- The Traces of Exile

- Gabriela Christie Toletti Talking with Dino Armas

(June 17, 2014) Drawings by Gabriela Christie Toletti

Photos by Charles "Chuck" Cody Christie, Jr.

Table of Contents

ACKNOWLEDGMENTS

I thank all my friends, relatives, and colleagues for their continuous emotional support and for their great love. Many thanks:

Special Acknowledgments

To our dear friend and *maestro* Dino Armas, whose playwriting has united everyone who contributed to this book in a shared effort of reflection, analysis, and love of our cultural heritage.

To my colleagues and friends Dr. Marcelo de León Montañés, Dr. Aida Heredia, Álvaro Loureiro, Lourdes Martínez Puig, María del Carmen Montañés Tejera, Susana Mosciaro, and Dr. Dolores Rangel, for the fascinating perspectives you have contributed in your interpretive essays for this book.

To my beloved husband, Charles "Chuck" Cody Christie Jr., for his great love, support, encouragement, enthusiasm, vision, and heartfelt work on this book. The graphic design, the captivating design of the front and back covers, and the pictures taken in Montevideo are Chuck's work. He is a multitalented person, excellent in everything he sets his mind to, be it as a businessman, financial counselor, and pilot, or in the areas of digital communication, graphic design, social media, and publication. He is always at the forefront of technology and media. Thanks, Chuck, for being my great love, my life companion, my best friend, and my husband. I feel lucky to share my life with you, and I am so proud of you!

To the editors of the original Spanish version of this book, Álex Omar Bratkievich and Dr. Marcelo de León Montañés, for their excellent, detailed, and careful labor in honor of our country, our dramaturgy, and our friend Dino Armas. The multidisciplinary and multi-regional work with Marcelo and Álex has been an extraordinary intellectual and emotional experience. Thank you, dear friends, for enriching this collection with your intellect, for teaching me so much, and for the beautiful friendship we have forged. It is a pleasure to work with both of you. I also thank Álex for his excellent translation of the essays included in this compilation.

To the lead editor of the English translation of the manuscript Dr. Amy Lindstrom and associate editor Lindsey Newbold. Thank you for your detailed, careful, and excellent work. This book is enhanced by your skillful editing skills and by your thoughtfulness. It has been a pleasure to work with both of you.

To my colleague and friend Dr. Frederick Lubich, in whom I found the initial inspiration to imagine the project and go through this fascinating creative process: It was not purely by coincidence that after many years, my friend Frederick Lubich and I had arrived at a shared crossroads. We soon embarked on a journey of transatlantic connections as Frederick shared with me the remarkable life and works of his friend, the recognized Jewish German-Argentine writer Roberto Schopflocher. I felt an instant connection with Schopflocher that inspired me to tell Frederick the amazing story of how I reclaimed my homeland and reunited with my Río de la Plata family. Frederick invited me to share my family story in the book he was compiling in honor of Roberto Schopflocher. My essay "El reencuentro de una familia del Río de la Plata"[1] was therefore included in this book on experiences of migration entitled *Transatlantische Auswanderergeschichten: Reflexionen und Reminiszenzen aus drei Generationen. Festschrift zu Ehren von Robert Schopflocher.*[2] It was in this capacity that I found my inspiration to compile a book— also examining topics of migration—in honor of my friend, Uruguayan playwright Dino Armas. Thank you, transatlantic friend Frederick, for our conversations, and for your inspiration.

To Dr. Juan Raúl Ferreira Sienra for his powerful, thought provoking, informative, and incredibly moving speeches at the presentations of this book both in Uruguay and in the United States. Thank you dear Juan Raúl for your support and help. Chuck and I are honored by your friendship.

To Dr. William A. Paquette for his advise, for his support, and for the interesting ideas and meaningful information that we shared about the history of Latin America and about the plays included in this compilation. Chuck and I are

---

[1]   TN: "The Reunion of a Family from the La Plata River."

[2]   TN: "*Transatlantic Stories of Emigration: Reflections and Reminiscences from three Generations. A Festschrift in Honor of Robert Schopflocher.*" This book compiled by Dr. Frederick Lubich and published by Königshausen & Neumann in 2014 is a commemorative compilation in honor of the Jewish-German and Argentine author Robert Schopflocher (1923-2016) who fled Nazi Germany in 1937 and started a new life in Argentina. The book includes essays in German, English, and Spanish.

thankful for your support and friendship always.

To my friend Gabriela Spera, for her work transcribing Dino Armas' plays and writings, her excellent disposition to work as a team, her continuous support of Uruguayan authors and artists, her sensitivity, and her sisterly love. I value greatly the friendship we have developed, which continues to grow.

To Hugo Ponce, for his hospitality, friendship, and support of this project. I also thank him for the interesting and instructive conversations we have had, and for the delicious delicacies that he prepares, which Chuck and I have had the pleasure of enjoying together with him and Dino.

To my dear parents, Ludovico Toletti Tammaro and Zulema Altieri Pereyra, who smile down from above, for having given me the emotional, intellectual, and spiritual tools to be analytical and to live in this interesting, conflictive, and fascinating world of ours.

To my dear cousins, who are like sisters to me: Dr. Claudia Toletti Flecchia and Virginia González Jiménez:

I thank Claudia Toletti for having helped me recover my roots and reunite with my family. Due to a series of family circumstances, Claudia and I only met as adults, at the funeral service for my dear father, Ludovico. Through Claudia, I found branches of our Toletti and Tammaro families that I had not known as a child. All of my "new" relatives immediately adopted me with joy, having found the lost relative they had never seen but had always missed. I got to know my living relatives and learned of those who are no longer in this world. Claudia told me stories about relatives who have passed on, and those stories magically penetrated my subconscious and became new family memories. Thank you, Claudia, for having opened this door to our family for me, and thanks for being such an important part of my life every day. Also, thank you for always being ready to give me professional advice, and for your continuous emotional support.

I thank Virginia González for including me in the family and being an exceptional role model as an enterprising and visionary businesswoman. Thank you also for delighting everyone with your insightful wit and intelligent sense of humor.

To both of you, thank you for always being there for me, for your great love, and for giving me beautiful family moments and memories that caress my soul. I am fortunate to have you in my life.

To my dear friend and soul sister, Carmen Álvarez Tejera, for her great emotional support, sisterly love, transcendent conversations, invaluable advice, the beautiful memories from when we were psychology students in college, our infectious laughter, and for being such a significant part of my life. You connect me every day with our motherland, you provide me with reinvigorating energy, and you always enrich me. Thank you, supportive and ambitious friend, for always being there for me and with me in spite of the distance. I am proud of your achievements, both as a professional and as a human being.

To my dear "North American brother," Randy Harrell, who always shows me and reminds me that there are many ways to create and to learn, since it is in the university of life where ultimately we learn the most important and transcendent lessons. And it is there, in the quotidian, from which the most fantastic, beautiful, captivating, interesting, emotive, and original stories, anecdotes, and works of art arise. You are an excellent artist and self-taught engineer. The genius of your creations shows your talent. I am very proud of you and I also know that *papá* Ludovico was very proud of you, and still is—from up above.

To all my dear uncles and aunts, who have given me family warmth, unforgettable memories and anecdotes; especially Dr. Carlos Altieri, Everton Toletti, and Dora Flecchia (in memoriam); María de los Ángeles "Lelé" Garay, and Klaus Zeissl.

To all my dear grandparents (in memoriam), who today accompany us from another dimension, for illuminating my path and for giving me unforgettable lessons and memories. I was able to know some better than others, but I deeply love every one of you, and all of you have contributed in one way or another to my life story.

To my dear mother-in-law, Marcia Christie, for including me and always making me feel included, for loving me, for believing in and supporting our projects, and for having influenced Chuck to be the wonderful human being he is.[3]

Gabriela Christie Toletti

---
[3] Introduction translated by Álex Omar Bratkievich.

PROLOGUE
Nearby Worlds

Álvaro Loureiro

The characters created by Dino Armas in a good many of his plays might be found on any city street. Circumstances might vary so as to allow those figures to go through difficult situations or find unexpected obstacles in their paths, which sometimes they themselves are responsible for disseminating, either consciously or unconsciously. As in life, human beings' characteristics, their virtues and defects, intertwine and blend in Armas' world. Thus, these virtues and defects converge in the deeds carried out by Juan and María (in the past and the present), by the charming Doña Mercedes, by those who visit the seashore in order to enjoy the sun Uruguayan-style, and even by those who have not yet assimilated the weight of a not-too-distant past. The shortcomings of *Present, Señorita's* teacher, meanwhile, almost completely hide her virtues, even if a second reading of the text shows the present to be just one phase in the existence of a woman who used to be very different. These recognizable figures talk and feel as do many other creations from the playwright's works, and each and every one of them reveals features also shared by those who listen to them in the audience. They are us.[1]

---

[1]   Prologue translated by Álex Omar Bratkievich.

INTRODUCTION
Origins and Objectives of a Project from the Heart

Gabriela Christie Toletti

**Dino Armas and Gabriela Christie Toletti in Montevideo
(July 17, 2014)**

This book contains works of Uruguayan playwright Dino Armas that deal with issues of migration and dictatorship, accompanied by interpretive essays written by authors who specialize in Latin American literature, theater, psychology, and history. The compilation also includes two interviews with the playwright about, among other topics, his creative process and the influences on his writing career. Examining this group of texts is a way to enter Armas' world in order to inquire into local and universal human conflicts. Each one of his works confronts us with human complexities that intertwine with social and historical realities to provide a profound and authentic commentary on migration and dictatorship.

Matías "Dino" Armas Lago is a multifaceted man: playwright, theater director, stage designer, actor, television scriptwriter, and also school teacher and principal. His plays reflect his interior world, but they are also instructive in the best sense of the word: they present situations without taking sides and invite the audience to analyze them so as to encourage critical thinking. Their open-endedness invites the spectator to complete them, so that the plays can keep evolving beyond the author's creative ideas and their staging.

In addition, Armas' plays reveal and investigate several aspects of Uruguay's culture, life, and history. Because the playwright uses them to express universal and timeless human conflicts, the plays have also found a wide multicultural audience beyond Uruguay.

It is a great honor and privilege to present a selection of Armas' works, accompanied by the interpretive articles which present a picture of part of Dino Armas' world through diverse opinions and ways of seeing. The works included in this collection are the following:

- *Juan and María; Yesterday / Juan and María; Today* (2006)

- *Doña Mercedes* (1992, published in 1993)

- *Beach Day* (2008)

- *Present, Señorita* (2011)

- *Sea Murmur* (2008)

- *Just Yesterday* (1987, premiered in 1995)

2

The order of presentation leads us, step by step, into deeper and more complex themes and conflicts. We start with the shorter literary pieces and progressively include longer and more elaborate plays. Regarding the essays, the criterion for their order within each chapter is to include first the ones coming from the theatrical realm and later those that examine the works from other perspectives (literary theory, history, and psychology).

We include texts from the author that allude to or deal with the European migration to Uruguay during the nineteenth century and the beginning of the twentieth century, as well as works that examine the realities of the more recent migrations from Uruguay to Europe, Australia, the United States, and other destinations. The former happened mainly as a way to escape the horrors of war and poverty in Europe. The latter happened primarily as a result of political issues (during the military dictatorship years: 1973-1985) and economic ones (during the '80s, and as a consequence of the 2002 crisis).

In Dino Armas' work, the subjects of migration and dictatorship are elaborated, and since they are two traumatic issues for the modern country, they complement each other. There appear, for example, the effects of an oppressive government on daily life, family, education, the collective unconscious, and society's future. Forced exile during dictatorial times is also discussed, as well as the resulting heartbreak for those who had to leave the country and for the relatives and loved ones who stayed. By directly or indirectly reflecting the effects of repressive institutions and situations on people, Armas' texts can be considered "committed literature," that is, literature in which the themes, characters, and settings reflect social and political conflicts with the intention of awakening and stimulating the collective conscience and the audience's analytical abilities.

In order to understand the origins of this compilation, it is necessary to go back to the past and tell the story of how I met Dino Armas.

Working as a Spanish and literature professor at Wingate University (Charlotte, North Carolina, U.S.), I was granted a scholarship to study Uruguayan theater, with the requirement that a professor and a student work as a team on a multicultural research project. This made possible my 1995 trip to Uruguay, my native country, where my assistant Kelly and I met and interviewed several playwrights. We were very cordially received by all of them, but I felt a special connection with Dino Armas. He welcomed us with enthusiasm and professionalism, but also with great warmth and affection. He immediately invited us to dinner at his home, to a rehearsal, and to the opening of his disturbing *La lujuria según Ramiro.*[1]

Dino Armas became a friend, and even though life took us on different roads and I was away from my country from a while, fate led me to a reunion with my homeland, my family, and my Uruguayan friends. This book is an homage to Dino Armas and to that reunion with my country and loved ones in the great *paisito.*[2]

It is a great honor and privilege to have in this volume the contributions of authors coming from various academic fields. The collection includes essays by Aida Heredia and Dolores Rangel, Latin American literature specialists who were fellow graduate school students at the State University of New York at Buffalo. They represent the beginnings of my career in literature studies, so it is fitting for them to be a part of this book, which represents the culmination of a period of professional development for me.

Heredia's participation in a study program in the Southern Cone broadened her understanding of Uruguay's culture, idiosyncrasies, and history. She helps us understand issues related to violence and alienation in contemporary society in general and in Uruguay in particular.

Rangel's essay combines the analysis of literary techniques with an investigation of the effects that a repressive government has on society.

It was also very important to give Álvaro Loureiro, Lourdes Martínez Puig, and Susana Mosciaro a voice in this compilation; they have been friends with Dino Armas for years and have written about or worked on his plays.

As a theater critic, actor and director, Loureiro—whom I have had the pleasure of knowing for a long time, first as an English teacher and then as a colleague at Alianza Cultural Uruguay-Estados Unidos[3]—provides a precise and succinct glance at the characters and conflicts in Armas' theatrical works.

Lourdes Martínez Puig is the foremost researcher and writer on Armas' work. In her essay, she poses the following questions: What are the effects of dictatorship and exile on the Uruguayan family? What consequences did the different decisions made during the dictatorial period have? Is it possible to heal

---

[1] Translator's Note: "Lust According to Ramiro."

[2] TN: El paisito (literally, "the little country") is an endearing term used by Uruguayans to refer to their homeland.

[3] TN: "Uruguay-United States Cultural Alliance."

the wounds caused by exile's uprooting?

It was also natural to include Susana Mosciaro in this compilation since she has directed and performed Armas' plays. In this book she delights us with an analysis, from her perspective as an actress, of the experiences and challenges in the Argentinean adaptation and staging of *Present, Señorita*.

It is also a pleasure to have the contribution of a historian, Marcelo de León Montañés, and a teacher, María del Carmen Montañés Tejera. Our friend, colleague and author Carolina de Robertis was the initial link that led De León to meet Armas, who then put us in touch. In this compilation, De León offers a deep, informative, and touching historical perspective on migration, exile, and dictatorship. He focuses on the conflicts and anxieties that those deeply affective, life-changing situations generate for the individual.

Through De León, I got in touch with Montañés, who had already met Armas many years before when Armas collaborated with a student theater group that Montañés and her colleague Mirella Izquierdo had founded in Maldonado. As a literature and theater teacher, Montañés provides an interpretation which explores a repressive government's impact on the educational sphere and emigration's effects on multigenerational family groups.

As for me, my goal is to apply literature and psychology to examine issues of migration, oppression, group and family dynamics, apathy, and mass media's role in contemporary society. After graduating in psychology, I was primarily interested in the study of Latin American literature and literary text analysis using a psychological frame of reference. This approach allowed me to explore topics which previously had been little investigated. Furthermore, I include my own illustrations as a way to provide artistic comment on Armas' work.

Finally, it is a pleasure and honor to thank Dino Armas for the fantastic plays he has given us in his first fifty years as a playwright. I will also be forever thankful to everyone who, in one way or another, has contributed to and helped me bring to fruition this project from the heart.

CHAPTER ONE
Immigrants from Yesterday, Today, and Forever

El Cerro Forever

Juan and María; Yesterday

Dino Armas

Translation by Gabriela Christie Toletti

(Several couples standing still in different positions. With traditional music in the background, the men and women say in different tones, volumes, and languages: "I love you," "Hello," and "Welcome." Later—when the director considers it necessary—they will repeat some of JUAN's and MARÍA's expressions and/or lines. These two, like the other couples, are also in a fixed pose. JUAN is lifting up MARÍA by her waist. She is noticeably pregnant. She may be carrying a basket or a bunch of clothes. She may be wearing a scarf and a long skirt. He is wearing a vest, shirt, rolled-up sleeves, and a hat or cap. At their feet there is a cardboard suitcase tied up with thick twine. The other couples have their own suitcases.)

MARÍA: *(With a suffocated laugh.)* Juan… put me down. *(He turns her around and laughs.)* You are going to drop me. We look silly. People are looking at us. Put me down. *(He squeezes her and slowly puts her down. Then he kneels down. The other couples repeat or imitate this movement.)* Juan…? What are you doing? *(The other women repeat her words in their own languages.)*

JUAN: Look at this land, María. The soil is soft and dark. It's good soil. They say that here wheat grows wild, and corn grows huge. Here, María, we will have our bread. *(She walks a few steps away.)* What's wrong?

MARÍA: I'm not sure. I feel a little cold… and I'm really scared. Really! *(He hugs her.)*

JUAN: Do you regret coming here?

MARÍA: Juan, didn't I follow you to the end of the world in that ship that scared me so much? Days and days through that never-ending ocean? Cramped together in that hold which was too small for so many people? Didn't I leave my parents, my brothers, and sisters to follow you? To come with you? To live with you?

9

JUAN: Yes, that's right.

MARÍA: So...?

JUAN: I love you, María.

MARÍA: I love you, Juan. (*They kiss and hug tightly. The other couples, with the same expressions, repeat in their own languages: "I love you, María," "I love you, Juan."*)

JUAN: (*Lifting the suitcase.*) In this land, in this place, we will have a new life. Now this will be our land, our home. Here we will work. Our kids will be born here!

MARÍA: The first one will be named after you. (*She touches her belly.*) I know it will be a boy. He will have the good luck that we never had. He will be born in peace. He will grow up without hearing the sounds of war and the screams of the wounded; he won't have to see the blood of the dead.

JUAN: My son will work with me. We will make the best of this land.

MARÍA: My hands and feet won't freeze anymore. Is it true that it never snows here? And that there are no big mountains? And no earthquakes?

JUAN: The tallest mountain is that hill you see there. (*Points at el Cerro de Montevideo.*[1])

MARÍA: That one? But it's very small... Juan, look at the sky. So many stars!

JUAN: Those are our stars. The stars we will have forever, from now on! Now we live under these stars!

MARÍA: But there is something here that...

JUAN: You suddenly look very serious. What's wrong, sweetie?

MARÍA: There, on the ship they told me something that... that I... If I tell you, you will laugh at me!

JUAN: No, María! I swear I won't. Tell me! What did they tell you on the ship

---

[1]   Translator's Note. (From the translator of the essays): El Cerro de Montevideo (literally "Montevideo's Hill") is a hill adjacent to the Bay of Montevideo. One of the neighborhoods located on it is called Villa del Cerro (literally "the Hill's Village") or, simply, El Cerro ("the Hill").

that scared you so much?

MARÍA: They told me that here people eat raw meat... rare meat! I don't want to eat that.

JUAN: Well, don't eat it, and that's that! No problem! OK?

MARÍA: OK.

JUAN: As far as I am concerned, I plan to eat beef until I am fed up with it! Raw, rare, medium, or well done! (*Looking surprised; he tells her.*) They say that people here eat beef every day, not just once a month! (*He extends his hand to her. The other men repeat the same movement.*) Shall we go? (*The other characters repeat the same words.*)

MARÍA: Where?

JUAN: To the hill. I want to see our world from up there. And when I get there, I want to lie on the ground and look at the sky, until I get tired of looking at the sky and counting new stars. And I will kiss you and hug you like never before! Come on, girl, let's go! We have to hurry! I want to be there so badly, I can't wait. Let's run! Let's get out of breath. We can't stop until we get to the top of the hill.

JUAN: I love you, María.

MARÍA: I love you, Juan.

(*The other couples repeat the poses and voices from the beginning of the play and the same music is played. Lights out.*)

THE END

Juan and María; Today

Dino Armas

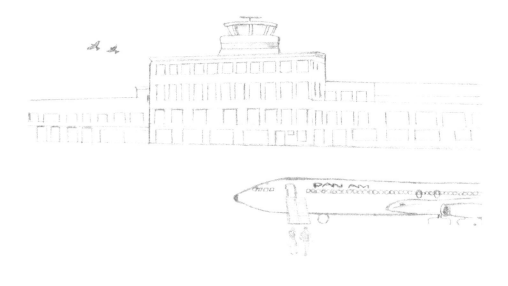

Departing From The Old Airport

(Again, several couples stand close to JUAN and MARÍA. Everyone is standing still. They wear modern clothes. The music is modern, too. A suitcase or backpack is by their feet. Here MARÍA is also pregnant. They are in a space that, from the sounds, seems to be an airport. The couples repeat in several languages: "Goodbye," "I love you," etc. JUAN walks a few steps away from MARÍA; he tries to cover his face and suppress the tears.)

JUAN: Son of a bitch… I never thought this would happen to me… to have to leave… for us to have to leave…

MARÍA: Juan… People are looking at us. What are they going to think of us?

JUAN: I don't care. I've been holding it in until now, María. With family, with friends, and even with neighbors. Now we are alone, you and me. *(The couples repeat: "Alone, you and me.")* With you I can allow myself to cry, to scream, to curse, to let out this feeling that is squeezing me inside, taking my breath, that is going to make my heart burst. I never thought I was going to leave the country this way! What about you? You didn't either, right?

MARÍA: No, but we don't have any other choice, Juan. You need to calm down. Let me see… let me… *(She wipes his tears with a handkerchief. He breathes heavily.)*

JUAN: Do you know what I want to see from the plane?

MARÍA: What…?

JUAN: El Cerro, the hill. Even though it is small, we will be able to see it, right?

MARÍA: Of course! You ask such funny questions…

JUAN: *(He fidgets with his passport and plane ticket. He looks doubtful.)* Do these passports and tickets grant us the way to a better world? Is that how it is, María? Is there a better and different world waiting for us beyond the ocean?

MARÍA: Juan, didn't we talk and discuss this night after night until we were exhausted? Didn't we save penny after penny and sell even the smallest things to buy these tickets? *(She touches her belly.)* Aren't we also doing

14

this for him? You told me, "María, this is the best that can happen to him... to be born abroad... to have papers from the country where we chose to start over again." If it helps, Juan, it's not easy for me either to leave this all behind, but I am following you. I told you I would go, even if it means to follow you to the end of the world, and live with other people with other customs. Aren't I leaving my parents, my brothers and sisters to follow you? To go with you? To live with you?

JUAN: Yeah, you're right.

MARÍA: So...?

JUAN: I love you, María. So much!

MARÍA: I love you, Juan. So much! (*The other couples repeat the same expressions and words in different languages.*)

JUAN: Where this plane takes us will be our country now. We will have a home there. And it will be his homeland too!

MARÍA: We will name him after you! At least he will have a very Uruguayan first name and last name! I'm taking the last sonogram with me.

JUAN: I'm sure my son will teach me to use the latest-generation electronics. He will be able to do and have what I was never able to have in my country!

MARÍA: They say that the winters are very hard where we are going. That the winds are very strong and there is so much snow that the people and cars can't get through... that there are terrorist attacks and earthquakes. But there is something even worse...

JUAN: Even worse? (*She nods.*) Why that serious face? What are you so scared of?

MARÍA: Everything is going to be harder for us. There they won't give us anything for free. They will call us "spics," "foreigners," "those people"! And we will have to work from dawn to dusk in whatever job we can find.

JUAN: (*He softly covers her mouth.*) Isn't the same thing happening to us here? Here we don't have jobs either. Here we are also "those people." I'm not scared of working. Not scared at all, even now that I have to work for the three of us. (*Sounds of the plane are heard in the background.*) That noise is our way out. Now is the time to find work abroad. Maybe someday we can come back...

MARÍA: Maybe... Tomorrow we will live under different stars. In that sky I won't be able to see the Southern Cross.

JUAN: There we will have different stars, all right! But they will be our stars, María. (*She looks startled.*)

MARÍA: Oh! Did I bring it...? I hope I didn't leave it... (*She looks in her bag or backpack.*)

JUAN: What are you looking for?

MARÍA: The notarized transcript of the last course I took in... Oh, here it is. Thank God! (*He laughs.*) Are you laughing at me?

JUAN: Well! You brought all those papers. Degrees, courses, diplomas, workshops... And what for?

MARÍA: What do you mean? To find a good job! And don't look at me with that face, with that smirk on your face, that I know so well, Juan. You think my first job will be cleaning bathrooms, right? (*JUAN makes a gesture meaning "I didn't say anything." The other men make the same gesture.*) That I am going to clean other people's shit?

JUAN: So, your cool Carrasco[1] attitude comes out! Your second skin!

MARÍA: More than one person has told me that they make immigrants do those jobs.

JUAN: So, you keep talking about cleaning other people's excrement?—See how refined I am acting? I said "excrement" and not "shit."—If you have a problem with that, I have the solution.

MARÍA: What is it?

JUAN: Thinking of that, without telling you, I bought you a pair of Funsa[2]

---

[1] Translator's Note: Carrasco is regarded as one of the most expensive and exclusive neighborhoods in Montevideo, Uruguay, located on the city's southeast coast. It features a wide variety of architectural styles.

[2] TN: Funsa is a Uruguayan factory and brand of rubber products. It manufactures several products, from tires to gloves.

rubber gloves. They're great! They last forever! And besides, the color is a beautiful red; they will go well with anything you wear!

MARÍA: What a coincidence! I got a pair for you too. Also Funsa, but these are black! A better color for men! (*They laugh, and the noise of the plane drowns their laughter.*)

JUAN: (*He stretches his hand.*) Let's go! The plane is about to take off.

MARÍA: Let's go! Yeah! (*They are starting to walk when he stops, covers his face, and suppresses the tears.*)

JUAN: Son of a bitch!

MARÍA: Again, Juan?

JUAN: It's just that I think when we fly over the Cerro, I'm going to cry. Am I going to see it, María? Can you see it from up there?

MARÍA: Of course. The sky is blue and clear.

JUAN: Shit! El Cerro… I never thought I would cry for El Cerro. God! You have to be a real tough man to cry for a hill, right?

MARÍA: (*María kisses him. The other couples do the same.*) I love you, Juan.

JUAN: I love you, María.

MARÍA: Let's go, tough guy! (*He stretches his hand.*)

JUAN: (*She takes his hand.*) Let's go!

(*They exit running. The other couples repeat in their own languages, "I love you," "Goodbye," etc. Musical background and final lights out.*)

THE END

Up and Down the Hill

Álvaro Loureiro

Through these two brief texts, *Juan and María; Yesterday,* and *Juan and María; Today,* Dino Armas takes a look at the story of two immigrant couples. In the first, set many years ago, a couple arrives in Uruguay, the promised land, the country of wheat and meat, where the young man will work and his wife will accompany him and raise their future children. The voyage has been tough; Europe, devastated by war, famine, and unemployment, recedes into their past. Juan and María have shared the ship's hold with fellow travelers from different places, who also disembark at the port of Montevideo to try to make it on their own. Juan and María know that the future will not be easy, but they are young and believe that this city, with its single nearby hill, will afford them the chance to shape a future for their family. Of course, even the stars will be different in the South American sky as seen from the top of that hill, which they now climb in order to contemplate the new world at their feet.

The second text finds a second couple, also named Juan and María, at the airport of the same city that long ago welcomed the first couple. The new Juan and María—simple names representative of countless Uruguayans—now abandon Montevideo in search of new horizons. They are not alone. María, as was her forerunner, is pregnant. The child will be born in a place where they might be called "spics," a place where they will have to get used to the sight of different stars. María follows her husband and knows that, at this new destination, she will have to find a job in addition to taking care of their future children. El Cerro is left behind, but they wish to see it once more from the plane, even through their tears.

Two similar stories about characters that have much more in common than their names mirror many other eras of one country in transformation. Thus, Juan and María's *Yesterday* shows their arrival in a land that welcomed foreigners wishing to find a place to settle, work, and start a family. The Cerro neighborhood, with its streets named after the different countries that the emigrants left to reach Uruguay's shores, also stands as a symbol of those traveling dreamers packed into the holds of transatlantic ships. The ironic *Today* of the current Juan and María,

19

on the other hand, declares that opportunities have run out. Juan and María leave the hill, the neighborhood, Montevideo, and Uruguay; they are about to take a plane that will lead them to the other side of the ocean, where they hope to rebuild their lives and raise their children without the increasing difficulties of their lives at home.

Will the story repeat itself on the other side of the Atlantic? The playwright wrote this second part some years ago and Uruguay's current economic recovery—although it is difficult to determine how long it might last—seems to attract immigrants, sometimes from origins different from those of Juan, María, and other past immigrants. In turn, Europe's current unemployment problems frighten off prospective immigrants. Therefore, it would not be strange if Dino Armas thought of a third text, which might be called *Juan and María; the Return*.[1]

---

[1] Essay translated by Álex Omar Bratkievich.

The Immigrant's Hopes and Longings Throughout Time: Parallels and Contrasts between
Juan and María; Yesterday and *Juan and María; Today*[1]

Gabriela Christie Toletti

My heart is looking to the South
and in my memory there is
a parade of remembrances
NÉSTOR SUÁREZ

This essay's goal is to explore the subject of migration in Dino Armas' *Juan and María; Yesterday* / *Juan and María; Today*. These plays deal with the subject in regards to the history of Uruguay, the Southern Cone, and other parts of Latin America; at the same time, they open a window to examine it from a more universal perspective. In all places and throughout time there have been migrations that change or even shape the cultures of countless countries and regions. By examining these plays we can learn about the history, culture, migration patterns, geography, and vocabulary of Uruguay, as well as the region surrounding the Río de la Plata. At the same time, the reader or audience member is invited to reflect on her/his own cultural heritage and establish parallelisms and contrasts with recent migrations.

The formation of many modern countries is intimately linked to immigration. In Uruguay and Argentina there were two important migratory movements to the Río de la Plata region: one during colonial times and the other in the second half of the nineteenth century. In both cases, the entry of foreigners into the territory—mostly Europeans, with a resulting fusion of cultures and ideologies—contributed to the formation of the nation. In the twentieth century there was a reverse migratory flow from Latin America towards other destinations for political, ideological, and economic reasons. During the Uruguayan military dictatorship (1973-1985), many Uruguayans were persecuted because of their political ideas and forced to live abroad in exile. Some eventually returned to live in Uruguay when democracy was reinstated, but others, already accustomed to their adoptive countries, never did.

---

[1] Translator's Note: The original Spanish titles are *Juan y María; ayer* and *Juan y María; hoy*.

In these two short plays, Armas tells two migration stories that represent two important migratory flows in Uruguay's history. In *Juan and María; Yesterday*, a couple emigrates from Spain to Uruguay, possibly during the second part of the nineteenth century, fleeing from the horrors of war and poverty in Europe, in search of a better life in a new land where they can start a family.

In *Juan and María; Today*, a similar couple leaves Uruguay in the twentieth century, in search of a better life abroad. They are likely forced to leave their country during the most recent dictatorship for political or economic reasons.

There are distinctly local elements in these plays, such as comments about el Cerro de Montevideo,[2] Uruguay's temperate climate, the importance of meat in the diet, the Carrasco neighborhood, the products of the local factory Funsa, and the slang from the Río de la Plata region. Nevertheless, the conflicts and issues are not exclusive to Uruguay's history, or to the Southern Cone's, but universal. Migration is a phenomenon present throughout human history and many cultures and religions have included in their origin stories some important kind of migration that contributed to their formation (for example, the Jewish exodus from Egypt). The causes of human migrations are varied, ranging from political, economic, or religious motives to natural catastrophes or environmental changes. Juan and María's feelings and emotions are, therefore, not only local realities but also universal experiences for immigrants: longing for the land left behind and hope for a better life in a new land.

Parallelisms between *Juan and María; Yesterday* and *Juan and María; Today*

There are several parallelisms and constants in these plays. The main constants are the love between the protagonists and their desire to find a better future for the family in a new land. There is hope in both stories and also some apprehension for what the future holds. Another factor that remains constant in both plays is the immigrant couple's names: Juan and María. Given that they are common names throughout the Spanish-speaking world, they can represent every male and female immigrant from yesterday, today, and forever. In addition, if we consider the symbolism of the name "María" (Mary) in the Christian tradition, we can find a parallel with the biblical story. In these plays, María is pregnant, and

---

2   TN: El Cerro de Montevideo (literally "Montevideo's Hill") is a hill adjacent to the Bay of Montevideo. One of the neighborhoods located on it is called Villa del Cerro (literally "the Hill's Village") or, simply, el Cerro ("the Hill").

the future parents' desire for their child to have a better life is mentioned in both plays. The main incentive for Juan and María to continue the struggle is their son; hope is placed in the new generation. In the same way that Jesus symbolizes the start of a new era, in Armas' plays Juan and María's son might symbolize the beginning of the process of forming a new cultural identity.

There are other couples in *Juan and María; Yesterday* / *Juan and María; Today* who appear on stage and repeat words or phrases in different languages. These characters might represent the diverse nationalities and cultural heritages that formed the Uruguayan people. Each of these couples has, like Juan and María, a familiar story of migration, struggle, and survival.

Another—distinctly local—feature that appears in both plays is the importance of El Cerro for the characters. In *Juan and María; Yesterday*, the hill symbolizes the future, the new land full of hope and opportunities:

JUAN: […] Shall we go? […]

MARÍA: Where?

JUAN: To the hill. I want to see our world from up there. And when I get there, I want to lie on the ground and look at the sky, until I get tired of looking at the sky and counting new stars. […] I want to be there so badly, I can't wait. […] We can't stop until we get to the top of the hill. (11)

In *Juan and María; Today*, the hill symbolizes the past and the land that is difficult to leave behind. Montevideo's hill is a national symbol in the minds of these characters, the people of the city of Montevideo, and every Uruguayan. Traditionally it represents strength and resistance, because on its summit is la Fortaleza del Cerro,[3] built between 1809 and 1811 in order to defend Montevideo and its port on the Río de la Plata. In fact, the hill and its fortress appear in Uruguay's national coat of arms's upper right quadrant.

Furthermore, Montevideo's hill is a symbol of the working class and the immigrants who built a new nation with their hard work. During the nineteenth-century migration period, many immigrants from different European nations settled in the Cerro neighborhood, which therefore also symbolizes the struggle

---

[3]   TN: "The Hill's Fortress."

and determination of immigrants.

El Cerro's presence in these and many other works by the author has a personal, autobiographical meaning as well. In fact, Matías "Dino" Armas Lago was born in the Cerro neighborhood, once known as Villa Cosmópolis.[4] He grew up in a place inhabited by immigrants from Spain, Italy, Armenia, Russia, Lithuania, and other countries. His parents, like many other Cerrenses,[5] were the children of Spanish immigrants. Therefore, the characters of *Juan and María; Yesterday* might represent Armas' grandparents and many other people like them, who arrived in a new land and settled in the Cerro neighborhood.

El Cerro was a working-class neighborhood—mainly comprised of workers at a meat-processing plant—with rich cultural and theatrical offerings. It was there that Armas became interested in theater in his youth. Armas greatly values his roots, hence the homage he repeatedly pays in his work to El Cerro and its people.

Contrasts between *Juan and María; Yesterday* and *Juan and María; Today*

We have examined some of the parallelisms between the two plays, but they also have marked contrasts and differences. In *Juan and María; Yesterday*, the immigrant couple arrives in Uruguay by ship; possibly, as mentioned before, in the second half of the nineteenth century. In *Juan and María; Today*, a couple emigrates from Uruguay by plane, in modern times, looking for a better life abroad. The differences in clothing, music, and set design indicate each play's historical period.

In both plays there is anxiety about the future; however, the predominant emotional tone in the first is one of joy, faith, and hope for a happy and prosperous future. Uruguay will be their home, their country, their homeland:

> JUAN: […] In this land, in this place, we will have a new life. Now this will be our land, our home. Here we will work. Our kids will be born here!

> MARÍA: The first one will be named after you. […] He will have the good luck that we never had. He will be born in peace. […]

> JUAN: My son will work with me. We will make the best of this land. (10)

---

[4]   TN: "Cosmopolis Village."

[5]   TN: Demonym used for the people of the Cerro of Montevideo.

In the second play, even though there is some hope, the future does not look as promising. Juan and María anticipate discrimination and difficulties in life abroad.

> MARÍA: We will name him after you! At least he will have a very Uruguayan first name and last name! I'm taking the last sonogram with me.

> JUAN: I'm sure my son will teach me to use the latest-generation electronics. He will be able to do and have what I was never able to have in my country!

> [...]

> MARÍA: Everything is going to be harder for us. There they won't give us anything for free. They will call us "spics," "foreigners," "those people"! And we will have to work from dawn to dusk in whatever job we can find. (15)

Juan and María; Today reveals a heartbreaking anguish at leaving the motherland. The characters cling to the idea of continuing traditions such as giving their son "a very Uruguayan name." The distress of leaving Uruguay is also clearly seen when Juan talks about El Cerro: "It's just that I think when we fly over the Cerro, I'm going to cry. Am I going to see it, María? Can you see it from up there?" (17).

Observing the contrast between the two plays, we wonder what happened in Uruguay during the years between *Juan and María; Yesterday* and *Juan and María; Today*. In the former, Uruguay is a promised land, and the characters are happy to make their home there. In the latter, there is a pressing need to leave Uruguay in order to survive. Much happened between one time frame and the other. Until about 1955 Uruguay was a prosperous country, considered "the Switzerland of the Americas," but around that year a recession began, which became entrenched in the '60s. This recession was the result of a series of interlocking factors, such as the dependence on international prices, the poor development of the national market, the devaluation of the national currency, political clientelism, and the weight of big bureaucracy. Without a doubt, the precarious condition of the economy, coupled with the horrors of the Uruguayan military dictatorship from 1973 to 1985, led to the bleak circumstances in which Juan, María, and so many like them found themselves. The only solution for many was to leave the country.

There is also a contrast in the speech of the characters, which can be observed in the original Spanish version of the plays. In *Juan y María; ayer*, the couple has just arrived in Uruguay, hence their Spanish has Peninsular features. By contrast, in *Juan y María; hoy*, the characters are typical Uruguayans, and this is shown in the vocabulary used. Some examples are *pitucada*, *bárbaro*, and *durar pila*,[6] common in Uruguayan speech.

The Spanish spoken in the Río de la Plata region has changed and acquired distinctive linguistic characteristics. This was caused largely by the influence of immigration into Argentina and Uruguay, composed primarily of immigrants from Italy, different regions of Spain (such as the Basque Country, Catalonia, Galicia, and Andalusia), and adjacent countries. Especially strong was the influence of various Italian languages; in fact, Rioplatense Spanish[7] has a great number of loanwords from the languages spoken in different parts of Italy.

The most characteristic phenomenon of Rioplatense Spanish, however, is probably the *voseo*, which consists of the use of *vos* (instead of *tú*) as a second-person singular pronoun, together with *vos*'s corresponding conjugational verb forms, most notably in the present indicative. There are variations in its use: full *voseo* (use of *vos* and its verb conjugation, e.g. *vos sabés*), pronominal *voseo* (use of *vos* with *tú* verb conjugation, e.g. *vos sabes*), and verbal *voseo* (use of the *vos* verb conjugation with *tú*, e.g. *tú sabés*).

As Norma Beatriz Carricaburo explains in "El voseo en la Historia y en la lengua de hoy,"[8] Spanish *voseo* can be traced back to the Iberian Peninsula in the fourth century, when *vos* was the preferred form to indicate respect towards an interlocutor of higher social status. In Spain, the use of *vos* changed throughout the centuries: originally used by a person from a lower social rank to address someone from a higher social status, it ended up being used in the opposite direction, i.e. by a person from a higher social rank to address someone from a lower social status. Later, towards the end of the fifteenth century, the completion of the Reconquista modified address formulas again and *vos* started being used between people from the same social status. Even though the *voseo* disappeared

---

6 TN: In *Juan and María; Today*, the English translations are "cool […] attitude" (16), "great," and "[t]hey last forever" (17).

7 TN: The Spanish dialect spoken in the areas in and around the Río de la Plata basin of Argentina and Uruguay.

8 TN: "Voseo in History and in Today's Language."

from Iberian Peninsula Spanish in the nineteenth century, it endured in regions of the former Spanish Empire, hence its persistence to varying degrees in Latin America: extremely restricted in Mexico; spoken in specific areas in Peru, Colombia, and Venezuela; distributed according to social class in Chile; and widespread in Central America, Paraguay, Argentina, and Uruguay.

Juan y María; hoy presents examples of pronominal *voseo* ("*Ahora estamos solos* **vos** *y yo*" [Armas 14]; "*Yo, previendo eso, compré —sin que* **vos** *supieras— un par de guantes de goma Funsa bárbaros*" [16]; "*Qué casualidad... Yo también compré un par para* **vos**" [16]) and verbal *voseo* ("*¿***Sabés** *lo que quiero ver desde el avión?*" [14], "**Hacés** *cada pregunta...*" [14], "*¿Qué* **buscás**?" [16], "*¿Te* **reís** *de mí?*" [16]).[9]

Conclusions

Dino Armas does not tell us how life unfolds for the modern Juan and María in their new land. The play ends before they board the plane. It is also not known what life was like for Juan and María in the past after settling down in Uruguay. These are open-ended plays that encourage the reader and the spectator to imagine what happens later in the characters' lives. Armas' plays generally have open endings, maybe as a way of expressing that, since we do not know what will happen tomorrow, our lives and our futures are open-ended. Every day until death we keep writing the script of our lives. Provided that the future is not written or predetermined, there exists a possibility to grow and to become better human beings and societies; however, the opposite could also happen. If life is like an open-ended play, Armas summons us to write our future and the future of our societies with responsibility, determination, intelligence, and compassion. Furthermore, in these and other works from the playwright, immigrants are the authors of the future in the societies in which they settle. The immigrant is thus the great writer of the Americas' social and political storylines.

Juan and María; Yesterday and *Juan and María; Today* deal with issues related to the culture, life, and history of Uruguay and, by extension, the Río de la Plata region and all of Latin America. In fact, though Armas' works generally depict local vignettes, they also present a universal vision; therefore, they are welcomed

---

[9] TN: In *Juan and María; Today*, the English translations are "Now we are alone, you and me" (14), "Thinking of that, without telling you, I bought you a pair of Funsa rubber gloves" (16-17), "What a coincidence! I got a pair for you too" (p.17), "Do you know what I want to see from the plane?" (14), "You ask such funny questions..." (14), "What are you looking for?" (16), and "Are you laughing at me?" (16).

not only by Uruguayans and Latin Americans but by a broad international and multicultural audience. They wonderfully depict immigrants' conflicts, hopes, and challenges that are universal, atemporal, simple, and complex at the same time: longing for the country that is being left behind and hope for a better life in a new land.[10]

Works Consulted

Armas, Dino. "Juan y María; hoy." *Migración y dictadura en escena: Un acercamiento interdisciplinario a la obra del dramaturgo uruguayo Dino Armas*. Dir. Gabriela Christie Toletti. Norfolk: New Dominion Press, 2017. 13-17.

Carricaburo, Norma Beatriz. "El voseo en la Historia y en la lengua de hoy." *Elcastellano.org*. October 10, 2016 <http://elcastellano.org/artic/voseo.htm>.

Keen, Benjamin, and Keith Haynes. *A History of Latin America*. Boston: Cengage Learning, 2012.

Schweizer, Nina. *El voseo en Hispanoamérica*. Norderstedt: GRIN Verlag GmbH, 2014.

---

[10] Essay translated by Álex Omar Bratkievich.

CHAPTER TWO
The Fascinating Immigrant Grandmother

The Magic of Doña Mercedes

Doña Mercedes

Dino Armas

Translation by Gabriela Christie Toletti

My grandmother was Doña Mercedes, the healer of El Cerro.[1] She was as good at curing indigestion as she was at bringing back an unfaithful husband.

Her line of customers was very long and competed with Dr. Ostria's line down the street on the corner. Both knew and respected each other: one healed the body; the other the soul. The women in the line—sitting without speaking to one another in respectful silence, some holding their babies tightly, others holding clothes or photos that belonged either to their beloved or to the one who had betrayed them—patiently awaited the words and the touch on the head from the woman who blessed these local *criollas*.[2]

Her hands were still soft, and they reminded me of that young girl who, many years ago, had left the Canary Islands to come to the Americas to follow her Pepe. The two of them never returned.

Her children were all born in Uruguay. I, her first grandson, would often go to see her and was used to walking past those women who waited all afternoon.

I liked seeing my grandmother work, leaning over those women, blessing scarves, ties, or underwear, or pulling the back skin of babies to cure indigestion, or using the edge of a blade to cure bumps or more severe pains.

My Sunday visits were primarily a result of self-interest. I knew that she was going to give me money for the matinées at the Apolo, the Selecto, or the Edén theaters.... From her robe, always black, always the same one, she would take out the coins that allowed me to spend all afternoon watching *convoy*[3] movies or Sandrini's[4] latest films. Gradually, my asthmatic bronchitis got worse. Coughing

---

[1] Translator's Note: El Cerro de Montevideo (literally "Montevideo's Hill") is a hill adjacent to the Bay of Montevideo. One of the neighborhoods located on it is called Villa del Cerro (literally "the Hill's Village") or, simply, el Cerro ("the Hill").

[2] TN: Criollo refers to a person born in Latin America or native to Latin America. Criollas is the plural feminine form of criollo.

[3] TN (From the translator of the essays): One of the common Spanish pronunciations for "cowboy."

[4] TN: Luis Sandrini (Buenos Aires, 1905-1980) was an Argentine actor, comedian, and producer.

and intense chest pain prevented me from running, made me miss school often, and my Sunday trips to the movies had to be abandoned for reading books and magazines at home.

Then she, the grandmother and the healer together for the first time, determined the remedy: I had to spit into the mouth of a live fish and throw it back into the waters of the bay. So, I was going to pass the asthma to the fish, which was going to take it with him far away, to the bottom of the sea.

My father borrowed a boat and together with a friend, both rowing hard, took me to the center of the bay, near the Isla de las Ratas.[5]

I do not know if we waited for an hour or a minute until he could catch a fish.

My father took in his hands that fish which was tossing more than the rowboat, and I gathered a lot of saliva, as much as I could, because I knew my grandmother's remedy would be effective.

Then my father threw it into the water and the fish sank fast in the gray waters. We returned to the shore amid lightning and the first drops of rain dampening our clothes. On the Round Stone my mother was waiting for us with a coat to cover me.

That night I slept without coughing, my chest open to the fresh air of the storm. And the remedy of my grandmother from the Canary Islands was successful. What injections and pills could not do, Doña Mercedes could.

I grew up and the asthma was left behind. That nervous and jumpy fish took it with him to the bottom of the bay forever. And now, when I hear the sound of the waves crashing against the old timbers of the pier, I say to myself that there, in that hoarse and repeating noise, is my childhood asthma.

---

[5]   TN: Isla de las Ratas (literally "Island of the Rats") is a small rocky island in the center of the Bay of Montevideo. It is also called Isla Libertad (literally "Freedom Island").

Autobiographical Elements in the Marvelous Real World of *Doña Mercedes*

Gabriela Christie Toletti

Doña Mercedes is a short first-person narrative in which Dino Armas tells a story about his childhood in Montevideo's Cerro neighborhood, involving his healer grandmother. This essay's goal is to examine the autobiographical elements in the story and to establish connections between them and the concept of the marvelous real (*lo real maravilloso*) in Latin American literature.

The events of *Doña Mercedes* transpire in the Cerro neighborhood when Armas was a child. In a 2014 interview, the author talked to me about his childhood. He explained that in that time, Villa Cosmópolis[1] (as El Cerro had also been known) was a very special working-class neighborhood with a lot to offer in the areas of culture and theater (*Conversation* 307). It was an area with unique characteristics, inhabited by immigrants from many European and Western Asian nations. During an informal, unrecorded part of the conversation, Armas mentioned that when strikes happened, the bridge over the Pantanoso River would be closed and nobody could enter or exit the village. However, the Cerro people had everything they needed to live: it was a self-sufficient neighborhood, with schools, churches, jobs (mainly provided by the meat-processing plants), a cemetery, doctors, and an excellent healer (the well-known Doña Mercedes). The Cerro neighborhood and its people, so distinctive, had a great influence on Armas and appear frequently in his work.

The author's grandmother Doña Mercedes, an immigrant from the Canary Islands (Spain), was a well-known figure in El Cerro. Very efficient at her work, she made a great deal of money as a healer (she ultimately had a two-story house, which was uncommon in El Cerro; she also bought other houses in the same neighborhood and one at a beach resort). Armas remembers that, as a general rule, there were more people waiting to see his grandmother than the neighborhood's doctor.[2] This short story about his immigrant grandmother and her achievements is an homage to the work, the originality, and the strength of nineteenth-century immigrant women: strong women who, along with their

---

[1] Translator's Note: "Cosmopolis Village."
[2] Conversation with Gabriela Christie Toletti. June 17, 2014: off-record comments.

husbands, left their motherland in order to start families in a faraway land. Armas' immigrant grandmother, once transplanted to the new land (Uruguay), adapts, raises her children, works side by side with her husband, and follows her calling using her great talent to help people.

The idea of writing *Doña Mercedes* was first suggested when a newspaper from El Cerro asked Armas to write a piece about his childhood or a notable figure in his life. He chose to write about his grandmother, who saved him twice as a child: once from asthma, and another time—when he was even younger—from convulsions (using hot bricks [*Conversation* 306]).

When Armas was a child, he was asthmatic and overly protected by his mother. He had an atypical childhood because he could not participate in common activities such as playing soccer with the other children. Asthma left its mark on him because he had to spend a lot of time in bed and medicated; it was also damaging to his schooling and even caused him to repeat a grade. Nevertheless, it is also possible to say that it helped him in some ways. Spending a lot of time in bed, Armas got into reading and developed observation and introspection skills that he was later able to apply to his writing career (*Conversation* 307).

Doña Mercedes is the work that best transports us to Armas' childhood in order to find the essence and the origins of his creative process. It is meaningful that Armas' grandmother always supported his interest in the dramatic arts: "I knew she was going to give me money for the matinées at the Apolo, the Selecto, or the Edén theaters…. From her robe, always black, always the same one, she would take out the coins that allowed me to spend all afternoon watching *convoy*[3] movies or Sandrini's latest films" (31).

When young Armas' asthma worsened and he had to spend more time in bed without being able to go to the movies as often, Mercedes became determined to find a cure. In the story, Armas explains that the remedy consisted of his spitting into a live fish's mouth; then the fish would be thrown back into the water in order to take the asthma to the bottom of the sea (32). The cure worked perfectly: he did not have asthma from then on (32). Thus, the story explores the power of faith and belief. If his grandmother's cure was effective, it was because young Armas had faith that the fish would take the asthma back to the deep: "My father took in his hands that fish which was tossing more than the rowboat, and I gathered a lot of saliva, as much as I could, because I knew my grandmother's remedy would

---

[3]   TN: A common Spanish pronunciations of "cowboy."

be effective" (32).

The perception of reality based on faith that we find in this autobiographical short story by Dino Armas takes us into the realm of the marvelous real. Alejo Carpentier became the founding father of the literary movement of magical realism when he posed the following question in the prologue to his novel *El reino de este mundo*,[4] first published in Spanish in 1949: "After all, what is the entire history of America if not a chronicle of the marvelous real?" (26). America's marvelous real is a vision of reality based on faith that has two aspects: on one hand, the extraordinary aesthetic quality of the Americas' reality; on the other, the writer's ability to perceive and have faith in this quality so as to transform it into literature. It is not only the writer's creative ability that allows her to capture in her work the America's marvelous real, but also her belief and faith originating in Latin American reality.

According to Carpentier, the marvelous real is *our* marvelous reality: what we find in its rough form, latent, omnipresent in everything Latin American, where the incredible is and has always been quotidian. In order to capture this extraordinary American reality, the writer has to get rid of rationalist prejudices and let herself go.

The release of the exclusively rational, the adoption of an attitude towards reality based on faith, and the belief in cultural, spiritual, and magical elements are essential features of the marvelous real which can clearly be identified in *Doña Mercedes*. In this work, the concept of *faith* is essential for healing. Without faith in his grandmother's magical and unusual cure, perhaps Armas would never have been able to heal, free himself, or grow.

The idea of healing is key in the author's creative process. According to Armas, the neighborhood's doctor healed bodily afflictions, while his grandmother healed afflictions of the soul (*Doña Mercedes* 31). Was his childhood asthma then an "affliction of the soul?" Was it more psychological than physical?

Asthma is a respiratory disease characterized by difficulty to breathe, which may even result in suffocation. Various psychological theories have attempted to explain asthma as a psychosomatic symptom, establishing a connection with an overbearing love or a tight smothering relationship that interferes with becoming an autonomous person. Taking into account that young Armas was

---

[4]   TN: "The Kingdom of this World."

overly protected by his mother, it is possible to see his grandmother's cure as a way to symbolically move him away from his overbearing mother and make him spit out everything that was stuck in his chest.

In this sense, we can think of his grandmother as a liberating maternal figure, while his own mother was a constraining maternal figure. His grandmother's role was to help him let go of the asthma as a physical illness but also as an emotional hindrance, which allowed him to break out and give free rein to his creative abilities.

If asthma symbolizes emotional asphyxiation and suffocation, breathing symbolizes liberation, independence, individuality, and creativity. Maybe his grandmother provided young Armas with a formula—that is, symbolic resources—to break his emotional chains and set out on a journey of growth which began by releasing his saliva into the fish. This process has continued throughout his life, as he has created and released texts, scenes, and words. These continue to be therapeutic to Armas, the audience, the actors, and the readers, who interpret his work and identify with the conflicts expressed therein. His grandmother's magic healed Armas' asthma, and literature's magic seems to have continued to heal him symbolically through the years.

Doña Mercedes, as a short story, is unlike most of Armas' work. However, the tale was turned into a play, because its subject, plot, and visual elements are conducive to staging. Actually, it can even be said that within the story Armas' grandmother stages a script written by herself. Armas, his father, and his father's friend become characters in a therapeutic play in which they perform roles assigned by the grandmother: his father and a friend take young Armas into the bay on a rowboat, in search of a live fish into whose mouth he has to spit. It is a scene which, when performed, magically heals young Armas. His healer grandmother seems to occupy the role of creator and director of a scene that helps Armas to symbolically throw his illness overboard and thus release himself of the conflicts that tie him down.

In the interview, Armas commented that everything related to theater (mainly writing plays, but also acting, directing, and attending the theater) has always had a healing, therapeutic, and cathartic effect in his life (*Conversation* 308). Through his plays, Armas perhaps not only heals himself but—also symbolically—attempts to cure the "asthma" of a people in a similar way to how his grandmother cured his own asthma. Is theater then a way to cure people's asphyxiation? Is theater a way to allow people to become independent, work through limiting conflicts, and reclaim the ability to breathe freely and peacefully? Is the writer, in some sense, a symbolic healer of human conflicts?

In *Doña Mercedes*, a symbolic meaning can be assigned to the fish and water elements of the story. Regarding the water, Juan Eduardo Cirlot explains in his *Diccionario de símbolos*: "From the waters and the universal unconscious arises everything living as from the mother" (69).[5] Water symbolizes the depth of unconscious knowledge and the origins of life.

The fish also has a rich allegorical meaning. Cirlot suggests that, given its connection to the sea and the *Magna Mater* (Great Mother, Mother Goddess), several religions and cultures have assigned a sacred value to the fish and have linked it to creation and the origin of life (*Dictionary* 101-02). For example, as Antonio Hermán explains in "el simbolismo del pez,"[6] there are ancient African myths that link the fish with creation in a story of the planting of the seeds of two fish in the cosmic uterus. The fish is also an object of worship in several Asian rites and in Greco-Roman mythology, where it has the symbolic meaning of change and transformation.

Cirlot points out that, given its abundance of eggs, the fish is also a symbol of fertility, plentitude, and spiritual development, according to Babylonian, Phoenician, Assyrian, and Chinese beliefs (*Dictionary* 101-102). Hermán additionally reminds us that within Christianity, "the fish is a symbol of abundance and faith, as can be observed in the biblical story of the fish and the loaves of bread" (1).

Hermán explains that, observing that certain fish swim in pairs, the Chinese use them to symbolize unity, harmony, and fidelity; in Buddhism, they symbolize happiness and freedom. Furthermore, in ancient Norse culture and in other European cultures, fish symbolize the flow of life and adaptation to the constant progression of life.

The symbolic values of fish in many cultures and religions seem to intertwine in Dino Armas' real-fantastical story. The faith placed in this "redeemer fish" that carried the asthma to the depths of the bay freed young Armas from his

---

[5]   TN: In the English translation of Cirlot's book, the phrase is rendered as follows: "The projection of the mother-*imago* into the waters endows them with various numinous properties characteristic of the mother" (*Dictionary* 365).

[6]   TN: "the symbolism of fish."

emotional chains, which produced a transformation that allowed him to display his creativity, determination, and ability to adapt in order to develop a fertile career as a playwright.

Marius Schneider, in his book *El origen musical de los animales-símbolos en la mitología y la escultura antiguas*,[7] suggests that fish "is the mystic Ship of Life, [...] spinning out the cycle of life after the pattern of the lunar zodiac" (cited in Cirlot, *Dictionary* 101). This beautiful and suggestive idea from Schneider can help us understand another aspect of Dino Armas' short story: for Armas, by making the healing of psychological and spiritual wounds easier, that fish might also symbolize a mystical vehicle towards a fuller and more productive life.

In this short story, Armas–and, by extension, his grandmother–invite us to embark on a spiritual journey of faith through the authentically Latin American and the marvelous in our daily life. In short, the story is about valuing what is authentically ours and returning to our roots so as to reunite with our cultural heritage, our identity, and our marvelous American reality. Perhaps this reunion is what can provide us with the recipe and the key to grow, create, breathe, free ourselves, and heal personal and collective wounds. Optimism and faith in change are essential qualities for growing both individually and collectively. We might conclude that, through the written word, Dino Armas attempts to heal symbolic wounds, putting together works of art for a nation feeling the pain of years of dictatorship and exile in addition to the pain caused by social, economic, and family-related hardships. Grandma Mercedes was a maternal figure that cured young Armas by providing him with healing and the emotional resources to move on and venture into the creative act. As a playwright, Dino Armas has kept on creating and healing personal and collective wounds.[8]

---

[7] TN: "The Musical Origin of Animal-Symbols in Ancient Mythology and Sculpture."
[8] Essay translated by Álex Omar Bratkievich.

Works Consulted

Carpentier, Alejo. *El reino de este mundo*. 2nd ed. Mexico City: Lectorum, 2013.

Chaparro Valdez, Teresa de Jesús. "Diferencia entre el realismo mágico y lo real maravilloso." *Respeto mutuo es libertad y yo soy libre de pensar* October 2009. September 10, 2016 <http://teresaeiou.blogspot.com/2009/10/diferencia-entre-el-realismo-magico-y.html>.

Christie Toletti, Gabriela and Dino Armas. "Conversation on Life and Theater". *On the Scene with Migration and Dictatorship: An Interdisciplinary Approach to the Work of Uruguayan Playwright Dino Armas*. Dir. Gabriela Christie Toletti. Norfolk: New Dominion Press, 2018. 305-319.

Cirlot, Juan Eduardo. *Diccionario de símbolos*. Madrid: Siruela, 2016.

---. *A Dictionary of Symbols*. Trans. Jack Sage. Taylor & Francis e-Library, 2001. July 18, 2017 <http://www.iausdj.ac.ir/ostad/DocLib71/J._C._Cirlot_Dictionary_of_Symbols__1990.pdf>.

Cortés, Rocío. "El Realismo Mágico en HCH de Luis Leal." *University of Wisconsin – Oshkosh*. September 20, 2016 <http://www.uwosh.edu/faculty_staff/cortes/classes/Spring2005/420/Magico.html>.

Hermán, Antonio. "el simbolismo del pez." September 27, 2011. September 15, 2016 <http://antonioherman.blogspot.com/2011/09/el-simbolismo-del-pez.html>.

Laplanche, Jean, and Jean-Bertrand Pontalis. *Diccionario de psicoanálisis*. Buenos Aires: Paidós Ibérica, 1996.

Padura Fuentes, Leonardo. *Un camino de medio siglo. Alejo Carpentier y la narrativa de lo real maravilloso*. México, D.F.: Tierra Firme, 2002.

Schneider, Marius. *El origen musical de los animales-símbolos en la mitología y la escultura antiguas*. Madrid: Siruela, 1998.

Tordjam, Gilbert. *Cómo comprender las enfermedades psicosomáticas*. Barcelona: Gedisa, 2009.

A Magical Word

Marcelo de León Montañés

In *Doña Mercedes*, the experience of a child in Uruguay in the times of "the Switzerland of the Americas—the peak of the wave of prosperity and high standards of living that turned Uruguay into an admirable example of development—is linked to memories of a no-longer-existing country and a transformed neighborhood. Narrated with a captivating simplicity and characteristic elements of the Latin American short story, the tale is an example of a literary source with historical content. Even its fantastical component is historical, since it stems from a complex Ibero-American historical identity in which the boundaries between the world and the hereafter are easily blurred, and in which the healer, "magical word that the people revere,"[1] occupies a prominent place.

Temporal Frame

Armas does not indicate the exact year of the fish incident, but he provides data that allow us to place it at an approximate time. We know that the author was born in 1941 and that he was a child at the time of the anecdote, since the asthma made him "miss school often" (32). At the same time, there are mentions of the Apolo (1915-1958), Selecto (1924-1954), and Edén (1905-1949) movie theaters. The curing of the asthma, therefore, must have happened between 1947 and 1952, in the last years of Uruguay as the "Switzerland of the Americas."

Spatial Frame

The story of Mercedes and her grandson occurs in the Cerro neighborhood. Mercedes' own story begins earlier, in the Canary Islands (Spain), but, except for the brief mention of her emigration, the account does not move away from the Cerrense[2] surroundings where Dino Armas was raised.

---

[1]   "… and which [the people] obey with the blind misfortune with which chaos obeyed the *fiat* of the Supreme Creator" (Navas and Pérez 225).
[2]   Translator's Note: Adjective used to refer to everything related to the Cerro neighborhood.

Maybe for Mercedes, as for other immigrants, her life preceding emigration was an already-closed past (as for Jhonny in *Beach Day*, a brilliant and caustic comedy by Armas) or a past imbued with nostalgia without the desire to return to it (as for Eduardo in *Just Yesterday*, also by Armas). From what is perceived in the short story, however, the healer did not get wrapped up in the alienating yearning of Beba and Pedro (*Beach Day*).[3]

This last point is deduced from what is not told: were it not for the author's clarification, the reader would not even know that Mercedes was a foreigner (unlike Beba and Pedro, who take care to maintain the languages heard in Uruguay— Spanish and Italian—and reject English). There is almost no information about her departure and none whatsoever about the emotional attachments she left behind, her *decires* ("sayings, proverbs"), her dialectal peculiarities, or life in the Canary Islands in general. There is only one emotional link with the motherland: Pepe, her husband who is also Canarian (Armas, *Doña Mercedes* 31).

In contrast to the children of the older characters in *Beach Day*, which deals with the emotional conflicts of a group of Uruguayan expatriates in Australia, all of Mercedes and Pepe's children were born in the family's new country, in their case Uruguay. This surely contributed to Mercedes' putting down deep roots in her adoptive land, since she must have loved it for being her children's homeland. Possibly, Beba and Pedro's adjustment to Australia would have been better had Luisito or Jhonny been born there. Uruguayan parents Pedro and Beba resent the detachment felt by their son Jhonny towards Uruguay, the country where he was born; but Pepe and Mercedes escape such an emotional shock regarding the Canaries since none of their offspring were Canarian: "Her children were all born in Uruguay" (Armas, *Doña Mercedes* 31).

In *Juan and María; Yesterday*, Dino Armas shows the arrival of an immigrant couple in Montevideo in an unknown time frame which includes the likely year of Mercedes and Pepe's arrival in Montevideo. Even though the play is not inspired by the author's immigrant grandparents,[4] their dialogue allows us to imagine the one Mercedes and Pepe could have had upon arriving. Juan says—and Pepe could have said —"This will be our land, our home"; "Our kids will be born here!" (10). If Mercedes and Pepe chose to leave the past behind, perhaps they did it in

---

[3]   Nona is not included since it is not clear whether she really yearns for Uruguay or simply goes along with the illusion of her son and daughter-in-law (after all, being Italian, Uruguay is for her what Australia is for the others: an emigration endpoint).

[4]   Armas, Dino. E-mail to the author. March 2, 2017.

order to overcome the grief of uprooting, accepting with resignation the reality that they might not ever return to their birth land (as indeed happened with Mercedes and Pepe), and embracing the promise of a future better than the past and the present. Isabel Allende expresses this last point very well by comparing the immigrant, who "looks towards the future, ready to take advantage of the opportunities within reach," with the exile, "who looks towards the past, licking his own wounds"(193)—as does Eduardo in *Just Yesterday*.

The bond between Mercedes and her grandson, the young Armas, was tight and communication frequent: "I, her first grandson, would go to see her and was used to […]," "I liked seeing my grandmother work," "My Sunday visits were […]"(Armas, *Doña Mercedes* 31). It can be assumed that if Mercedes had resented her life as an immigrant, some of her rancor would have seeped through into the short story or some of the author's other works. This is not the case, at least in those that form this compilation: Uruguay is the promised land (*Juan and María; Yesterday*); the place that one regrets leaving even if fate offers the promise of a good standard of living abroad (*Juan and María; Today*); the country with which there is an unbreakable emotional tie; whereas Spain—Mercedes' own land—only offers a material connection (Eduardo, *Just Yesterday*). The emotional tie with Uruguay is so strong that it can lead to fantasies as an antidote to the pain of being apart from the homeland (Beba and Pedro, *Beach Day*), in a way that neither Spain nor Italy seems to have achieved in Armas' work (Nona, *Beach Day*).

El Cerro

If one place in Uruguay were to be sought as representative of its history as a country of immigrants, there would be agreement on choosing El Cerro. Since its establishment (1834), it was already expected that foreigners arriving in Montevideo would choose the town to settle in. For this reason it was marketed as "Villa Cosmópolis"[5] along with the official name of "Villa del Cerro,"[6] and its streets were given the names of countries (1867).

The realization of the expectations for El Cerro was not immediate, but in the following decades more townspeople and industries settled there, bringing progress and prosperity. Meat-processing plants formed a sizable part of the

---

[5] TN: "Cosmopolis Village."
[6] TN: Literally, "the Hill's Village."

productive engine of the cattle-ranching country of Uruguay, and three of the most important ones operated in El Cerro, maintaining the dream of the Switzerland of the Americas. The latter was so linked to the former that in later years the definitive collapse of the ideal country was brought about by the fall of the meat-processing industry, turning El Cerro from the paradigmatic example of a nation of fat cows into an omen of the decades of lean cows that would follow.

In the short story there are indirect indications of that golden era in the absence of news about social upheavals, in the placid atmosphere conveyed by the narration, in the mention of moments of leisure (movie theaters), in the hints of the low cost of living ("those coins […] allowed me to spend all afternoon watching […] movies" [31]) and safety in the streets. Even though the child's parents cared about his physical well-being ("my mother was waiting for us with a coat to cover me" [32]), it would seem that Armas used to go to the movies without them, since the money he would get from his grandmother was only for his ticket.

At the time of the story's setting, El Cerro was not simply a conglomerate of nationalities (Greeks, Russians, Poles, Spaniards, etc.), but had its own identity as well. A large portion of the residents used to work in the meat-processing plants, which provided jobs with good salaries and additional benefits (meat allocations, for example). In this way, an occupation that would have been seen with disdain in other places was appreciated and even coveted in El Cerro. Whole families could be employed in the same sector.

Its social awareness, diversity of origins, and shared goals; its model prosperity as a predominantly working-class village; and its life-enriching heterogeneity made El Cerro an enclave so self-sufficient that a resident from those times would say, in reference to the city to which the neighborhood belonged, "How beautiful Montevideo is… pity it was made so far from El Cerro" (Turcatti and De León 446).

Even the movie theaters young Armas attended—which in the eyes of a child were probably only a place where movies were projected—would transcend their purpose of entertainment, blend with Cerrense idiosyncrasy and, at the same time, contribute to molding it. The Apolo was born as a live-performance theater and inaugurated with zarzuela, dramatic musical theater of the same origin as one of the main immigrant groups of that period (Spain). The Edén was the meeting place for the assembly that in 1942 founded the Federación Obrera de la Carne y Afines[7] (Porrini Beracochea 72-73). The Selecto was born within the economic boom that would dedicate a palace as seat of the legislature, and it died at the beginning of the economic decline (Saratsola).

Mercedes, Immigrant

The short story reveals more than it seems about the co-protagonist and her relationship with the demographic history of the country. Mercedes "had left the Canary Islands" (31). Setting aside precise time periods, Italians and Spaniards constituted the majority among the foreign minorities which settled in the country until the middle of the twentieth century. For Spanish immigrants, surely the common Hispanic ancestry, the open border agreements between ex-mother-country and ex-colony, and—above all—the common language and culture, made Uruguay attractive.

The Canarian immigration laid the foundations of the Spanish Uruguay of the Eastern Strip[8] in colonial times, continued during the years of the independence movement, and further continued in the established republic. Aside from the contingent that founded Montevideo, ships full of Canarian immigrants arrived in Maldonado (birthplace of the writer of this text, who has Canarian people among his ancestors) and, of course, in Canelones, where even today people who are born there are known as Canarians, regardless of their ancestors' roots. Canarians left a deep mark on the Uruguayan way of farming, the rural buildings, the food, customs, beliefs, vocabulary, and more. Surely Mercedes also contributed in carrying the legacy of her people to Uruguay.

Contigo, gofio y cebolla[9]

Historically, there has been more than one reason to emigrate to Uruguay, but the most common one has been economic. Another common reason to immigrate was to escape the lack of physical safety caused by wars, political instability, or

---

[7] TN: "Workers' Federation of Beef and Related Products."

[8] TN: Banda Oriental ("Eastern Strip" or "Eastern Bank") was the name given to the land east of the Uruguay River and north of the Río de la Plata, comprising most of the modern Uruguayan nation as well as the modern Brazilian state of Río Grande do Sul. It was the easternmost territory of the Viceroyalty of the Río de la Plata. In 1813, under the name of "Provincia Oriental" ("Eastern Province"), it became a separate administrative unit of the Provincias Unidas del Río de la Plata ("United Provinces of the Río de la Plata"), first name for the independent nation of Argentina.

[9] TN: "With you, *gofio* and onions," traditional Canarian saying. *Gofio* is a Canarian staple ingredient, a flour made from roasted grains, traditionally corn, wheat, or barley.

both (in the case of Spain, the fall of the First Republic in 1874 and the Civil War from 1936 to 1939). There were also more personal motives of a different order (a desire for adventure; evasion of debts; and avoiding discrimination of any type, including religious persecution). Mercedes' history fits into what has been called "matrimonial emigration" (*Domestici et al.* 116), since she left "to follow her Pepe" (Armas, *Doña Mercedes* 31).

Once more, the fiction of Juan and María in the past helps us imagine Mercedes' words to Pepe: "Didn't I leave my parents, my brothers and sisters to follow you? To come with you? To live with you?" (Armas, *Juan and María; Yesterday* 9).

Nothing is known of Pepe in the short story, which barely mentions him, be it because Armas had less contact with him than with Mercedes, because he was not particularly relevant to the anecdote, or for some other reason. Perhaps he departed the Canary Islands for economic motives, as did the majority of emigrants. In any case, his absence from the tale highlights the presence of the healer as an executive, dynamic, autonomous, professional, self-reliant woman. In other words, Mercedes embodies a model of success able to overcome not only the challenge of being a foreigner but also that of being a woman in a patriarchal society. Concerning this last point, it should be remembered that vigorous women like her contributed to the fight for women's equality, and that she herself witnessed a changing country: the first female vote in Latin America (a local plebiscite in Cerro Chato, Uruguay, 1927), the law of women's suffrage (1932), the elections of 1938 (when women voted for the first time at a national level), and the law of Civil Rights of Women, contemporary to the short story's events (1946).

There is something else to note about Pepe, who is truly conspicuous by his absence. After all, he set into motion the events that ultimately allow the reader to enjoy a magical and emotional story superbly evoked by his grandson. It is impossible not to relate "her Pepe" from *Doña Mercedes* (31) with "my Pepe," partner of the pseudo-Melchora Cuenca in *Present, Señorita*, another play by Dino Armas (106). The historical figure "Pepe" (José) Artigas,[10] hero of Uruguay's independence, was his partner Melchora's beacon; she would have figuratively sailed unknown waters and even gone as far as a second expatriation[11] for him ("I will follow you even to ostracism" [Armas, *Present, Señorita* 106]). The other Pepe

---

[10] TN: General José Gervasio Artigas (1764-1850) is considered the main Uruguayan national hero due to his role in the fight for independence against the Spaniards.

[11] Melchora was born in Paraguay; therefore, she was already an expatriate when she met Artigas.

was Mercedes' beacon in a less metaphorical sense, since she actually crossed an ocean following him and became an expatriate for him. The Canarian version of the well-known Spanish saying *"contigo, pan y cebolla,"*[12] adapted in the first ingredient to *gofio*, the traditional staple food on the islands, could well have been Mercedes' reply to Pepe's decision or proposal to immigrate to America.

A Canarian—the modern Pepe; a grandson of Canarians—the Pepe of the Independence Movement: both had enough charisma so that their partners followed them out of love, as revealed by the possessive pronouns "her" and "my" used by Armas, and not because of promises of well-being. Both are the absent presences in the literary moments of their significant others, but both of them changed the course of the lives of these two women, who were their own masters even in the devotion they voluntarily granted.

Mercedes emigrated very young ("young girl," says Armas [*Doña Mercedes* 31]), as did the majority of immigrants. The reasons are logical and pertain equally today: labor markets are more receptive to young labor; jobs are usually hard and require health and physical energy. There is a certain intrepidness (indispensable for endeavors with high risk due to many unknowns) easier to find in youth than in maturity (when experience moderates impetuosity), and there is a flexibility that comes with less depth of rooting in the native surroundings (compared to that felt by older people).

As a married woman, Mercedes was not part of the majority of expatriates, since migration cast out mainly single young men (even though the percentage of females increased with time and, in Uruguay, reached 44% by the mid-thirties [Cagiao Vila 4]). She must have faced both the challenges of emigration itself and also those of being a woman in a patriarchal society. It was customary in the Spanish/Spanish-American society of the time (the beginning of the twentieth century) for women to remain at home and under the tutelage of male blood relatives (fathers, brothers) until leaving the home to enter a convent or to get married. Masculine tutelage continued then under the ecclesiastical head or the husband, respectively.

This surveillance and control was claimed to be justified by the alleged weakness, vulnerability, or inferior ability of women. In actuality, it revolved more than anything around the concept of family sexual honor (for which the "purity" of women had to be maintained—in contrast with men's—which ultimately was

---

[12]   TN: "With you, bread and onions."

47

related to the transfer of the patrimony, since blood relationships could only be guaranteed by the woman's progeny) and around control of labor (women as caretakers of the home, the children, and the elders). In *Doña Rosita la soltera*[13] (1935), a play by Federico García Lorca, it is the boyfriend who immigrates to America, not Rosita. Similarly, in *Las medias rojas*[14] (1888), a short story by Emilia Pardo Bazán, Ildara's dream of leaving Spain is ravaged along with her face because of the violence inflicted on her by her father in order to prevent her from going.

Gender, therefore, must have influenced Mercedes when considering her departure. It could have been such a determinant that perhaps she followed "her Pepe" not only out of love but also in order to avoid the disintegration of the marriage out of which her descendants were expected to be born. "Many emigrant's wives, girlfriends, mothers, or daughters, keen to reunite with them, took the road of emigration guided on many occasions by their intention to maintain their cohesive role within the family group," writes Cagiao Vila (2-3). Setting aside the love between the two, if Pepe left without her, Mercedes would be condemned to spend the rest of her years tied to an absent husband, watched by the cruel eyes of a society that would not allow her to rebuild her life or to engender children with another man, in an undefinable state (neither single nor married nor a widow) like so many other "Canarian daughters of Penelope" (as María Victoria Hernández Pérez calls them), trapped in a marital status that did not correspond to any acceptable role for a woman.

Mercedes followed Pepe out of love; perhaps she also thought about the integrity of the conjugal union on which she would establish her family; maybe she got frightened at the prospect of becoming a daughter of Penelope. All these assumptions imply a voluntary departure, but we should ask: was she legally free to refuse to depart if Pepe had already decided to do so? Both canonical and civil law in Spain restricted the free will of wives and established the duty of obedience of the wife to her husband.[15] The Spanish Civil Code forced the wife to follow the husband to wherever he would take up residence, except if it was in an overseas

---

[13] TN: "Doña Rosita the Spinster."

[14] TN: "The Red Stockings."

[15] Encyclical *Arcanum Divinae Sapientiae*, 1880: "Therefore, as the Church is subject to Christ, so also let wives be to their husbands in all things" (León XIII, "Carta encíclica *Arcanum Divinae Sapientiae* del sumo pontífice León XIII sobre la familia." *La Santa Sede*. March 15, 2017. http://w2.vatican.va/content/leo-xiii /es/encyclicals/documents/hf_l-xiii_enc_10021880_arcanum.html). TN: English translation available at http://w2.vatican.va/content/leo-xiii/en/encyclicals/documents/hf_l-xiii_enc_10021880_arcanum.html. August 28, 2017. Spanish Civil Code, 1889: "The husband must protect the wife and the latter obey the husband" (Art. 58).

position or abroad. In order to get an exemption from her obligation, a woman had to resort to the court and prove just cause for not accompanying him (Art. 58). The Church went so far as to protest against even this limited opening before the approval of the article that enacted it: "Why would not the husband be able to relocate Overseas [capitalized in the original] or abroad whenever it is in his interest and in the interest of his well-being and his family's? Why ought he not have the right to take his wife?" (Carbonero and Sol 360). Mercedes, therefore, could not actually count on the same opportunities as her husband at the moment of deciding her fate, independently of the love that motivated her to follow him. That was the world of the "young girl" of the time.

La mujer que no vela no hace larga tela[16]

Mercedes' children were born in Uruguay, her first grandson (Armas) was born in 1941, and she emigrated at the beginning of her youth, which leads us to assume that she was born around 1900 and arrived in Uruguay circa 1915-1920. Even though the Canary Islands were far from the physical stage of the Great War that ravaged Europe for four years (1914-1918), their economy was negatively affected (Ponce Marrero) and perhaps this drove Pepe and Mercedes to emigrate. The only transoceanic means of transport in those times was by ship; therefore, their approach to Montevideo, the bay, and El Cerro must have been similar to Juan and María's (*Juan and María; Yesterday*). Their emotions and expectations could also have been similar: "In this land, in this place, we will have a new life. Now this will be our land, our home. Here we will work" (10).

In an interview carried out by Gabriela Christie Toletti, Armas said that Mercedes "made a lot of money" and came to acquire several properties (one at a beach resort), including her residence in El Cerro, a two-story house (*Conversation* 307). Even though she was born when the welfare state was beginning to form both in Spain and Uruguay, there were still many risks of becoming destitute.[17] Owning property could guarantee a roof over her head, an income, or both. A "very efficient [woman] in her work" (Armas, *Conversation* 308), it seems that Mercedes managed to secure both: the large house provided

shelter, and we might imagine that all or some of the other properties generated

---

[16] Spanish saying. TN: "The woman who does not stay up late does not make a long cloth."
[17] Life expectancy was shorter, social security was in an embryonic state, medicine was still fighting diseases that are eradicated today, the risk of accidents was higher (for example, Montevideo would not have traffic lights until the '50s, the same decade in which seatbelts were invented), etc.

income. The house at the beach resort, even if it was destined for personal use, undoubtedly constituted an investment of increasing value in a world where the pleasure of summer holidays had become permanently established (there have been tourists in Punta del Este since the end of the 1880s, Piriápolis was formed in 1890, Atlántida in 1911, Carrasco was established in the '20s, and Salinas came into existence in 1937).

The aforementioned suggests business acumen, prudence, managing skills, and more, qualities that were questionable in women at the time. In this way, the healer stands out again and, considering everything that has already been stated, perhaps this Melchora surpasses her Pepe in heroism.

For some immigrants, a house not only provided refuge but also served to publicize their success. Either in their adoptive land or their native land—if they returned—they would erect mansions that bore witness to their wealth (Spain even coined the term *indiano* for the emigrants who returned rich). Mercedes did not go that far, perhaps because the economic investment was not worthy, because the times were different, because it would have been jarringly offensive in El Cerro, or simply because she was not interested.

Nevertheless, her prosperity was visible in the two-story house, something only people with high purchasing power would have (Armas, *Conversation* 307). Was it a variant of the "austere ostentation" that Alcides Beretta Curi detected in nineteenth century immigrants in Uruguay? Probably not, given a clue that contradicts the suspicion of material boasting: "her robe, always black, always the same one" (Armas, *Doña Mercedes* 31). What would drive Mercedes to keep wearing the same garment? Maybe the restraint of those who have known hard times and maximize their prudence even in favorable times, or the experience of having been raised in an economy of durable assets (a wise attitude to face fluctuations in fortune).

Restraint, however, does not mean stinginess. Mercedes never denied her grandson money for recreation ("I knew she was going to give me money for the matinées" [Armas, *Doña Mercedes* 31]), even if someone stricter in home economics would have dismissed it as a frivolous expense.

From some perspectives, the ownership of properties would have cancelled out any grief the immigrant might have suffered, as if material success wiped away the pain of expatriation. In *Just Yesterday*, Daniel dismisses at a single stroke the long and heartfelt speech of his brother, who has just bared his soul speaking about the grief of exile: "But in the end you did well" (253). Hidden beneath the material success are—as it must have been for Mercedes—the loss of friendships, family, customs, community, and even personal identity; and the new sorrows of solitude, despair, anxiety, emptiness, frustration, and fear. Given that in the healer's time the contact between the native country and the new one was reduced to sporadic epistolar communications, and that transoceanic trips were costly and long, it was known that the separation would be most likely for life, which made the losses irreparable. "They never returned," writes Armas in reference to his grandparents (*Doña Mercedes* 31). Eduardo's words in *Just Yesterday* (shortly before Daniel's aforementioned questionable remark) may well have been Mercedes': "It was a very high price I had to pay" (251).

In the face of this reality, the achievement of the goals that led to emigration could balance the scales to a certain degree. Let us hope that it was like that for Mercedes and Pepe.

The Healer

The main baggage for an emigrant is that of her/his talents and virtues. Most Canarians that arrived in Uruguay came from rural areas and small villages with a distinctive language, customs, dwellings, tools, food, and beliefs. This cultural legacy, which must have been Mercedes' as well, traveled with the expatriates. If she did not practice in the Canary Islands the profession that would make her renown, surely at the very least she knew of it.

Traditional healing was very popular in the social setting of Armas' grandmother. Canarian researcher José Pérez Vidal wrote in 1945, "it is odd in the Canary Islands the region or village without an old man who is a healer—old man or woman, it does not matter [...]. [...] Furthermore, aside from those old *santiguadores*,[18] healers, and herbalists, it is odd in rural areas the person of some age who does not know countless homemade remedies and advice against all kind of illnesses" (20-21).

---

[18] TN: *Santiguar* means "to make the sign of the cross"; *santiguadores* are people who allegedly cleanse or heal by making *santiguados* (i.e. ritual cleansings and/or healings consisting of repeatedly making the sign of the cross while intoning some prayer or chant).

According to Armas, Mercedes was not *a* but *the* healer of El Cerro. It is unlikely that he might have meant she was the only one; therefore, it must be understood that she was the best during her time, the healer par excellence (at least that is how her grandson considered her). Perhaps she even prevailed over the masculine competition due to being a woman, since, according to Pérez Vidal, female healers seemed "more loaded with witch-like knacks and mysteries" (20).[19]

The Spanish Royal Academy distinguishes two meanings for the word: in the first, a healer is a person who practices (Western) medicine without an official title; in the second, it is one who, "without being a doctor, follows empirical or ritual healing practices" (*Diccionario de la Real Academia Española*, 2014). The second meaning is the one which applies to Mercedes, and it is the older meaning as well, since there was a time when even the predecessor of the modern doctor would resort to both rituals and herbs or other treatments in his profession. Today, as in Dino Armas' grandmother's times, traditional healing coexists with scientific medicine, in spite of the competition and scorn from the latter.

What is true is that, aside from the fact that healers apply treatments both effective and ineffective, a great difference between their treatments and doctors' is found in the sphere of treatment. The healer believes s/he is able to influence not only the physical world but the supernatural as well, in the last case through *santiguados*, prayers, blessings, etc.; s/he attends to the problems of the body as well as those of the spirit and ultimately replaces the doctor when the latter is absent or does not find a remedy, or when the root of the illness does not come from the physical sphere.

Canarian people took their popular medicine with them when they emigrated, and maybe Mercedes did too. The healers' catalog of diseases and remedies was long. Uruguayan readers will be able to recognize more than one belief and remedy among the following examples of the Canarian healer's baggage: sties were healed with a key and the sign of the cross, or by touching them with the tail of a cat; counting stars caused warts, which were healed—among other ways—by burying a string of thread with as many knots as warts the affected person had, or by fictitiously "selling" them; willow tree bark and stem broth would alleviate headaches; hiccups were stopped with a scare or seven swigs of water.[20]

---

[19] The passage speaks of old female healers, but it does not aim at age but gender, since it attributes more resources to them than to old male healers.

[20] Numerous healing practices and beliefs are found, with or without variation, in other parts of Spain and Europe. The fact that the practices described are part of the Canarian cultural legacy does not mean they are exclusively Canarian.

Canarian folk medicine drew from the knowledge of the indigenous people who populated the islands before the Spaniards conquered them, from the popular medicine of these conquerors, and from contact with America. The knowledge Mercedes applied in her profession, provided she had acquired at least some of it in her homeland, must have come from that variety of sources. In El Cerro, she may have received the contribution of other cultures' popular medicine; after all, the neighborhood was living up to its original advertising name, and immigrants from a number of countries coalesced (even within the same block). In that environment, the fusion and interchange of knowledge among cultures must have been a habitual phenomenon.

Of the bodily maladies Mercedes used to treat, Armas remembers indigestion, head lumps, and "stronger pains." As remedies, he mentions using the dull edge of a knife (for head lumps) and tugging the skin of babies (to treat their indigestion [*Doña Mercedes* 31]). As curious as these treatments may seem, and in spite of their singularity, medical science might agree on the effectiveness of both treatments.

Many treatments had an important magical component; in Armas' case, it was spitting into the mouth of a live fish to cure his asthma. I have not found information about this particular remedy, although I did find another remedy for the same malady, which consists of drinking black cat broth (Sánchez Pérez 49), so it is possible that the fish treatment—more humane and less disagreeable than the cat-broth one—was Mercedes' own creation.

Truth be told, the magical ingredient in Mercedes' treatment was not very different from religious beliefs. Let us remember, for example, the relics of the saints, holy water, novenas,[21] the laying of hands, etc. (all this within Catholicism alone, but present in one way or another in other religions). Traditional healing methods shared elements of the predominant religion, Christianity (Mercedes did *santiguados*), but they diverged enough from it so as to cross a thin boundary between official religion and superstition, magic, or sorcery. This line is typically drawn by the politically or spiritually dominant creed, which turns the unapproved practices into the target of criticism and anathemas.[22] Mercedes' profession did not escape the censure of the Catholic Church (the majority Christian denomination

---

[21] A series of prayers lasting nine days or nine weeks which includes a personal petition for help.

[22] A current example about how hazy the line can be between what is accepted by organized religion and what is not is an Uruguayan good-luck ritual that requires a plastic cup, garlic, sugar, cinnamon, clove, incense, honey, parsley, a candle, a coin, and a little plate, plus a specific prayer. The addressee is St. Cono (Porzecanski 53).

in Uruguay) and possibly of other churches already established in the country, such as the Methodist, Anglican, Mormon, and Russian Orthodox churches.

In *Just Yesterday*, Armas shows this conflict between spiritual alternatives when Amalia confesses to having resorted to a healer (in order to separate her son Antonio from Marisa, her prospective daughter-in-law) using words that reveal that she did something unthinkable given her faith: "Do you even know what I ended up doing? I went to a healer." Marisa's reply is as ironic as it is incredulous: "You? You, such a believer?" (241). More than one of Mercedes' clients must have felt similar conflicts of conscience. The posture that the grandson observed in the women that waited for their turn—"without speaking to one another, in respectful silence" (Armas, *Doña Mercedes* 31)—perhaps was due to their reverence towards the healer, their distress, or their pain because of the physical or emotional sickness that afflicted them; but it could as well have been the result of their guilt stemming from contravening doctors, priests, and pastors.

Since the second half of the nineteenth century, health care improved considerably in Uruguay. Aside from the worldwide advances in the knowledge of diseases and treatments, there was an increase in the number of doctors, hospitals, and community organizations that provided health care. Surely all this, along with legal limitations on the non-professional practice of medicine,[23] gradually restricted the healers' scope of operation upon the natural world and, as a reaction, enhanced their role in the realm of the paranormal. It is not surprising, therefore, that by the time of the story, the doctor "healed the body" and the healer "the soul" (Armas, *Doña Mercedes* 31). And, since their spheres of treatment collided less than in the past, it is not strange either that they respected each other, as Armas remembers.

More than a century before Mercedes, a Spanish surgeon complained, "The healers that have more reputation around here [...] have more patrons than all the surgeons, and without knowing at what school they have studied" (Barrera 29). By the time of Armas' story, the scene—in Montevideo this time—had not varied except in the vocabulary: "The line of customers was very long and competed with Dr. Ostria's line down the street on the corner" (31). The difference between

---

[23] Decades before the time of the story, one of the ancestors of the writer of this text experienced firsthand the force of the law: "The neighbor and businessman of this city Don Pablo Miret has been apprehended and placed as well at the disposal of the Departmental Court, for being accused of practicing medicine, illegally" (*El Conciliador*, Maldonado, July 23, 1891, p. 3). Apparently, he refused to be intimidated by the bad experience: decades after dying, Miret (a Spaniard like Mercedes, if national idiosyncrasy is relevant) was remembered as a healer by profession.

the Spanish doctor and Ostria is that the latter respected the healer, perhaps because, as mentioned, their respective areas of expertise overlapped less than in the past.

In corroboration of this last point, the short story abounds in references to an area removed from the physical plane: "to bring back an unfaithful husband," "clothes that belonged either to their love or to the one who had betrayed them, or otherwise, photos" (obviously to carry out passes, prayers, or rituals), "the touch on the head," "blessing scarves, ties, or underwear" (31).

References to a spiritual plane appear again in *Just Yesterday*. Antonio intends to marry Marisa, ex-girlfriend of his brother Eduardo, who is exiled. Amalia, mother of the young men, considers Marisa a bad influence. In order to protect Antonio, as mentioned before, she transgresses the stipulations of her religion so as to separate the couple: "I went to a healer. I brought her some stockings and underwear so she would make the sign of the cross over them" (241). The incident reveals, in addition, that the power of *santiguados*, just like the power of prayers, is relative, since Amalia's attempts do not succeed in preventing Antonio's marriage to Marisa.

The Clientele

A 2000 article on magical practices in El Cerro published in Montevideo's *La República* newspaper notes that most of the followers of the practices were women. A 2009 study highlights that the percentage of female believers in the supernatural in Uruguay surpassed—and in some instances far exceeded—that of male believers (Ferré, Gerstenbluth, and Rossi). At the end of the nineteenth century, the situation was similar enough to that of the present day that the Catholic Church appealed to women to counter the increasing secularization of society. An example of the response to their request for help is the 1883 collection of signatures from Uruguayan ladies in order to Christianize their children's school and teach them "to save their souls" (*La exposición-protesta* XVI, XXIII).

Mercedes' times, halfway between those of the 1883 Uruguayan ladies and the 2009 study on religiousness, seem to have been characterized as well by a greater participation of women in matters related to the supernatural: the clientele mentioned by Armas was all female. Of all the believers mentioned, including the women that young Armas used to see in the consultation room, as well as the healer and the author's mother (who approved the faith cure); only the author's father was male (we do not know about the child's beliefs and, in any case, he was too young to form an opinion on the validity of the practices).

Epilogue

A literary piece is more than a work of fiction since it reflects—even if only at an unconscious level—the cultural background that informed the mind of its creator. When that literary piece is of an autobiographical nature, its historical value increases exponentially due to the express will of the narrator to reproduce actual events that he experienced directly or indirectly.

One of the appeals of *Doña Mercedes* is that the subject of the story and its magical realist content seem to move the personal account into the realm of fiction, where stories are born out of the imagination but contain glimmers of truth. This would brand it as a literary source with historical value limited to the background or the surroundings of the story. The asthma incident and its unorthodox cure, however, actually took place, which returns the story to the realm of autobiographical testimony and confers it full value as a historical source. This peculiar sequence of events is entirely salvaged in its value as a historical source due to Armas' prudence in presenting the events without pronouncing a verdict: his grandmother helped women hurt by a romantic betrayal, but we do not know whether the *santiguados* had an effect; he narrates that he suffered from asthma, his grandmother prescribed a remedy, they put it into practice, and he got cured, but a careful reading of the account makes it clear that the author avoids connecting the events in a cause-effect relationship. As he does in his plays, Armas lets the reader provide the ending and decide whether it was Mercedes' remedy that cured the boy, whether the fish-healing had a placebo effect, or whether the asthma disappeared for some completely different reason that we do not know about.

As a historical source, *Doña Mercedes* is an example of both the testimonial value of a story's setting and of the secondary characters in relation to the main one. It also shows the multiplicity of research paths that a single work can offer. The tale may be used to supplement studies about El Cerro, childhood in Montevideo in the '40s and '50s, leisure in the Little Silver Cup,[24] popular

---

[24] The nickname "tacita de plata" [TN: "Little Silver Cup"] is recorded for Montevideo since at least the 1900s. Perhaps because of a cross with "perla del Plata" [TN: "Pearl of la Plata"] and "coqueta del Plata" [TN: "Charming [City] of la Plata"], nicknames also recorded for Montevideo, by the time of the tale's events, it

medicine, Uruguayan beliefs, or immigration to Uruguay, because it provides interesting data on any of those subjects. In this essay we have touched on the latter three points and skimmed some of the former ones.

Doña Mercedes also sheds light on Dino Armas and his dramaturgy. Thanks to the short story, we understand why El Cerro is a frequent reference in his work (among the plays in this compilation, it is mentioned in *Juan and María; Yesterday* and *Juan and María; Today*). A descendant of immigrants, raised in a cosmopolitan neighborhood, it is not surprising that he created a story about Spaniards (the use of *vale*[25] in the original Spanish version [Armas, *Juan y María; ayer* 11] indicates the protagonists' origin) and included an Italian woman in *Beach Day*, since those nationalities correspond to the two main groups of European immigrants in Uruguay.

Armas has said that all his works contain something of himself: "I put a little bit of me or my family history, or my neighborhood" (*Entrevista* n.p.). This includes not only this autobiographical story. There existed in fact a Chancha Colorada (*Sea Murmur*), a Tapia School (*Present, Señorita*), an insane relative (*Just Yesterday, Present, Señorita, Beach Day*), and Canarian grandparents (*Doña Mercedes*). The same applies to other plays by Armas outside of this compilation.

As regards Mercedes herself, woman and immigrant, she inspires us to say, as is heard in the islands where she came from in allusion to people that know how to navigate the vicissitudes of life with determination and wisdom: "*A esa no se le quema el tostadero.*"[26] She is an example of the many stories of those who, with their virtues and talents, face the eventualities of uprooting and start again in an unfamiliar world.

Like many of them–although not everyone–Mercedes triumphed with her own resources. Her assets were largely her skill (as shown in the practice of her profession) and her passion. She demonstrated her passion by having left her land to follow her beloved husband and–if we fuse her story with Juan and María's–to give their eventual children a better future. Armas' perception that Mercedes was *the* healer of El Cerro, provided it is not distorted by subjectivity,

---

was occasionally called "tacita del Plata" [TN: "Little Cup of la Plata"]. With this name it was immortalized on the song *Montevideo* by Romeo Gavioli, Uruguayan singer to whom Dino Armas pays homage in Amalia's evocation in *Just Yesterday*.

25 TN: "That's right" (literally "it is valid, worthy")

26 TN: "Her toasting does not get burnt." *Tostadero* ("toaster") refers to a receptacle for toasting millet and is also used metonymically to refer to the toasted millet itself. The saying describes a woman who is skilled at toasting the millet (and, by extension, any endeavor) without overdoing it.

indicates that Mercedes commanded her field so well as to become a paradigm of her profession. Evidently, she knew how to reach the souls of her clientele.

What the story does not reveal is to what extent her success was due to life's hard lessons. Surely the healer had to heal herself of many common wounds among emigrants: the separations, the difficulties of the new beginning, the bifurcation of paths between her and those who remained on the Canary Islands, the periodic news of the death of a relative who had not been seen again, the ever more prolonged silences....

"They never returned," Armas narrates (31). This in and of itself surely hurt. There were no reunions with the native land. If she felt nostalgia, Mercedes did not find relief in a temporary return. The wounds provoked by leaving, which are sometimes partially healed by returning, in her must have remained open.[27]

---

[27] Essay translated by Álex Omar Bratkievich.

Works Consulted

Allende, Isabel. *Mi país inventado*. Barcelona: Círculo de Lectores, 2003.

Armas, Dino. "Beach Day". *On the Scene with Migration and Dictatorship: An Interdisciplinary Approach to the Work of Uruguayan Playwright Dino Armas*. Dir. Gabriela Christie Toletti. Norfolk: New Dominion Press, 2018. 65-77.

---. "Entrevista en 'La Commedia'". Interview with Lorenna Esposito, Nicolás Paciello, and Alejandro Fleitas. September 2006. February 26, 2017 <http://dinoarmas.tripod.com/id17.html>.

---. "Juan y María; ayer." *Migración y dictadura en escena: Un acercamieto interdisciplinario a la obra del dramaturgo uruguayo Dino Armas*. Dir. Gabriela Christie Toletti. Norfolk: New Dominion Press, 2017. 9-11.

---. "Just Yesterday". *On the Scene with Migration and Dictatorship: An Interdisciplinary Approach to the Work of Uruguayan Playwright Dino Armas*. Dir. Gabriela Christie Toletti. Norfolk: New Dominion Press, 2018. 201-270.

---. "Present, Señorita". *On the Scene with Migration and Dictatorship: An Interdisciplinary Approach to the Work of Uruguayan Playwright Dino Armas*. Dir. Gabriela Christie Toletti. Norfolk: New Dominion Press, 2018. 103-121.

Barrera, Francisco. *Tratado sobre los cirujanos, médicos, boticarios, y falsedad de los curanderos*. Madrid: Imprenta de E. Aguado, 1822.

Barrios Pintos, Aníbal. *Montevideo: Los barrios (I)*. Nuestra Tierra 4. Ed. and dir. Daniel Aljanati. Montevideo: Editorial Nuestra Tierra, 1971.

Beretta Curi, Alcides. "Los hacedores de milagros: familias de inmigrantes italianos y empresariado industrial." *Historias de la vida privada en el Uruguay*. Dir. José Pedro Barrán, Gerardo Caetano, and Teresa Porzecanski. Vol. 2. Montevideo: Taurus, 1996. 278.

"Brujos del Cerro". *La República* [Montevideo] June 26, 2000. March 12, 2017 <http://www.lr21.com.uy/sociedad/14738-brujos-del-cerro>.

Cagiao Vila, Pilar. "Una perspectiva histórica de la emigración de las mujeres españolas". *Acogida – Cuaderno de la emigración española y el retorno* (June 2008): 2-5. March 8, 2017 <http://www.espanaexterior.com/upload/pdf/50-acogida4.pdf>.

Carbonero y Sol, León. "Comentario católico al proyecto de ley del llamado Matrimonio Civil (3)." *La Cruz – Revista religiosa de España y demás países católicos.* Vol. I. Madrid: 1870. 349-379.

Christie Toletti, Gabriela and Dino Armas. "Conversation on Life and Theater". *On the Scene with Migration and Dictatorship: An Interdisciplinary Approach to the Work of Uruguayan Playwright Dino Armas.* Dir. Gabriela Christie Toletti. Norfolk: New Dominion Press, 2018. 301-315.

Domestici, M.-J. et al. *Geopolítica y ayuda humanitaria.* Serie Ayuda Humanitaria, Textos básicos. Vol. 5. Bilbao: Universidad de Deusto, 1999.

Ferré, Gerstenbluth y Rossi. "Religión y religiosidad en Uruguay." Cited in: Porzecanski, Teresa. *El Uruguay religioso.* Montevideo: Nuestro Tiempo (MEC), 2014. 7, 17.

Hernández Pérez, María Victoria. "Ni solteras, ni casadas, ni viudas: las hijas canarias de Penélope en el siglo XX". *BienMeSabe* 669 (July 25, 2011). March 8, 2017 <http://www.bienmesabe.org/noticia/2011/Julio/ni-solteras-ni-casadas-ni-viudas-las-hijas-canarias-de-penelope-en-el-siglo-xx>.

La exposición-protesta de las damas uruguayas sobre enseñanza religiosa. Montevideo: Laurak-Bat, 1883.

Navas y Pérez, Tiburcio. "El curandero." *El pabellón médico: Revista científica y profesional de medicina, cirugía y farmacia* (Madrid) XI n. 478 (May 21, 1871): 225.

Pérez Vidal, José. *Contribución al estudio de la medicina popular canaria.* Santa Cruz de Tenerife/Las Palmas de Gran Canaria: Idea, 2007.

Ponce Marrero, José. "Canarias, Economía y Guerra: 1913-1920." *Aguayro* (Las Palmas de Gran Canaria) 204 (July/October 1993): 10-14.

Porrini Beracochea, Rodolfo, "Experiencia e identidad de la nueva clase obrera

uruguaya: la huelga frigorífica (montevideana) de enero de 1943."
História Unisinos (São Leopoldo, Rio Grande do Sul, Brazil) N° 6 (July-December 2002): 63-96.

Porzecanski, Teresa. *El Uruguay religioso*. Montevideo: Nuestro Tiempo (MEC), 2014.

Sánchez Pérez, José Augusto. *Supersticiones españolas*. Madrid: S.A.E.T.A., 1948.

Saratsola, Osvaldo. "Cinestrenos: El cine en Montevideo desde 1929." *UruguayTotal.com*. October 24, 2016 <http://www.uruguaytotal.com/estrenos/salas/salas_estreno8.htm>.

Turcatti, Dante y Marcelo de León. "Recovering the Identity of Neighbourhoods in Montevideo and the Interior, In and Since the Forties." *Communication Experience*. Gotenburgo: IX International Oral History Conference, 1996. 444-450.

Vidart, Daniel y Renzo Pi Hugarte. *El legado de los inmigrantes (II)*. Nuestra Tierra 39. Montevideo: Editorial Nuestra Tierra, 1969.

CHAPTER THREE
Uprooting and Memories of the Motherland

Memories of Playa Ramírez

Beach Day

Dino Armas

Translation by Gabriela Christie Toletti

Characters:

    Beba
    Nona
    Luisito
    Pedro
    Jhonny

(*The audience can see the characters dressed in shorts, cover-ups, and/or bathing suits. They start to display the following items: beach umbrella, beach blanket, cooler, fishing rod, pail, etc. Finally, they add a floor lamp without a shade, with only a lit lightbulb. When all these items are placed on the beach blanket, they all sigh with satisfaction in unison. All except BEBA.*)

Beba: Oh, the sand is hot… hot as can be… burning up!

Nona: (*Dressed in black from head to toes. Soft voice.*) Like you….

Beba: What did she say?

Pedro: You two, don't get started like you always do ….

Nona: To the beach one has to come prepared. For the wind, the sun, the jellyfish, and the sand… (*Looking at BEBA*)… hot sand.

Luisito: (*Talking to his father.*) What did grandma say? The sand is hot? In heat? (*He pants. Spasmodic gestures with one hand.*) What's that, Dad?

Pedro: Come on, Nona. Talking that way you already got the idiot going. Fix it, could you?

Nona: Look, Luisito. I meant that the sand, with so much sun on top …

Luisito: (*Repeats*): On top….

65

NONA: … It gets hot….

LUISITO: *(Repeats)*… hot….

NONA: Do you understand now?

LUISITO: Then, if the sun is on top, the sand is hot, in heat. Then, the sand is like people? Like when Mom and Dad…?

BEBA: You see, Nona? With so many weird explanations, you put ideas in the boy's head….

LUISITO: *(Scared.)* Mom, what does grandma want to put in me?

PEDRO: *(Putting on his head a hat that covers even his eyes.)* Nothing, idiot. Nothing. Play with your little pail.

BEBA: The idiot—I mean, the boy—has a name. Luisito, in case you don't remember.

NONA: *(Soft voice, talking to PEDRO.)* Ugh, "Luisito"… she didn't even name him Pedro like you. No one in our family is called Luis, and no one in hers either. Have you taken a good look at that kid?

PEDRO: Do you think she cheated on me?

NONA: Oh, I don't know. I was never under her bed.

BEBA: *(With the thermos in her hand. Stretching her arm.)* Who will go get some hot water?

PEDRO: You will, who else?

BEBA: Oh, no. I won't step on that hot sand again. You go!

PEDRO: No, not me! I work all week long, and on top of that I have to run errands today? The idiot should go.

BEBA: No, not him. What if he gets lost?

PEDRO: I wish.

NONA: It's OK, Pedrito. I will go. There is a reason why I came prepared.

(Shows her socks and sandals.) Hand me the bath towel, baby. *(PEDRO gives her the towel. She puts it on her head like some old ladies do at the beach. She exits. BEBA looks at her with hatred as she leaves.)*

BEBA: She is dressed as if she were going to the North Pole. People are going to think that we took some crazy person from Vilardebó[1] out for fresh air.

PEDRO: I forbid you to refer to my little old sainted Mom as crazy. *(Turns on the tape recorder. Sounds of a tango sung by Gardel.[2] He sings, whistles, or hums it.)* Sweet tango to dance to.

BEBA: Don't count me in. I never liked making a fool of myself.

LUISITO: Daddy…. Can you teach me to dance tango?

PEDRO: *(Happy.)* Why do you want to dance tango, kid? Because of the Uruguayan blood running through your veins?

LUISITO: *(Deep voice.)* Tango is like sand….

PEDRO: Like sand…. I don't understand….

LUISITO: *(With deeper voice.)* Tango is hot, it turns me on.

PEDRO: We'll have to keep our ears cocked with this kid. And does he already shave?

BEBA: Since he was nineteen. Ten years ago already. *(NONA enters.)*

NONA: Here's the hot water.

PEDRO: That's my sweet old Mom. *(He stretches his arms towards her and they intertwine in a tango dance with breaks. BEBA, trying to hide, puts on black glasses, looks away, and fans herself with a newspaper.)*

---

[1] Translator's Note: *Vilardebó* is a psychiatric hospital in Reducto, Montevideo, Uruguay. It opened in 1880 and it is named after the physician and naturalist Teodoro Vilardebó Matuliche.

[2] TN: Carlos Gardel (born Charles Romuald Gardes; (Dec. 11, 1890 - June 24, 1935), was a tango singer, songwriter, composer and actor, and the most prominent figure in the history of tango. There are three countries that claim him as their own: Uruguay, Argentina, and France. Some claim that he was born in France and that there was a French birth certificate in his name. But he had a Uruguayan passport that stated his birthplace as Tacuarembó, Uruguay. Argentina claims him as his own because it was there that he was raised and rose to stardom. His name is most often associated with the long tradition of tango music and dance of Argentina and Uruguay.

BEBA: Luisito, if someone comes and asks about them, you just tell them that you don't know them.

PEDRO: *(Caressing his mother.)* Who is Pedrito's sweet Mommy?

NONA: I am your sweet Mommy. Who is my baby boy?

PEDRO: I am! Oh, I feel like…. Please say something in Italian.

NONA: *Io sono la mafia.*[3] *(He cheers.)*

PEDRO: More, more.

NONA: *Mascalzone. Figlio di puttana. Io ti ammazzo.*[4] *(Cheerfully, he embraces her and takes the final steps of the tango. It ends with the mother making a* sentadita[5] *on his legs.)*

BEBA: *(Loud enough so that others around can hear.)* Luisito, those who see and hear them will say that we brought not one, but two crazy people out for some fresh air.

NONA: Don't call my son crazy.

PEDRO: Don't worry, my sweet Mom. Turn a deaf ear to stupid comments.

LUISITO: Mom…. What is this place called?

BEBA: Ramirez Beach….

PEDRO, NONA, LUISITO: *(Angry. Almost violently angry.)* Beba!

BEBA: What?

PEDRO: You said "Ramirez Beach" instead of *Playa Ramírez.*[6]

BEBA: Oh, well…. Anyone can make a mistake. It was a slip of the tongue.

PEDRO: *(Talking to NONA.)* A slip of the tongue, a slip. She'll do anything to ruin such a nice moment.

---

[3] TN: *Io sono la mafia.* Sentence in Italian. In English it means: I am the mafia.

[4] TN: *Mascalzone. Figlio de putana. Io ti ammazzo.* Expressions in Italian. In English the meaning is: "Scoundrel. Son of a bitch. I kill you."

[5] TN: *Sentadita* is a tango move in which the woman sits on the man's lap.

[6] TN: *Playa Ramírez* is Ramirez Beach in Spanish.

NONA: I told you so. I told you so since the minute you brought her home. "I don't like her. You deserve better," I said. And your deceased father also said the same. If he were alive, he wouldn't let me lie to you. He would be brutally honest.

BEBA: Why do you have to involve the dead? Why don't you let the dead rest in peace?

NONA: Oh, oh…. Did you see? She yelled at me, Pedro. She yelled at your mother. At me, at your mother. I'm the one who carried you in my womb; I'm your mother! She disrespected me. Aren't you going to do something?

PEDRO: *(With raised fist or finger.)* Look, Beba. You're going to make me lose it. And I know myself. I get angry and I can't control myself….

BEBA: *(Covers LUISITO's ears or pulls his hat down further.)* Shut up, Pedro. It's not good for the child to see and hear his parents arguing.

PEDRO: The child… that useless dumbass, you mean. He is almost thirty years old already.

BEBA: Thirty. He is thirty.

PEDRO: Twenty-nine or thirty is the same. Watch him with the pail. It's painful to watch. What a punishment from God to have a fool for a son.

BEBA: Punishment? It's not a punishment for me. I'm going with the baby to the shore. And if you want to drink *mate*,[7] she can pour the water. Come on, Luisito. *(They both exit.)*

NONA: *(Pouring hot water into his mate gourd. Sounds and looks intriguing.)* In our family we never had idiots. Pedro, have you taken a good look at his face?

PEDRO: Well, sure!

---

[7] TN: *Mate* is a traditional South American bitter infused drink, found particularly in Uruguay, Argentina, Paraguay, and Brazil. It is made by an infusion of dried leaves of the *yerba mate* plant. It contains the stimulants caffeine, theophylline, and theobromine, which are also found in tea, coffee, and chocolate. It is usually drunk with friends and served hot in a hollow calabash gourd with a special metal drinking straw called a *bombilla.*

NONA: Because I think he looks more and more like…. Every time I look at him he reminds me more and more of…. No. No, I shouldn't… I shouldn't tell you anything…. (*Trying to change the topic.*) Are there any sandwiches?

PEDRO: Yes, salami and mortadella. But don't change the subject. Keep talking to me.

NONA: Give me a salami sandwich. (*Playing dumb.*) What was I talking about?

PEDRO: You said that the idiot reminds you of someone. He must remind you of me!

NONA: No. You two are like oil and water. Take this. (*She hands him another sandwich, or her own sandwich.*) Some news should not be heard on an empty stomach.

PEDRO: I eat and you tell me, OK?

NONA: Swallow first. (*He does.*) Remember that you insisted I tell you, OK? Pedro, did you ever notice that the idiot looks just like the butcher?

PEDRO: (*With his mouth full.*) The butcher? What butcher?

NONA: The one who lived on the corner of our block. Coco was his name. Remember how many times your wife came home with a kilo of short ribs, a tip roast, a beef tenderloin…! Those must have been gifts from the butcher ….

PEDRO: You think, Mom?

NONA: Shh, shut up. The adulteress is returning with her bastard son. (*They stop talking and pretend they are just drinking* mate. *Awkward silence.*)

BEBA: What were you talking about?

NONA: About how crazy the weather is. How's the water?

BEBA: Very nice.

NONA: Is it cold? (*LUISITO is going to answer. BEBA stops him.*)

BEBA: Not at all. It's warm.

NONA: Any jellyfish? (*LUISITO tries to answer. BEBA doesn't let him.*)

BEBA: No.

NONA: Then I'm going to the water. I'll get a little wet and then come back. (*She turns back as she walks away.*) Oh, Pedro.... (*Making a gesture*)... Think about what I told you. Then you tell me. (*She exits.*)

BEBA: Your mother is acting strange....

PEDRO: Strange?

BEBA: She looks happy. She must be up to no good.

LUISITO: Mom... I'm hungry. (*She gives him a sandwich.*)

PEDRO: This one is always hungry. Who does he take after? Not me. I eat like a bird. Let's see, tell me kid, what's your favorite food?

LUISITO: *Milanesas.*[8]

PEDRO: (*Looking suspiciously at BEBA.*) Did you hear? He said *milanesas*. And what do you want to be when you grow up?

LUISITO: I want to be a....

PEDRO: No. It's better if you don't tell me. (*He whispers as he fixes his fishing rod.*) If he says he wants to be a butcher, I could walk into the water and keep going until I drown. (*Looking towards where NONA exited.*) What's that?

BEBA: (*Pointing scared.*) A shark! A shark![9]

PEDRO and JUIS: (*Looking at BEBA angrily.*) Again?

BEBA: (*Corrects herself.*) I meant to say: ¡*Un tiburón!*[10] ¡*Un tiburón!*

---

[8] TN: *Milanesa* is a South American variation of an Italian dish (in Italian *cotoletta alla milanese*) that consists of breaded thin slices of meat (beef, veal, chicken, etc.) The *milanesa* was brought to the Southern Cone by Italian immigrants during the mass emigration between 1860 and the 1920s. Beef *milanesa* is the most popular type in Uruguay. It is also similar to the Austrian *Wiener Schnitzel*.

[9] TN: The original play is in Spanish. When Beba uses English words the other characters get upset because by using English words she contributes to breaking the mood of being in Uruguay.

[10] TN: *Tiburón* is shark in Spanish.

PEDRO: Where?

BEBA: That black thing hovering over the water....

PEDRO: Is that Mommy drowning? (*Exits running.*)

BEBA: I have such bad luck, I bet they'll take her out of the water alive. That old woman is like a cat. She has nine lives. (*NONA and PEDRO enter. He is scolding her. Strangely, her clothes are dry.*)

PEDRO: But what were you doing in the water up to your neck?

NONA: The water was freezing, and I got a cramp.

PEDRO: And why didn't you scream?

NONA: I wanted to, sure. But I opened my mouth and it filled up with jellyfish. I could only make signals.

BEBA: Oh, the problem with Playa Ramírez is that it changes from one moment to the next. Now the water is warm, and then suddenly it gets cold. No jellyfish and then all of a sudden, jellyfish.

NONA: I brought this for the baby.

LUISITO: What is it, Nona? Let me see; give it to me.

NONA: *Una concha*[11]. (*LUISITO turns his eyes and begins to shake. She puts the shell in his hands.*)

BEBA: Why not use the correct name? You brought *una almeja.*[12]

NONA: In Spain they call it *concha*. (*LUISITO sits with his back to the audience. He manipulates the clam making strange gestures.*)

BEBA: But here we are not in Spain. We are here in.... (*Stops.*) We are in Playa Ramírez, in Montevideo. (*Looking at LUISITO.*) But what are you doing, Luisito? You're not supposed to put it there. Here, you can just hold it against your ear...

---

[11] TN: *Concha* means conch or sea-shell. In Uruguay, Argentina, and some other Latin American countries *concha* is a slang word for female genitals. Depending on the context, it can (although not always) be an offensive word similar to *cunt* in English.

[12] TN: *Almeja* is "clam" in English.

LUISITO: My ear? (*He tries to stick it in his ear with jerky movements.*)

BEBA: (*To NONA.*) See what you get? Boy, give me that *concha…* that *almeja*. Mom will keep it for you.

LUISITO: (*Pouting.*) No. I don't want to. Baby doesn't want to.

NONA: (*To PEDRO.*) Look at that profile. He looks like a portrait of the butcher.

BEBA: Ok, you can have it. But don't put it anywhere in your… anywhere.

PEDRO: (*Looking at Luis and talking to NONA.*) Luckily I have another son. Juancito didn't turn out dumb.

NONA: But your other son… that one is really yours, but he is not normal either. He looks down on us. He thinks he's different from us. We can't even call him by his name—Juancito. He wants to be called Jhonny.

PEDRO: Do you think that he really is like that? That he is not going to change?

NONA: Deep down, I hope; but…. Weren't you going to fish?

PEDRO: I don't feel like it anymore.

NONA: What a pity. I wanted to eat fried fish. (*Pause. No one speaks. Everyone sighs deeply facing forward.*)

BEBA: I like to look at the color of the water of the Río de la Plata[13]…. There is a reason why they call it the "lion-colored river"….

PEDRO: And the smell? That mix of salt and iodine….

NONA: And the sun… you can almost touch the sun here….

LUISITO: And the sky? It has the colors of the flag: sky blue and white…. (*They

---

[13] TN: *Río de la Plata* (literally: "River of Silver") is translated as "River Plate" in British English and the Commonwealth and "La Plata River" (Occasionally "Plata River") in other English-speaking countries. It is formed by the confluence of the Uruguay and Panamá rivers and empties into the Atlantic Ocean. Depending on the geographer, the Río de la Plata may be considered a river, an estuary, or a marginal sea. In Uruguay and Argentina it is usually considered a river and therefore the widest river in the world with a maximum width of 140 miles.

all sigh in unison.) And the shells… these here are unique. (*JHONNY enters breaking this idyllic atmosphere. He is wearing yankee-type clothes.*)

JHONNY: Not again, all of you with that same thing?

BEBA: Juancito… Come to the beach with us.

JHONNY: Jhonny, mother. Please call me Jhonny. And there's no beach! Stop this nonsense. You are in the middle of the living room of our house in Sydney.

PEDRO: He burst the bubble again.

JHONNY: When are you going to quit this Third-World therapy? You have to stop harping on *el paisito*[14]….

BEBA: (*Almost crying and wiping away a tear.*) But doesn't it break your heart when you think about Dieciocho de Julio[15]?

JHONNY: No. Because here I have Oxford Street. You cannot compare it with the boredom of Dieciocho de Julio.

PEDRO: And if I tell you, "the Mercosur[16] building"? Look, think: Montevideo, the Mercosur Capital.

JHONNY: (*Laughing.*) Then I tell you "the General Government house, the Admiralty House".

BEBA: And don't you feel nostalgic for el Teatro Solís,[17] our first coliseum?

JHONNY: Miss that, having the Sydney Opera House?

---

[14] TN: (From the translator of the essays) *El paisito* (literally "the little country") is diminutive of *país* which means country in Spanish. *El paisito* is an affectionate term used by Uruguayans to refer to their motherland.

[15] TN: Dieciocho de Julio (literally: "July 18th") is the name of the most important avenue in Montevideo. It crosses the downtown and other neighborhoods. It is not the widest or longest avenue in Montevideo but the best known as a commercial center and for important landmarks along its length. It is named after the first Constitution of Uruguay which was written on July 18th, 1830.

[16] TN: *Mercosur* is the acronym for *Mercado Común del Sur* (Southern Common Market). It is a sub-regional bloc founded in 1991 with headquarters in Montevideo, Uruguay. Its purpose is to promote free trade and the fluid movement of goods, people, and currency. Its full members are Argentina, Brazil, Paraguay, and Uruguay.

[17] TN: Teatro Solís (Solís Theater), which opened in 1856, is Uruguay's most important and renowned theater. It is located in Montevideo's Old Town.

LUISITO: And Parque Rodó[18]? You don't like Parque Rodó? With its Ferris wheel and the bumper cars....

JHONNY: Oh, come on, that little piece-of-shit park can't ever beat Centennial Park.

NONA: And Santa Lucía Bridge? They just finished it and it looks beautiful, beautiful.

JHONNY: Then I say, Sydney Harbour Bridge, which has been on TV everywhere, but Santa Lucía, who has ever heard of that bridge?

NONA: I have.

PEDRO: And I have too.

BEBA: And me too.

LUISITO: And how about me?

JHONNY: You four are four whiners.

PEDRO: (*Gesticulates to the others.*) Leave it to me. This can't fail. (*Walks forward. Looks into JHONNY's eyes and says with great emphasis.*) Estadio Centenario.[19]

JHONNY: (*Immediately, without any hesitation.*) Sydney Cricket Ground, or the SCG, whichever way you want to call it.

PEDRO: Uruguayan soccer....

JHONNY: (*Immediately, without any hesitation.*) Australian football. (*JHONNY, louder and louder, and PEDRO softer and softer.*)

PEDRO: The fierce fighting spirit of *la garra charrúa.*[20]

---

[18] TN: Parque Rodó (literally: "Rodó Park") is the name of both a neighborhood and a park in Montevideo. Apart from the main park area, *Parque Rodó* includes an amusement park. The characters in this play refer to the amusement park area. The name *Rodó* was given in memory of *José Enrique Rodó*, an important Uruguayan writer whose monument is in the southern part of the main park.

[19] TN: Estadio Centenario (literally: "Centenary Stadium") is the best known stadium in Montevideo, Uruguay, used primarily for soccer. It was built between 1929 and 1930.

[20] TN: *La garra Charrúa* (literally: "the claw of the Charrúa") refers to the ferocity and fighting spirit of the Charrúa indigenous people. That tenacity has been embraced as a national spirit by Uruguayans.

JHONNY: Ticker: heart, old man… tick-tick-tock… tock….

PEDRO: Nacional….[21]

JHONNY: Sydney Swans….

PEDRO: Peñarol…

JHONNY: Melbourne Demons….

PEDRO: (*In a desperate last attempt.*) Our mascots! *El charrúa del Mundialito!*[22] *La Vaca de Rocha.*[23]

JHONNY: Kangaroos, koalas. (*PEDRO lowers his arms in defeat.*)

BEBA: Let it go, man. He is lost.

JHONNY: Do you know what all of you are? Some disgusting spics.

PEDRO: I disown you. You are no longer my son. You're a xenophobe.

LUISITO: (*With the clam in his hand.*) A xenophobe in heat.

JHONNY: Bye, everyone. And take that crap out of the living room and put back the computers and twenty-inch televisions. Ridiculous. Oh! And think about this. Uruguay is so Third-World that the New Year starts here in Australia first. You are so backwards. You are such babbling idiots. (*Exits.*)

PEDRO: (*Rebellious. Comes forward with a raised fist.*) We won't take anything out, and that's it! We will not move!

BEBA: You're right, old man. (*They hug.*)

PEDRO: (*Kissing her forehead.*) Thank you, partner.

---

[21]   TN: Nacional and Peñarol are the two most popular first division soccer teams in Uruguay.

[22]   TN: *El charrúa del Mundialito* was the Uruguayan mascot and logo of a special international soccer tournament held in Uruguay in 1980-1981. El Mundialito (literally "Little World Cup") was held in commemoration of the 50th anniversary of the first World Cup Tournament, which took place in 1930 in Uruguay.

[23]   TN: *La vaca de Rocha* (literally "Cow of Rocha"). The famous Vaca de Rocha was a real cow, mascot, and good luck charm for the second professional division Rocha soccer team named Rocha Fútbol Club, from the city of Rocha, Uruguay, in the homonym department. La Vaca de Rocha walked into the Mario Sobrero Stadium in 2005 when the Rocha Fútbol Club won a championship by defeating Rampla Juniors soccer team.

NONA: (*Joins the family group.*) At least we have the idiot.

PEDRO: He is a real Uruguayan. Should we dress him with everything we brought? (*The women nod and the three rush to dress him in the blue poncho, something from the Frente Amplio[24], a hat from Nacional or Peñarol; and they put in his hand a Uruguayan flag that the boy waves back and forth. The women embrace and step away to look at him fondly. PEDRO steps back visibly moved. He stands in the middle. He prepares a gesture, perhaps the hand forming the "V" for victory or a clenched fist, and with a faltering hoarse voice cries.*) Uruguay… ¡¡¡*Viejo y peludo, nomás!!!*"[25]

THE END

---

[24]   TN: Frente Amplio (literally "Broad Front") is a Uruguayan center-left to left-wing coalition of political parties. It was founded in 1971; it was declared illegal during the 1973 *coup d'état*, but it emerged again in 1984 when democracy was restored in Uruguay. It has been the governing coalition of Uruguay since 2004.

[25]   TN: *Viejo y peludo, nomás* (literally "Just old and hairy") is an expression that is used in Uruguay and Argentina to encourage someone, to show approval, or to cheer. It can be used for example in soccer games to encourage and support soccer players or a team. Similar to: "Go, Uruguay, go!" or "Long Live Uruguay!"

Back to the Past

Álvaro Loureiro

Everything looks like the typical summer outing of a Montevidean family, whose five members are sketched by Dino Armas in the hues of a costumbrist comedy with occasional grotesque shades. It is true that, on one hand, *Beach Day*'s characters never stop naming well-known places in Montevideo, such as Playa Ramírez[1] (located near the downtown area), Hospital Vilardebó (such an elegant name for a psychiatric hospital!),[2] Parque Rodó,[3] Avenida 18 de Julio,[4] and Estadio Centenario.[5] It is equally true that there can be no omission of references to the name of iconic tango artist Carlos Gardel[6] or the strength of the mythical *garra charrúa*[7] that gives Uruguay an air of eternal champion—even if it is only in soccer—and helps its inhabitants tolerate the bad times. On the other hand, the insertion of some Italian terms cannot be missing either, given the heritage of a good number of Uruguayans, who—little wonder—often call their grandmothers "Nona."

Between the quotidian features of the conversation between husband and wife, their two sons—so wittily differentiated—and the scheming grandmother, slip through some aggressive words and incidents. The playwright uses them to create delightful connections for the reader/spectator to uncover, not only with grotesque style but also with the most sophisticated absurdism and even a certain surrealism. None of this is gratuitous, since the beach foray of this very typical Montevidean family of past decades holds in reserve a sudden plot twist used by Armas to conjure memories of the recession that propelled a considerable

---

[1] Translator's Note: "Ramírez Beach."
[2] TN: Montevideo's main psychiatric hospital.
[3] TN: "Rodó Park." An urban park (which includes an artificial lake, an amusement park, a theater stage) located next to Playa Ramírez, close to the city's downtown.
[4] TN: "18th of July Avenue." Montevideo's main downtown avenue.
[5] TN: "Centenary Stadium." Montevideo's main soccer stadium, built for the first ever World Cup in 1930. Its name celebrates the hundredth anniversary of Uruguay's first Constitution.
[6] TN: The most iconic of tango singers in the Río de la Plata region (1887-1935).
[7] TN: "Charruan courage." The Charrua were one of the tribes living in what is now Uruguay before the Spanish invasion. They fiercely resisted colonization and assimilation until their extermination by the independent Uruguayan government in 1831. Ironically, Uruguayans refer to themselves as having "garra charrúa."

number of Uruguayans to pack, leave, and attempt to settle in such faraway places as the U.S., Spain, and Australia. It is worthwhile to find out the precise aim with which the author alludes to all this.[8]

Nostalgias: Brief Essay on *Beach Day*

María del Carmen Montañés Tejera

A Personal Note: Introduction

In 1987 I had the privilege of meeting Dino Armas, author of commendable relevance in Uruguayan dramaturgy, who, when asked by the also-renowned theater director Gustavo A. Ruegger, did not hesitate in heeding the call of two unknown literature teachers at the Liceo Departamental de Maldonado,[1] Mirella Izquierdo, and the writer of this text.

Being passionate about theater, we had set ourselves the goal of creating a hall suitable for this type of performance and tenaciously alternated teaching with the refurbishment of a great assembly hall (almost fallen into disuse by then), at the same time as we encouraged a group of students to take their first steps onto the stage.

Armas understood the effort, the enthusiasm, and the dream of these teachers who were determined to allow a group of very young pupils to express their experiences in front of an audience through gestures, words, movement, tears, or laughter. He wrote a play for them based on texts by Molière and Shakespeare, which he titled *Te quiero, che....*[2] The author left aside his renown so as to support a dream that was developing by fits and starts, but which became a reality with his unconditional support, rewarded only with the audience's applause and the satisfaction of the novice actors.

Today, at 87 years old and with the same love of theater as always, I feel happy to have been included in this beautiful volume of deserved recognition of Armas' work, and I am gratified by the mere fact of knowing that age does not matter to making a dream come true: in this case, that of publicly recognizing once more Armas' generosity and telling him, "Thank you, Dino, thank you for that *Te quiero, che....*"

---

[1] Translator's Note: "Departmental High School of Maldonado."
[2] TN: "I Love You, Pal...."

Beach Day

Armas' characters are life itself. With their defects or virtues, their laughter or tears, realities or fantasies, love or hate, they are… what life is: an accumulation of opposite and conflicting emotions. And the author catapults them onto the wonderful world of the dramatic stage.

Beach Day is a brief play that prompts reflection, even in the passages that provoke laughter. Its plurality of themes (intertwined in a natural and sometimes almost imperceptible way) undoubtedly captivates even the most demanding audience member.

The *mise-en-scène* sparks our interest from the very beginning, since the characters themselves are the ones who, dressed in summery clothing and in plain view of the audience, start placing on stage the elements that re-create what without a doubt will be the setting of a family beach day.

Everything seems simple and normal until they add a floor lamp—without a shade but with the light on—that appears to preside over this sort of beach camp. That is when the first questions arise: What does the author want to express? What does that lamp on the beach suggest: is it a glimmer of hope in the face of something we do not know about yet, but will be performed later? Perhaps something does not match reality? Are we dealing with an example of the theater of the absurd? These are questions without answers yet.

Sensuality

Already installed on the beach blanket, a traditional family composed of father, mother, grandmother, and grandson starts a conversation through which the author unravels, in a natural, spontaneous, and frank way, various topics that flow almost inadvertently.

One of them is eroticism, first insinuated by the grandmother (the character one would least expect it from) when talking, upset, about "hot sand." Luisito, the son with mental disabilities, absorbs with interest his grandmother's comments and asks, gesticulates, wants to know, and even compares the "hot sand" with his parents' matrimonial intimacy (65-66). An interesting word game thus ensues in which the young man's misinterpretation prompts the intervention of his mother (Beba).

At one point, Beba explains to her husband, Pedro, that their son's name is not "idiot" but "Luisito" (66). Sharp and methodical, Armas subtly introduces a new topic, the derogatory manner of a father towards his disabled son—the first manifestation of domestic mistreatment and abuse within this family (we will return to this point later).

Infidelity

Since everything is finely woven in this play, this is the moment in which the author has been preparing to introduce us to another topic: marital infidelity. Nona, cold and sarcastic witness of Pedro's indifference towards Luisito, listens to and watches the young man closely, then takes advantage of the precise moment to make mordant comments to her son: Luisito does not look like him at all, her daughter-in-law did not even name him Pedro, nobody in her or his family is called Luis…. The slanderous character of the old woman and the influence she exerts on Pedro, interwoven well in the plot, unleash the beginnings of suspicion in Pedro.

The image of the disabled son is like a puppet that the grandmother manipulates with the strings of her malicious insinuations when she suggests to Pedro that the "idiot's" face reminds her of the butcher's. The creative genius of the author slowly transforms the incipient doubt from the preceding moment into a humiliating accusation as Nona, bluntly, points to her daughter-in-law as the "adulteress" (70).

The passiveness and self-restraint that Pedro shows draw our attention; he only expresses (and without becoming angry) a minimum of interest in the truth through a conversation (trivial, given the underlying issue) with Luisito, a conversation that is interrupted and dropped for the remainder of the play.

Family Tensions

Without doubt, Armas' rich theatrical career allows him to go in depth into the virtues or defects, goodness or hate of ordinary people. Thus he outlines with acuity the generational and affective gap between mother-in-law and daughter-in-law. Beba criticizes Nona, calls her "crazy" (67), is ashamed of her warm clothes on the beach, and is upset by her relationship with Pedro. On the other hand, Nona never misses a chance to criticize (and we might even say infringe upon) the values that, in spite of her, her daughter-in-law may have.

Armas divests his characters of all artifice: they flow naturally, they are as their counterparts in daily life would be. In this play, as in others, they do not act according to the theories and ideas of the author, but as they would in real life were they actual people: Nona and Beba cannot stand each other; Pedro favors his mother; while Luisito watches, learns, and acts according to what his disability allows.

Abuse

The playwright very skillfully outlines his characters and stealthily leads us to other topics, such as gender violence. The topic grows gradually, but it starts with the apparently insubstantial comment made by Beba to Luisito that they are on "Ramírez Beach" (68). These two words infuriate the young man, Pedro, and Nona. The latter—quick-witted and cunning—takes advantage of the opportunity to criticize his son for his choice of wife. Through the nuances of this argument, Armas escalates the altercation to a verbal and gestural threat by an already-furious Pedro.

Gender violence, terribly robust and still existing in Uruguay's contemporary society, is a recurring theme in Armas' dramaturgy. In *Present, Señorita*, for example, the main character even boasts of the blows her father would inflict on her mother. In *Sea Murmur*, Santiago routinely assaults his wife. Armas' wit shows, without stridency or wordy expositions but also without circumlocution, the social reality in which we live.

Mistreatment

Back to *Beach Day*, in order for Luisito not to hear the argument, which includes the father's threat of physical assault towards the mother, the latter protects him by covering his ears. He is a 29-year-old man whom she calls "boy" or "baby" and the father "dumbass" (69) or, as before, "idiot." This exchange is part of a deeply rooted and painful topic: the father's indifference and lack of affection towards the different son (in this case, different from the cognitively normal Jhonny).

Pedro's indifference becomes evident in his ignorance of his son's exact age.

With regard to the lack of affection, we have already mentioned Pedro's scornful treatment, which will continue throughout the play (Pedro goes as far as to say, "Luckily I have another son" [73]). It will only change slightly in the end, for his own sake, when he realizes that he needs his despised offspring as a symbol of his beloved Uruguay. At this point, he supports Nona's words with actions, which contradict what he himself expressed earlier, "At least we have the idiot" (77).

Nostalgia

Armas guardedly places a little mystery within the dramatic action when the grandmother returns from her bath in the sea but, "[s]*trangely, her clothes are dry*" (72). It is a foreshadowing of the events that explore what, all in all, can be considered one of the most important topics in the play: the immigrant's nostalgia.

We are introduced to it almost without realizing, but for the characters it has as much presence as the sensations evoked by a landscape, even one that only exists in their memories. Engrossed now in a peaceful chat, they allude to the "lion-colored" waters of the Río de la Plata, to its smell which is a "mix of salt and iodine," to the sun which "you can almost touch," to the sky that has the light-blue and white colors of the flag (73) and not the other way around (as if they meant that Uruguay is so special that even nature adapts to it), recollections that culminate in a collective sigh.

Suddenly, the spell of the idyllic moment is broken with the appearance of Jhonny, the other son, the "normal" one, who will be in charge of the great revelation: the beach setting is unarguably false—it is only the made-up living room of their house—and the family's actions, as he asserts contemptuously, a "Third-World therapy" (74).

The author has been pointing out to the audience, nimbly and gradually, timeless topics. At this point, he finally changes the focus to emigration and longing for the *paisito* (affective form used by Uruguayans to refer to their country, which, in Jhonny's lines, can be interpreted both genuinely and sarcastically). The presence of these topics among the others hints at the fact that, except for expatriation itself, the emigrant essentially goes through the same joys and sorrows as her fellow country-people in her land of origin.

85

Jhonny is the antithesis of the other family members since, willingly or not, he has made his home in the country where they had to emigrate (they are in Australia, more precisely in Sydney). He has his feet on the ground, he knows that they can live better there, and, in a sort of question-and-answer table tennis match with the family, he explains the reasons for his viewpoint, based on comfort and the natural, technical, and cultural wonders that can be enjoyed in Australia.

But the other family members do not want to or cannot resign themselves to this, and their emotional conflict leads them to highlight the iconic places of their distant Montevideo (Avenida 18 de Julio,[3] Parque Rodó,[4] Estadio Centenario,[5] the bridge over the Santa Lucía River[6]) and, in short, everything that still ties them to their homeland. They unavoidably come up against his drastic, precise, and appreciative replies about what they are able to enjoy where they are now.

Perhaps many will find Jhonny presumptuous, smug, and insensitive, and they will think that, in emphasizing the beauty and advancements of his new land, he is devaluing the ones from his native land. Nevertheless, if we speculate about the motives this family had for emigrating, it is possible to take up the cudgel for him. We consider that perhaps he is not cold and indifferent, but rather wants his family to react and adapt to the place that took them in. He feels this way possibly because he knows or intuits that they have forgotten the dire reality that forced them to abandon the country, leaving behind an entire life history. The pain of emigration is so intense that they go as far as to fabricate a collective fantasy, which suggests that they saw themselves forced to emigrate as the result of a desperate situation.

With pragmatic skill, the playwright has been leading the reader or audience member to reflect on current realities of our society and consider that many times, dazzled by a glimmer of hope—even an imperfect one, like the lamp in the living room—we come to a halt and fail to act.

This strengthens the point made at the beginning: *Beach Day* is a play that prompts reflection. How many women and how many men have had to endure

---

3   TN: "18th of July Avenue." Montevideo's main downtown avenue.
4   TN: "Rodó Park." An urban park (which includes an artificial lake, an amusement park, and a theater stage) located next to Playa Ramírez, close to the city's downtown.
5   TN: "Centenary Stadium." Montevideo's main soccer stadium, built for the first-ever World Cup in 1930. Its name celebrates the hundredth anniversary of Uruguay's first Constitution.
6   TN: The Santa Lucía River marks the westernmost border of the department of Montevideo, where Uruguay's homonymous capital city is located. The bridge referred to in the play was inaugurated in 2005 and replaced an older structure.

being uprooted from their family? How many parents have said goodbye to children who had to leave because they understood that the political, social, and economic reality of their country was, and still is, a mask that hides incompetence or intolerance? I understand Jhonny. I have lived much and I believe I can intuitively sense his inner conflict. But Pedro cannot.

In a last attempt at forced persuasion, and in some kind of counterpoint to induce in Jhonny the feeling that "break[s] their heart" (74), the father focuses on sport. Not on just any sport, but soccer, which at least in the Río de la Plata region tends to fill a bigger role than mere entertainment. When personal or national reality frustrates or disappoints, soccer provides both escapism and catharsis; it unifies beyond political parties (and, in a way, even beyond social classes) and temporarily allows the forgetting of present problems ("bread and soccer" would be the Uruguayan equivalent to Juvenal's phrase). Surely it is because of this national unifying value that Pedro brings up soccer, almost in desperation, in a litany of references well known to any Uruguayan: Estadio Centenario, *la garra charrúa*,[7] Nacional,[8] Peñarol,[9] the mascots, *el charrúa del Mundialito*,[10] and *la vaca de Rocha*[11] (76)—the only reference missing is the Maracanazo.[12]

Perhaps the vivid memories of the father and the passionate enumeration of soccer references causes an unsettling duality in the boy, a painful and difficult doubt. But even if that is the case, the reality and tangibility of the present comfort are stronger. His replies, therefore, are firm, concise, downplaying, and end with the merciless comment: "And take that crap out of the living room and put back the computers and the twenty-inch televisions. Ridiculous" (76). With these words, Jhonny actually levels an accusation of hypocrisy at his relatives,

---

[7] TN: "Charruan courage." The Charrua were one of the tribes living in what is now Uruguay before the Spanish invasion. They fiercely resisted colonization and assimilation until their extermination by the independent Uruguayan government in 1831. Ironically, Uruguayans refer to themselves as having "garra charrúa."

[8] TN: One of the two main soccer teams in Montevideo.

[9] TN: The other main soccer team in Montevideo.

[10] TN: The official mascot of the 1980 Mundialito (literally, "Little World Cup"), a special soccer tournament held in Montevideo to celebrate the 50th anniversary of the first World Cup.

[11] TN: In 2005, for the first time a soccer team which was not from Montevideo won the National Cup. The Rocha Football Club was a team from the homonymous city which adopted as their mascot a cow that used to graze close to the place where they would train. When, against everyone's expectations, they won the National Cup, they paraded the cow around the stadium and took it along with the team to Montevideo to the medal ceremony. The episode is remembered as an emblem of the "small" team that managed to win.

[12] TN: In the 1950 World Cup final, Uruguay beat Brazil at Estádio do Maracanã in Rio de Janeiro. Since Brazil only needed a draw to win the World Cup whereas Uruguay needed to win the match, and the game happened on Brazil's own turf, Uruguay was clearly not the expected winner. The upset is remembered to this day by soccer fans worldwide.

who weep from nostalgia and yet do not return to Uruguay, because in the end they know that it is not the best solution if they aspire to enjoy the advantages of their current standard of living.

Jhonny's arrival has sped up the fast and sharp dialogue of this multifaceted play even more, and has caused the characters to define their own feelings and to show how they have taken one of two different stands in the face of the same challenge of emigration: one, nostalgically creating an escapist fantasy; the other, being harshly realistic.

Through his behavior, his feelings, and the conviction in his words that can get insulting (he brands them as "disgusting spics" [76]), Jhonny has let his family know that he already feels completely Australian and that the true foreigners are his parents. This explains Pedro's broadside: "You are no longer my son. You're a xenophobe" (76). Pedro, then, defeated, goes as far as to repudiate his son before declaring his longing for his birth country. Even after the arguments have run out, his nostalgia is left intact and almost deified, since the rejection of his son resembles a believer's repudiation of an apostate. He feels that the boy has abandoned his roots to such an extent that he accuses him of being a xenophobe despite the incriminated being a foreigner; the apostate has been accused not only of being such but also of persecuting his parents' faith.

This father who is trapped in the memories of his land, however, has not examined—not even understood—the likely true intentions of the son: to ease the difficulties of adaption to the new land, to shake off the sorrow tied to the idea that "there is nothing like Uruguay"[13] (implicit in Beba, Nona, Luisito, and Pedro's defense), and to assimilate without nostalgia since, as the Spanish poet Antonio Machado said, "the path is made by walking"[14] ("Proverbios y Cantares," in *Campos de Castilla*, 1912).

The symbolism in the set design, wordlessly depicting the longing for the homeland, can be touching, from the lamp without a shade (the nostalgia that is not concealed?) and the lit light bulb (the sun on the beach? the hope of returning?) on the made-up beach, to the sky-blue poncho, the sports cup, the little Uruguayan flag, and the emotional embrace of the characters joined by the memory of what they left behind. It all culminates in the father's hoarse

---

[13]   TN: In Spanish, *como el Uruguay no hay*. Phrase oft-repeated by Uruguayans both in the country and abroad.

[14]   TN: In the sense that the path is made as you go.

and faltering outburst when evoking his *paisito*: "*Uruguay... ¡¡¡viejo y peludo, nomás!!!*"[15] (77).

Pedro's scream, which closes the play, resembles the grunt of an overpowered animal that has lost his territory to a younger one. Beba's "You're right, old man" can be interpreted as a compassionate gesture of affection or as confirmation that age has caught up with her husband and has taken away his position in the hierarchy. Perhaps for this reason Pedro, who before threatened to hit his wife, now puts her on the same level as himself by calling her "partner" (76). The roles have reversed to such a point that the father is "[r]ebellious" (76) towards the son and not vice versa.

The collapse of Pedro as a strong man makes him cling even more—out of sincere attachment or obstinacy—to one of the few things that holds him up after losing the dialectical battle with Jhonny. Ironically, what holds him up is the same thing that has destroyed the integrity of the family: the exacerbated nostalgia and the refusal to assimilate to the adopted country. Jhonny is the only one who does not participate in the fantasy of Playa Ramírez; Jhonny is the only one who distances himself from the family. What neither infidelity nor mistreatment nor domestic violence could achieve is accomplished by the uprooting effect of emigration. As was said before, everything is finely woven together.

Closing

As in some of his other plays, Armas makes it possible for past and present situations in the lives of Uruguayans to be placed in an artistic context and to prompt reflection in the audience.... *Beach Day* touches upon and explores universal topics ranging from erotism to chauvinist patriotism. Many of them constitute lateral ways (suitable to having a life of their own) out of a main thematic avenue that the audience member or reader traverses throughout the plot, imperceptibly in the beginning, and more overtly later. This "18 de Julio" (to use one of Beba's references) can have more than one name: Uruguay, emigration, uprooting, longing, nationalism, integration, roots, family....

---

[15]   TN: Literally "Uruguay... old and hairy, yeah!!!" In this context, *nomás* (literally "nothing more") is an expression used in Latin American Spanish for emphatic purposes. The *viejo y peludo* phrase is used to encourage or cheer someone; therefore, the pragmatic meaning of the phrase is similar to ¡*Viva Uruguay!* or "Long live Uruguay!"

Armas is characterized by his open endings, which do not answer all the questions he raises, but encourage the readers or audience members to answer them on their own. Thus, the play grows on its own, separate from the playwright, fed by the personal experiences of those who come into contact with it. Does the final scene challenge exaggerated nationalism? Do Nona's aggressive words in Italian, masked by affectionate gestures, show rancor against Pedro, who perhaps dragged her to Australia, forcing her to experience a second uprooting? Does Jhonny's Yankee clothing in Australia reveal some inner confusion in a young man adrift between the world he knew (Uruguay), the one where he lives his daily life (Australia), and a third (the U.S.) which is perceived by many as an ideal emigration destination?

A bigger question revolves in the background and crystallizes towards the end. In the play, Beba poses the question regarding a specific point and directs it towards her son, but it transcends both the addressee within the play and the emigration frame of reference to reach the audience, evoking any aspect of life capable of generating memories: "And don't you feel nostalgic […]?" (74).[16]

---

[16]   Essay translated by Álex Omar Bratkievich.

Metadrama with Family:
Cultural Identity and Group Dynamics in *Beach Day*

Gabriela Christie Toletti

In *Beach Day*, Dino Armas uses highly effective metadramatic techniques to show the difficulties of adapting to a new country and to the identity conflicts caused by emigration. The goal of this essay is to examine these conflicts and the survival strategies developed to cope with emigration, as well as the family dynamics of the play's characters.

At the beginning of the play, a family appears to be at Montevideo's Playa Ramírez.[1] Their clothing and the objects surrounding them transport us there. We feel like we are in Uruguay because of the distinctly Uruguayan variety of Spanish spoken by the characters (e.g., the use of *vos* instead of *tú* as a second person singular pronoun), the customs of the Río de la Plata region (drinking *mate*, eating regional food: mortadella sandwiches and *milanesas*, and listening to tango), and the references to other Uruguayan places (e.g., the mental hospital Vilardebó).

For most of the play, we are watching the interaction of Pedro, Beba, Nona, and Luisito. We meet, then, three generations: Nona (the grandmother, of Italian ancestry), Pedro (Nona's son), Beba (Pedro's wife), and Luisito (Pedro and Beba's son). Luisito seems to have a mental disability and acts like a child in spite of his 29 years. Later, Beba and Pedro's other son, Jhonny, will appear on stage.

Even though initially everything points to the characters being on the beach in Montevideo, some incongruities give us clues that suggest something different. For example, together with the ordinary beach items (umbrella, mat, fishing rod, etc.), there is also a floor lamp. Another curious detail is that when Beba says "Ramírez Beach" instead of "Playa Ramírez" (68) and "shark" instead of "tiburón" (71), the others get upset, and Beba apologizes for using English words. In addition, it is mentioned that Nona comes back from the water with dry clothes.

Later, when Jhonny appears, we understand the reason for these apparent incongruities. We find out that, actually, they are not on Playa Ramírez but in

---

[1]   Translator's Note: "Ramírez Beach."

the living-room of their house in Sydney, Australia, role playing an "enjoyable" family beach day at Playa Ramírez.

It is clear, then, that the entire play is full of metadrama or drama-within-the-drama. Richard Hornby, in his book *Drama, Metadrama, and Perception*, defined "metadrama" thus: "Briefly, metadrama can be defined as drama about drama; it occurs whenever the subject of a play turns out to be, in some sense, drama itself" (31). Hornby identifies five varieties of metadrama: play within the play, ceremony within the play, role playing within the role, literary and real-life references, and self-reference (32). The different types of metadrama rarely occur in an isolated way; on the contrary, they generally appear intertwined, as it happens in *Beach Day* (in particular, the first three types are the most clearly identifiable in the play).

The characters repeatedly carry out this game of role playing a beach day in Montevideo. The scene on Playa Ramírez is, then, a case of role playing within the main play, which is set in Sydney. This situation corresponds to Hornby's first type of metadrama: the play within the play.

In examples of this type, the main play works as a frame in which the secondary play is inset. According to Hornby, in the past the main and the secondary plays were clearly delineated (47). In contemporary theater, on the contrary, it is more difficult to determine which the frame is and which the central figure within the frame or background is. The borders are diffuse, as happens in *Beach Day*. After watching the entire play, we could think that what happens in Sydney is the frame and that the Playa Ramírez role playing is the secondary play within the main one. However, that would entail that the play is named after the secondary play.... In fact, we have here a gestaltic game in which figure and ground can be alternately perceived because they can be reversed over and over.[2]

In presenting us with a play in which figure and ground are not clearly delineated, perhaps Armas is sending a message about the fluidity of figure and ground in the *cambalache* of the contemporary world—in its Rioplatense

---

2   The theory of figure-ground is the main principle of the Gestalt school. Within a space or field, the *figure* stands out in its reciprocal relation with other elements or objects. *Ground* refers to what is not figure; it is the area of space that contains those interrelated elements which are not part of the main center of attention. The ground holds and frames the figure. There cannot be a figure without a background or frame to hold it. Depending on where we focus our (visual or psychological) perception, different figures can emerge in what previously was background or frame. The figure-ground configuration forms a whole or Gestalt.

Spanish[3] meaning of 'hodgepodge' or 'junkshop'[4]—as well as in the immigrant's complicated internal world and cultural identity, where judgments and influences can repeatedly reverse. In the immigrant's new cultural reality, up can become down, figure can turn into ground and vice versa.

In this play, there also appears to a certain degree of the metadramatic device known as self-reference, which intertwines with the previous device of play-within-the-play. Self-reference occurs when the play itself alludes to the fictionality of what is represented, destroys the illusion of reality, and reveals that what we are seeing is just a representation. In *Beach Day*, Jhonny is the one who destroys the characters' illusion (i.e. pretending to be in Uruguay) as well as the audience's:

BEBA: Juancito…. Come to the beach with us.

JHONNY: Jhonny, mother. Please call me Jhonny. And there's no beach! Stop this nonsense. You are in the middle of the living-room of our house in Sydney.

PEDRO: He burst our bubble again. (74)

With these comments, Jhonny (or "Juancito") "burst[s] [their] bubble," that is, destroys the illusion they are experiencing. But the illusion also breaks for the audience, who suddenly gets hit with a bucket of cold water—to use an expression compatible with the scene—that makes them open their eyes and realize that the scene at Playa Ramírez is no more than a game of the imagination.

Jhonny's comments, however, are not an example of pure self-reference since Jhonny questions the reality of the play within the play but he does not question himself nor the "reality" of Nona, Beba, Pedro, and Luisito's existence (in an example of pure self-reference, the reality of the entire play would be questioned, not just the secondary play's reality).

---

3 TN: The Spanish dialect spoken in the areas in and around the Río de la Plata basin of Argentina and Uruguay.

4 TN: The original meaning of the word *cambalache* is "barter or exchange of things of little value" (*Diccionario de la Real Academia Española*, 2014). In parts of the Southern Cone, the meaning was extended to refer to a second-hand store. In 1934, Armando Discépolo wrote his famous tango *Cambalache* and gave the word a new sociopolitical sense by comparing the twentieth century to the "disrespectful window" of a junkshop where you can find anything and nobody cares where it came from or how it got there: "Twentieth century, *cambalache*, troublesome and feverish […] Stop thinking, sit aside, that nobody cares if you were born an honest person! It's all the same: the person who works day and night like an ox, the one who lives off of others, the one who kills, the one who heals, the one who's outside the law."

Jhonny's comments do make clear that he despises these role-playing games, which he calls "this Third-World therapy," and adds, "You have to stop harping on *el paisito*…" (74).

It is true that this game or ritual of pretending to be at Playa Ramírez could be likened to some kind of group therapy that the characters resort to in order to reaffirm their Uruguayan cultural identity when they need to feel immersed in their motherland.

The pseudo-therapeutic game reveals a certain level of alienation, which can be linked to the play's references to insanity and the "local" (i.e. Montevideo's) mental hospital:

> BEBA: She is dressed as if she were going to the North Pole. People are going to think that we took some crazy person from the Vilardebó out for fresh air.
>
> PEDRO: I forbid you to refer to my little old sainted Mom as "crazy." […] (67)

Maybe the author is thus alerting us that the emigrant's profound anguish and existential conflicts might even lead to insanity.

The scene or illusion game at Playa Ramírez can also be analyzed as another variety of metadrama: the ceremony within the play. Representations of various ceremonies can be found in plays from all eras. These ceremonies may include parties, weddings, religious rites, funerals, coronations, games, initiations, contests, and competitions. Ceremonies promote stability because they carry the meaning of 'expectable and repeatable'. Their purpose, then, is to provide order and stability and to foster group unity. The scene at Playa Ramírez becomes for the characters a ceremonial ritual they perform over and over, using what is known (Montevideo's beach) in an attempt to find order, unity within the family, and a certain degree of emotional stability in a world (Australia) that is still unknown, confusing, and frightening. It is a way of preserving the Uruguayan cultural identity that they fear losing.

Pretending to be at Playa Ramírez, however, is also a ceremony of denial and evasion in the face of the distressing reality of emigration. Denial is a psychological defense mechanism which leads to rejecting those aspects of reality considered unappealing or painful. The characters in this play, then, use denial as a desperate strategy to preserve their cultural identity and cope with the great pain of having been uprooted.

By using denial as a psychological resource, Nona, Pedro, and Beba not only attempt to face the pain of exile but they also isolate themselves from their new surroundings, which makes adapting to the reality of living in Australia more difficult. They would rather isolate themselves because the prospect of having to adapt causes fear and uncertainty. They fiercely cling to a purely Uruguayan cultural identity because they feel threatened in the new environment.

A question arises: why choose a beach instead of any other place in Montevideo? Water is the primary medium where life originated. Imagining that they go to the beach, where they will be in contact with water, seems a symbolic attempt to return to the origins of the maternal bosom, an attempt to go back to the motherland, Uruguay. By letting the "waters" of the unconscious flow, the characters mentally transport themselves to the actual Playa Ramírez and, therefore, to the motherland. Each representation of the scene rekindles the hope of being in Montevideo again as a family. But the beach day is not a harmonious beach day. The group displays troubling family dynamics, given that its members constantly argue, accuse, and criticize each other. In their fantasy, they go back not only to their land but also to arguments and unresolved family conflicts from the past, maybe as a way of processing them, maybe as a way to repeat them ad infinitum just to feel like they are in Uruguay again. Maybe they feel nostalgia even for these conflicts of the past.

Armas also uses another metadramatic device, the role playing within the role, which usually reflects existential identity conflicts within the characters. Several of *Beach Day*'s characters portray two roles: on one hand, immigrants in Sydney; on the other, Uruguayans who would not even dream of living elsewhere. What are Beba, Nona, and Pedro's authentic identities? For example, in the case of Beba, which identity is more real: the typical Uruguayan woman enjoying a beach day in Montevideo, or the immigrant who is aware of living in Sydney but clings to her past cultural identity?

Armas' play prompts existential questions not only about the characters but also about ourselves, our own identity, and the cultural identity of emigrants throughout time: "Who am I? Of all the roles I have in my life, which is the real one? Of all the influences and experiences I have lived and of all the places I have considered my home, which define me? Or am I perhaps a mixture of all the experiences and roles I have had and continue to have in life?"

Jhonny resists becoming a part of the Playa Ramírez role playing. He does not value what is Uruguayan, he repudiates his past, and he does not want to get close to his native land through this ritual. Moreover, he rejects his mother calling him "Juancito"; he has adopted a misspelled English version of his name. Once Jhonny bursts his relatives' bubble, they name places in Montevideo which they believe should prompt his nostalgia, but Jhonny substitutes each one with another in Sydney that he believes to be superior. The following is one of many examples:

> BEBA: And don't you feel nostalgic for Teatro Solís, our first coliseum?
>
> JHONNY: Miss that, having the Sydney Opera House? (74)

Jhonny tries to cut his ties with Uruguay and convince himself he does not feel anything for the country. Through this acculturation process, he succeeds in erasing his feelings for the motherland and he denies the importance of his cultural heritage and his memories. It is also likely that his family's strong insistence to cling to what is typically Uruguayan has the opposite effect on him and only accentuates his rejection.

Jhonny is a representation of the immigrant who tries so hard to assimilate to a new land that he loses his roots, even to the point of despising his native country. Rejecting our roots does not lead to a healthy adaptation to a new place, however. Adapting does not mean erasing the past. The person who rejects her own culture, her history, and her identity will be able to contribute very little to a new culture. Adapting is shaping oneself, not becoming a clean slate. Jhonny represents the members of the younger generations who try to dismiss their cultural heritage in an (often failed) attempt to completely assimilate to the new environment. At the same time, among members of the older generations (such as Nona, Pedro, and Beba) there is a tendency to resist the adaptation to a new land, and often they do not make the effort to learn the new country's language. These groups tend to form subgroups or closed cultural islands that idealize their own culture and traditions.

None of the characters seems to be able to adjust to the reality of immigration. Nona, Pedro, and Beba idealize Uruguay, while Jhonny puts it down. The former would rather deny that they are abroad, while the latter attempts to repress any positive feelings for his motherland and denies having a past that defines him.

Beba's use of some English words might indicate her first attempts at interior negotiation (in the psychological sense) or adaptation to the new land. Nevertheless, even Beba unites with Pedro and Nona to defend the Uruguayan cultural identity and oppose Jhonny's acculturation process. In the face of Jhonny's insults, therefore, the others react with rebellion, defiance, and determination:

> JHONNY: Bye, everyone. And take that crap out of the living room and put back the computers and twenty-inch televisions. Ridiculous. Oh! And think about this. Uruguay is so Third-World that the New Year starts here in Australia first. You are so backwards. You are such babbling idiots. *(Exits.)*

> PEDRO: *(Rebellious. Comes forward with a raised fist.)* We won't take anything out, and that's it! We will not move!

> BEBA: You're right, old man. *(They hug.)*

> PEDRO: *(Kissing her forehead.)* Thank you, partner.

> NONA: *(Joins the family group.)* At least we have the idiot. (76-77)

Pedro, Beba, and Nona place their hope of preserving the Uruguayan cultural identity in Luisito, the mentally disabled son, who can be easily influenced. So they dress and decorate him with a sky-blue poncho (ponchos are typical of gauchos, and sky-blue is one of the colors of the national flag and of the Uruguayan Football Association), some swag from the popular socialist political party Frente Amplio, and the cap of one of the two main soccer teams (Nacional or Peñarol), and they place in his hand a little Uruguayan flag. Luisito, thus, becomes a kind of emblem symbolizing everything Uruguayan.

In an attempt to resist acculturation, Pedro, Beba, Nona, and Luisito will go on interpreting variants of the scene at Playa Ramírez over and over, including in their scripts plenty of additional Uruguayan references. In this version, the characters mention several places in Montevideo (Hospital Vilardebó,[5] Avenida

---

[5] TN: Montevideo's main psychiatric hospital.

18 de Julio,[6] Teatro Solís,[7] Parque Rodó,[8] Estadio Centenario,[9] etc.), typical food and beverages (*mate, milanesas*, mortadella sandwiches), and well-known Rioplatense music (a tango sung by Carlos Gardel[10]). The inclusion of typically Uruguayan references—such as music, places, objects, and speech—in many of Dino Armas' plays has led him to be criticized for being too localist. However, even though someone who has knowledge about Uruguay and the region surrounding the Río de la Plata will obviously understand and experience *Beach Day* in a much more intimate way than someone without it, it is also true that this play (like others by the playwright) deals with conflicts that, beyond the local allusions, are ultimately universal.

Armas explores the conflicts of a Uruguayan family abroad, but these are also universal conflicts: the family members experience reactions, conflicts, and dilemmas which are typical of people from any place and any time. Armas uses metadramatic resources to depict the characters' complexities and the different levels at which they engage with each other. For the audience, the metadramatic experience produces a feeling of unease, confusion, and perceptive alteration. The audience is forced to accept that the play within the play is an illusion, as is, ultimately, the entire play, every play, and possibly even life itself. Using metadrama, Armas suggests that life is in fact a play and that we all belong to many different scripts at once.

There is another interpretation to the use of metadrama in *Beach Day*. As was mentioned before, by presenting us with a play in which figure and ground are easily reversed, Armas may be making a comment on the fluidity of the contemporary world, where figure can become ground and vice versa. This leads us to reflect upon the value of perceiving the main play and the inset play as integrated totality. In regard to the notion of totality, Guillermo Leone, in his article "Leyes de la Gestalt," explains that Wolfgang Kohler's famous phrase "the whole is other than the sum of its parts" summarizes the claim by Gestalt theoreticians that human beings perceive totalities and, therefore, when a part is removed from the context, that part loses the value it has in that context.

---

6   TN: "18th of July Avenue." Montevideo's main downtown avenue.

7   TN: "Solís Theater." Montevideo's main theater, built in the mid-eighteenth century.

8   TN: "Rodó Park." An urban park (which includes an artificial lake, an amusement park, and a theater stage) located next to Playa Ramírez, close to the city's downtown.

9   TN: "Centenary Stadium." Montevideo's main soccer stadium, built for the first-ever World Cup in 1930. Its name celebrates the hundredth anniversary of Uruguay's first Constitution.

10   TN: The most iconic of tango singers in the Río de la Plata region (1887-1935).

Role-playing a day of leisure at Playa Ramírez and living in Sydney are parts of a totality within the context of *Beach Day*. The play, along with the play within the play constitute, then, a totality or *gestalt*. Maybe the immigrant's maturing process necessitates achieving a totality and accepting herself as a whole being who has developed a new identity out of her experiences. These experiences throughout life alternate between figure and ground until they become whole, a new identity that is different from the sum of its parts.

Beach Day's characters have not yet achieved this integrated identity. They seem lost in an ocean of opposing currents that keep them adrift between Playa Ramírez in Montevideo and Australia's waters. Dino Armas' writing affects the audience and makes them feel uncomfortable so as to invite them to process conflicts, heal internal wounds, and find the whole of an integrated personality that differs from the sum of its parts.

The use of metadramatic techniques is especially effective in portraying the immigrant's conflicts and hardships. In the same way that there is a play within a play, the immigrant's identity displays different degrees and shades of a cultural identity within one person. There is a sort of poetic parallelism between the concept of drama-within-the-drama and what I would like to call "identity-within-the-identity." Some immigrants will achieve a new integrated or semi-integrated cultural identity, while others will live forever with two or more cultural identities that alternate between figure and ground in the immigrant's internal world.[11]

---

[11] Essay translated by Álex Omar Bratkievich.

Works Consulted

Cirlot, Juan Eduardo. *Diccionario de símbolos*. Madrid: Siruela, 2016.

Hornby, Richard. *Drama, Metadrama, and Perception*. Cranbury, NJ: Associated University Press, 1986.

Laplanche, Jean, and Jean-Bertrand Pontalis. *Diccionario de psicoanálisis*. Buenos Aires: Paidós Ibérica, 1996.

"Mecanismos de defensa." *Grupo de Estudios Sistémicos* June 5, 2013. January 12, 2016 <https://teoriasistemica.files.wordpress.com/2013/06/mecanismos-de-defensa.pdf>.

Leone, Guillermo Daniel. "Leyes de la Gestalt." July 1, 2004. October 11, 2016 <http://www.guillermoleone.com.ar/2004/07/leyes-de-la-Gestalt.pdf>.

CHAPTER FOUR
Teaching and "Patriotism"?

Susana is our Perla

Present, Señorita

Dino Armas

Translation by Gabriela Christie Toletti

(An empty space; a white or pink background, which later on will be removed. A spotlight on PERLA's body, still; at first glance, it seems as if there was just a pile of clothes and hair on the stage.)

PERLA: *(Crouched down, her forehead touching the floor, dressed as a nineteenth century countrywoman from the Southern Cone; she wears an obviously coarse wig with braids; she bangs her palms rhythmically, repeating the following indigenous words in a hoarse voice that gets louder and louder until she almost screams.)* Ibirapitá... Tupí... Arerunguá... Nambá... Guaraní... Ibicuy... Tacuarembó... Arapey... Camba Cuá... Inchalá... Nambááá.... *(She gets a half-moon spear beside her.)* This is my signal. *(She starts to get up.)* This is my sign.... I am the lancer.... José Gervasio Artigas'[1] woman. I am Melchora Cuenca. When they see my spear lying by the gable of the general store, the countrymen know that I am there and, behind me, the very same Artigas. Oh... if my daddy Gaspar Cuenca, the Paraguayan, saw me right now.... If mommy Martina were here.... *(With pride.)* "You have come a long way, girl...." I am the legal wife of Artigas. The second one, yes. But I didn't miss the dance, right? I earned it with pure courage. We got married at the Purification Chapel. Some of his priests and friends united us before the Law and the Church. I knew how to be a silent companion when he was immersed in thought, discreet regarding his duties of governor, and heroic and a guardian during brawls. By my side he went from being chief of the *Orientales*[2] to Protector of the Free Peoples. Quite a title, right? And all thanks to

---

[1] Translator's Note: José Gervasio Artigas (June 19, 1764 - September 23, 1850) is a national hero of Uruguay; he is considered the father of Uruguayan nationhood.

[2] TN: Orientales is a way of referring to people from Uruguay. It refers to its location to the east or orient of the Uruguay River. During colonial times, La Banda Oriental del Uruguay was the name of the territory east of the Uruguay River and north of the Río de la Plata. Later on, the Provincia Oriental was created. The official name of Uruguay is República Oriental del Uruguay.

whom? To this servant. To Melchora Cuenca, better known in Corrientes, Misiones, Santa Fe, and Entre Ríos as *la prienda de Artigas*.[3] They will say that behind every great man there is a great woman. He chose me for being a fierce and beautiful woman. So much respect he had for me that he wrote, "If Melchora were to get bored of being around and wanted to go elsewhere, let her make the arrangements she sees fit. She is not a woman for routine, for daily tasks." Eat your heart out. *(Ironic.)* And how about the others? Did he say the same about them? No way! I am out of their league. Neither Rosalía Villagrán *(she crosses herself,)* nor Matilde Borda, nor Isabel Velázquez… and, even less those whose names don't get recorded by History. The Guaraní who gave birth to María Escolástica, the mother of the Caciquillo,[4] the other one who mothered Pedro Mónico…. *(She gets more excited.)* Mine, yes. *(With gestures writes the capital H in the air.)* History records my full name and last names and those of my parents and of the children I had with Artigas: María Artigas Cuenca and Santiago Artigas Cuenca. *(A loud cell phone rings. She acts doubtful. She grabs the spear and advances.)* Ibirapitá… Tupí Nambá…. *(The telephone rings again. She, pressing her lips, takes a cell phone out of her skirt. With hoarse voice.)* Melchora speaking. Watchword. *(She changes back to her normal voice.)* Oh, it's you, Amanda. Nooo… you must have misunderstood. Melchora…? That's weird! Do not be surprised if someone is listening to us and getting into our conversations. I myself sometimes feel listened to, watched. Come on, speak with confidence. Oh… our plans to go to Cinemateca?[5] They were showing the Iranian movie today? The one which won so many awards? The Lion of Venice, the Shell of San Sebastián…. I say, who would have thought about giving that name to an award? Can you imagine, Amanda, you and I receiving, for being retired teachers, a shell as an award? It is in bad taste. You know that today I cannot go to Cinemateca. *(Amanda mutters loud. Perla pushes the*

---

[3] TN: La prienda de Artigas is equivalent to Artigas' darling or Artigas' woman.

[4] TN: El Caciquillo refers to a son of Artigas and a Charrúa woman. The Charrúa were an indigenous people of South America. They inhabited the areas of what today is Uruguay, adjacent areas in Argentina, and southern Brazil. They were a semi-nomadic people who sustained themselves through fishing, hunting, and gathering.

[5] TN: Cinemateca, established in 1952, is a non-profit civil organization in Uruguay that supports and develops cinema, culture, and art in general. It consists of five movie theaters in Montevideo, a cinema library, a school of cinema, and film archives.

phone aside. She waits. She holds the phone again.) Shut up and listen to me. I have a commitment. A date. No, not with a man. Nor with a woman. *(Brief murmur.)* How can you think of an animal? What do you mean there isn't anything else? There are men, women, and former students. You would do the same, Amanda. We carry the teaching profession in our veins. For a student we postpone everything. And for alumni, even more. And here... he comes to my house. Sebastián. What do you mean "which Sebastián"? You cannot ask me that question, Amanda. *(Ironic.)* Of all, but all my students, which one could Sebastián be? Yes, that one. The same one. He wants to see me. He insisted so much.... "Señorita Perla, I have to see you." The thing is that teachers are second mothers to the students. And you know what, Amanda? It was a mutual desire. I also wanted to see him, to meet with him again. And when he told me that he had dreamt about me, everything came together. I also dreamed about him.... *(With sour tone.)* What do you mean "nightmares"? If it was a joke of yours, Amanda, it's a really bad one. Okay, yes, yes, I forgive you. Anything else? What was I doing? Nothing. I was getting ready to meet with my former student. You just go to Cinemateca and enjoy the membership card and the film... although I read the review and it says that, like every Iranian movie, it is slow. And when critics say "slow," it is really slow. Yes, it lasts about three hours. Oh, but what are three hours for a retired teacher? It's a blessing. You're busy for three hours and not thinking about anything, watching a slow Iranian movie. Oh, and all that for what? So that the boy, after going through plagues and dramas of all kinds, dies.... Oh, Amandita, I told you the ending. I didn't mean to. It came out without me thinking. Yes, it doesn't make so much sense to watch it now. But go anyway. In all Iranian films there are many sheep and flowers in the foreground and you like that a lot. Oh, but be very careful. Dieciocho de Julio[6] is a little crazy lately. Squeeze the wallet under your arm or, better yet, put the money in your bra. And if you see someone shady, get inside the casino across the

---

6   TN: Dieciocho de Julio (literally: "July 18") is the name of the most important avenue in Montevideo. It crosses the downtown and other neighborhoods. It is not the widest or longest avenue in Montevideo but the best known as a commercial center and for important landmarks along its length. It is named after the first Constitution of Uruguay which was written on July 18, 1830.

street. Or, otherwise, go inside the temple on the corner. "Stop suffering"? No! It's better not to go there, because you have to leave ten percent of what you carry for the "tithe," as they call it. So, in any case, it's better to just take only what you need, Amanda. And why wouldn't you go? To stay locked in your house...? Look, if I were you, I would go. But take an umbrella. The newscast forecasted strong winds and heavy rain for the night. Ah, you're right, take a Plidex and go to bed.... OK, yes. We'll talk tomorrow. *(She smiles happily as she hangs up the phone.)* She deserves it for interrupting me when I was in the best part. *(Gets the spear.)* Ibicuy... Tacuarembó... Arapey.... The war separated us. Ramírez was close by. So close that my Pepe had to mobilize in the middle of the night. "I will follow you even to ostracism," I said. But he made me go back to the *Banda Oriental.*[7] And I just turned around. Carrying the pain with me. Alone, without a man, I managed the best I could: I washed, sewed, and ironed for myself. Poets sang to me. About me they said, "Melchora was the General's wife and hers the hand which brandished the spear to liberate and secure the land. And it was the same hand which squeezed, with all the force of love, the body of her man." *(Quickly one of the curtains in the background is drawn and a poster appears with the lyrics of the song* To Don José.*)* And now let's all sing. *(With one hand she holds the spear and points to the lyrics and with the other she directs the choir.)* Music, please. *(A recording of the song can be heard, sung by a chorus of very angelical children. She rallies the spectators to sing along. At the end of the song, a recorded applause, and she takes off Melchora's clothes as she speaks.)* How wonderful those school choirs.... My choirs.... Oh, the voices of the boys before they become brutalized, when they still sound like sexless angels, and are equal to the girls, forming together a single choir. My hands... my hands guiding them. Those little eyes and heads attentive to each of my gestures. *(She makes the gestures and hums.)* Pianissimo... the raising and lowering of the voice without dissonance. Finishing the song in unison. All at once. Everyone at the same time. Everyone responding to my energetic and beautiful gesture. *(She does and stays suspended in the gesture.)* Not

---

[7] TN: During colonial times, La Banda Oriental del Uruguay was the name of the territory east of the Uruguay River and north of the Río de la Plata. Later on, the Provincia Oriental was created.

everyone…. Not everyone. He… always out of time. I got tired of telling him, year after year, "No, Sebastián, no. You do not have to sing. Just move your mouth without making any sound. You should just lip-sync." But not him. And it seemed as if he did it on purpose. Everyone had finished the song and then his voice uttering the last word of the hymn. And that, of course, provoked laughter, mockery, sarcasm. Parents looking and hearing, my colleagues also, and… and the highest authorities. And, of course, the one who looked bad in front of everyone was me. The dumb ass was me and not him who had brayed. The clumsy one was the teacher who had failed to unify the choir. *(With the phone in her hand.)* Oh, I could be capable of calling him right now to ask him to move forward the time of his arrival. But no, no. *(Takes a deep breath.)* Calm down, Perla, calm down. Here you have to be the strong one. You, the serene one. Annotating in my diary calms me down, gives me peace. *(Looks for a notebook that has a pencil attached to it. To write, she lies down on the floor and adopts a typically childish pose. She says the date of the performance as she writes it down.)* Point one: my contact with the Holy Father of our nation Artigas was stronger today than ever. More sensual. I felt my flesh burn and almost… I almost reached… sorry for the word, dear diary, I felt that I reached orgasm. Point two: inopportune call from silly Amanda. She cannot help her condition of having been a kindergarten teacher. *(She presses firmly on the paper as she gets to the final period of the sentence, without writing, imitating Amanda.)* "Perlita, we had made plans to go to the little Cinemateca Theater…." The only thing she did not say is "little cute theater *Cinematequita*,"[8] or she would have completed it. *(The telephone rings.)* Could it be him? *(Creeping and distressed.)* Maybe he is not coming. Maybe he changed his mind. *(On the phone.)* Hello. Hello. Oh, is that you, little Amandita?[9] I never called you "Amandita" before? I don't know. I must have gotten it from someone else, must have heard it somewhere. What's the matter, my dear darling? *(Ironic.)* Do you have to ask me a little question, a little inquiry?

[8] TN: Cinematequita is the diminutive of Cinemateca. The most common diminutive suffixes in Spanish are -ito/-ita. Diminutive suffixes can be used to indicate small size, youth, affection, or contempt. In this case, Perla is using the diminutive suffix to express contempt and irony.

[9] TN: Amandita is the diminutive of the name Amanda. In this case, Perla is using the diminutive suffix to express contempt for Amanda.

I'm listening. I'm all ears. Oh… you decided to go to the movies alone. Nooo, I'm not offended. No, please, no problem. Plus, they will show the movie again, right? Only one showing? Then you do very well in going, my dear. In your place, I would do the same. Me, angry? Not at all. To each his own. Tomorrow morning, you call me early and tell me all about the little movie. Every little detail. Bye, little Amandita. *(Hangs up, waits for a second, dials, with hoarse and deep voice.)* Ass…. *(Gasps exaggeratedly.)* Tits. *(She pants.)* Tit. Ass. *(Hangs up and waits with a half-smile. The phone rings, she answers with a sweet voice.)* Hello…. You sound distressed, girlfriend! What happened? *(Murmur.)* Did the satyr call you again? The one with the bad words? The one who tells you that he's going to follow you…? Oh, this time he did not tell you that he's going to follow you? It must have slipped his mind. Oh, and why aren't you going to go to Cinemateca? Yes, it is better, Amanda; lock your door and go to bed. It's for the best, Amanda. There are so many crazy people running loose in Montevideo. You have been a virgin for sixty-five years. It would be very sad to lose your virginity to a satyr. Because a spinster can lose her virginity to a cousin, to a neighbor, and even to the building's doorman, but to a satyr it looks bad. They would even expel you from the Association of Teachers of Uruguay. Until tomorrow, my dear. Sweet dreams. *(Hangs, sighs deeply, writes down.)* Point three: silly new talk with Amanda. I had to read her the riot act. Point four: Sebastián is coming. *(Smiling, underlines point four with two or three strong streaks. Turns the pages of her notebook backwards.)* Amanda on the phone, Amanda at the fair, Amanda at the Sodre Auditorium[10] Oh, my God. This woman is in all the days of my life. *(Serious. She reads.)* Visited Mommy at the nursing home. *(Reads the date.)* Two months ago already. I should go see her. Well… if anything had happened, they would have called me. That's what I pay them for. And quite expensive it is. Mommy is so strong. When she was admitted in the nursing home, they told me that she wouldn't last past that weekend. And she has been there for six years now. *(From the box from where she took the diary, she now pulls out two puppets that she will use and a wooden egg.)* Old woman who is admitted,

---

[10] TN: Sodre Auditorium (Auditorio del Sodre) is a cultural center in Montevideo containing theaters, exhibit halls, and conference rooms.

old woman who dies. But not Mommy. She is always there, relentless. In strength, I took after her. In beauty and intelligence, I took after Dad. I remember the faces of the two of them when I told them I was going to be a teacher. I have present here *(she touches her head)* that familiar picture: Mommy sewing stockings with the help of her wooden egg; Dad reading the newspaper. I walked in and told them that I had discovered my true calling, that I would be a teacher. Mamita, without looking away from the stocking, said: *(PERLA makes the puppet act, she will do the same with the father's lines and later on with their fight.)* "You chose well. The elevator doesn't go all the way to the top. There's not much else you could do." Dad set aside his newspaper and said, "Actually, there's not much else you could do... because you have inherited all the stupidities of your family. In your family you have alcoholics, mentally-ill people, and syphilitics." And Mommy, the good Mommy, who was and is very stubborn, always without raising her head, and always sewing that wool sock on the wooden egg, replied: "Before talking about my family, why don't you look at yours? Wasn't it your grandmother who ended up crazy at the Vilardebó?"[11] And one answer brought another one. A strong word brought a worse word. And the insults and the threat of hitting. When I left them, in the best part of the discussion—as I was leaving the dining room—the wooden egg struck the head of one of the two. Luckily, it was Mommy's head. She was diagnosed with head trauma. But just as my saint father—may God have him in his glory—always made her swallow her words with blows, I also shut her up with my brilliant teaching career. *(The background changes. Boxes can be seen. From the ground up to the ceiling, the boxes have numbers of years ranging from 1966 to 2006. In some of these boxes the numbers appear complete, in others only the beginning or the end of the numbers can be seen. The boxes form a labyrinth through which PERLA will move. Each box that she takes out will let a light go through that will make the environment feel more unreal. At regular intervals there are white tunics that she has worn throughout her teaching career and that are hanging like white shadows.)* Whenever the two of them fought, Mommy was upset

---

[11] TN: Vilardebó is a psychiatric hospital in the Reducto neighborhood of Montevideo, Uruguay. It opened in 1880 and is named after the physician and naturalist Teodoro Vilardebó Matuliche.

with me. *(If the director considers it appropriate, it can continue–or not–with the game of the puppets, now incorporating PERLA's.)* With the pretext of combing or braiding my hair, she pulled it so hard that my temples hurt. If she wet my hair, the water was too cold or burning hot. When she put brooches on my hair, she always pricked me until I bled. "I didn't mean to," she said. Her hand also went unintentionally and fell heavily over my head or over one ear or behind my neck. Then her advice muttered under her breath: "If you tell your father anything, you can't even imagine what will happen to you"; "If he finds out, you go directly to boarding school." She would have liked to see me cry, but I never gave her the satisfaction. Of the two, I was the strongest. When my father arrived, tired of working, he greeted me first. He pushed me up, above his head, and asked me, in a routine that he never broke: "And? How did the two women in my house behave today?" Knowing that she held her breath waiting for my answer, I delayed it on purpose. I would run my tongue wetting my bottom lip or playing with one of my braids. Then I would answer, "Okay, Dad. All right." Then I could hear her breathing deeply, as if she had been holding her breath. When I realized that this ceremony did little harm to her, I learned a thousand and one ways of provoking quarrels between the two. Fights that always ended in beatings that I only heard because Daddy, surely to take care of my education, closed the door. It is not that I am bad; I am fair, which is very different. And Mom deserved every one of those beatings. Only one time he sided with her. Just once. And it was something so... so.... *(Not finding the term, she makes a gesture as if pushing the word away.)* It was summer... I was feeling so hot... I was alone in the backyard. I had been given a Pomona.[12] I took little sips and put the top back on the bottle so that it would last longer. I took off my dress and fresh air ran down my chest and back. Why not do the same with the panties? In doing so, I discovered that part of my body as if I had never seen it before. And my hand went to that place that should always be covered. A tremor, which I did not know where it came from, ran through my body. I took a long sip from the drink and the apple smell and taste filled my nose and

---

[12]   TN: Pomona was a type of apple cider.

throat. Then I started to play with the little bottle top on my body. I made marks on my arms, I put it on my nipples, the belly button, and on that place that always had to be covered. That's how she found me. I did not see her until she lifted me by one arm, so strong that she made me scream with pain. Her eyes, her words, which she screamed repeating them over and over again: "That's nasty. It's a degeneration." And the blows on my hand causing the bottle of Pomona to break into a thousand pieces and splatter us, leaving us both with a sticky apple smell. Just as I was, without clothes, she locked me in my room. And like that, without clothes, my father, because of her stories, hit me for the first and only time. That incident was never talked about again at home. None of us three ever mentioned it. Neither Dad nor me... nor her. Never. It was then that I redoubled my abilities to provoke their fights. (*She shrugs.*) Well... it was so easy. They had not changed, but I had. Now I spied on how Daddy beat her. I am not spiteful, I just have a good memory. Every time I go to the nursing home to see Mommy, I take the wooden egg and a sock. I make her look at me and I put the egg inside the stocking slowly. Then I hit her here and there... on the head, on the mouth of the stomach, on the bony knees, and I whisper, "Do you remember, Mommy? Do you remember?" In the end, what I'm doing is family therapy. Something that is good, both for her and me. More than one psychology book–of the many I have read–says so. (*Enraptured, with short drowned exclamations, she points at the boxes and engages with the audience more and more.*) My whole life as a teacher.... How many beautiful memories.... I am moved to tears.... The white tunics that I wore as a teacher.... Ah.... (*She can have a staircase with wheels and circulate through the maze of boxes reading some years out loud. When she gets to 1966, she stops. She brings the box down and leaves it on the floor, and takes the robe that is hanging closer to her.*) My first tunic. That one I wore during my first five years working as a teacher. (*She smells it, presses it against her.*) It still retains the stiffness of the starch. Starches were things of the past. (*On an impulse.*) I'll put it on. (*She puts it on. It's too small. She cannot button it up.*) What a great figure I had. So slim.... (*She goes to the box, caresses it.*) My first job... that rural school in Tapia Station.

Those were good times! I had to take the train, get off at an open field which was actually the station, and then walk about a mile to get to school. But in that mile there was a stream with a flimsy bridge. When one crossed it, the logs would move like crazy. Every time they announced rain in Canelones,[13] I did not go to the school because, as the countrymen would say, the bridge was not passable. The one who did not give me... enough rope was the principal of the rural school of Tapia Station. I must have her here. *(Quickly looks, takes several pictures out, mutters as she goes through them.)* Oh, what a young girl I was here.... This one, with the president of the Development Commission.... Oh, I found you. That false smile... Martirio Martínez Borda de Palazzo. Her name was longer than her intelligence. She had a stamp: "Because I want people to know that I'm married." She would stamp every sheet, notebook, and card that got in front of her and then doodle on it. She was a doodle herself. When Martirio and I met, we felt hatred at first sight. She looked me up and down and said, "You just graduated. In this type of school we need people with experience. Did you know that here you will not have a single class but several in the same classroom?" She sighed and released an "Anyway..." She kept the smaller classes with fewer children and dumped on me third to sixth grades. What Martirio Martínez did not know.... Ugh, I refuse to say the whole name because... holy shit... my throat gets dry for nothing. Oh, it came out without me thinking. I was going to say "for goodness sake", but "shit" has more to do with Martirio Etcetera of Etcetera. What this good lady did not know was that, ever since my mother dropped the bomb about whether or not I was going to have the wits to become a teacher, I had declared war on the teaching career. It was a constant struggle at the Teaching Institute with the principals, the teachers, and my colleagues. And I was not going to lose that war in the first battle and even less against a teacher whose name was Martirio.[14] Ugh. *(Takes out another photo.)* The schoolhouse. Now that I look at it, it was like an old shed. And lunch was good, rich. *(Another tone.)* Rich in fats, rich in cholesterol, rich in calories. But, deep down, I did not care

---

[13]   TN: Canelones is a department of Uruguay located in the south of the country. Its capital is also named Canelones.

[14]   TN: The name Martirio literally means "Martyrdom."

about anything. Neither about the principal nor the shed nor the food. When I got off the train and walked that mile to school in the middle of shrubs, thistles, *carqueja*[15] plants, and dung, I felt like Julie Andrews in *The Sound of Music* and, instead of singing like her *(humming the film's song)*, I sang with all my strength *My Flag.*[16] *(Finds a poster with the lyrics. Illustrates her walk and rallies the audience, imaginary companion to PERLA, to accompany her singing. Like the other theme, this one is also sung by children with high-pitched voices. The choreography of PERLA singing* My Flag *is an imitation of what Andrews does in the film.)* I was very happy, yes. So much…. Of course I was, since "he" hadn't appeared in my life yet…. Sebastián. Sebastián Cuenca. Nor had there been a clash with Martirio. She fell into the trap all by herself. She did not know what she was getting into. I had spent years trying to be the strongest, the best, the only one. And in doing so, I was able to use every possible method at my disposal. The good ones and those that are not so much. Martirio Etcetera de Etcetera appeared one day in my class and, with that typical smile of hers, said to me, "Sorry, teacher, for intruding. But, unintentionally, from my classroom I heard that you were doing conversions." "Yes," I said, sounding all innocent, imbued with the pedagogical spirit of José Pedro Varela,[17] and feeling protected by the immaculate white of my tunic. And she said, loud enough for me and the students to hear, "I think you are making a pedagogical mistake. See. Here." And her index finger, which ended in a long red nail, pointed at the blackboard, where the meters, the decameters, the hectometers were…. I did not hear anything else she was saying because, among the murmur that the principal's observation produced among the students, stood out Pedrito's voice, the son of the Promotion Commission President: "Señorita Perla is a dumb-ass." She heard it too, and before she left, she stroked his head as to approve what that son of… the president had said. It took me a whole week to think what would be the worst punishment for the two of them.

---

15 TN: Carqueja is a shrub-like plant native to South America. Carqueja tea is used to treat pain and indigestion, to protect the liver, to prevent ulcers, etc.

16 TN: My Flag (in Spanish, "Mi bandera") is a patriotic song dedicated to the Uruguayan flag. It is considered to be an anthem of the Uruguayan Flag. It is commonly sung in school ceremonies and in patriotic events.

17 TN: José Pedro Varela (1845-1879) was a Uruguayan sociologist, journalist, politician, and educator. Uruguay adopted free, compulsory, and secular education thanks to his efforts.

With Pedrito it was very easy. I sent a short note to his father telling him that I had found him copying and that he should be punished, but that I—as a teacher—could not do it, but that he as a father could. The father, before using force, brought him to me. Pedrito had the nerve to swear in front of me that I was lying about him copying. Poor guy…. It was his word against mine. And as a good father, who would he believe, the son or the teacher? Of course he believed me. After three days, Pedrito returned. There were still some bruises on his face. Regarding Martirio's punishment, it was almost Mommy's idea. She asked me to buy her a laxative because she was constipated. I went and, with the bottle in hand, suddenly had a brilliant idea. I bought two. A small one for my mother and another one—the biggest one in the pharmacy—for Martirio. *(Background music. Maybe the theme of Julie Andrews's movie.)* That day as I walked to school with the laxative in the briefcase, the field seemed more beautiful than ever. I felt… I don't know… I felt like poet Juana de Ibarbourou[18] and I started to gather herbs and, since I did not have a fig tree close by, as I walked by the only skeletal old ombú[19], I said, "Beautiful. Today they have told you that you are beautiful." Steps from school, I looked up at the sky and I saw a cloud in the shape of Artigas' profile: his clear forehead, his aquiline nose, his prominent chin. And I knew that was a sign from him. Artigas was with me. He supported me in my case against Martirio. Feeling more confident than ever, I went to school. Like every day, we started with our task: preparing breakfast. I was the one in charge of heating the milk and Martirio served it. She didn't realize that I put half a bottle of laxative in her cup. I think she even liked it. "Mrs. Principal…" (I never said "hey," "Martirio," or anything like that, neither to her nor to any principal; I always knew how to maintain distances and to respect ranks… I mean, hierarchies) "Mrs. Principal, after lunch, would you like to come to see the History lecture that I prepared for today's class? And, by the way, you can also look at the notebooks to check everything about Mathematics and see if I followed your directives

---

[18] TN: Juana de Ibarbourou (1892-1979), also known as Juana de América ("Juana of the Americas"), was one of the most popular Uruguayan poets of Spanish America, nominated for the Nobel Prize in Literature four times.

[19] TN: Ombú is a large evergreen with an umbrella-like canopy typical of the Southern Cone Pampas grasslands. It can be found in Argentina, Brazil, and Uruguay.

accurately." "Of course, my dear–said the fake one–"It's good for me to attend so that I can write the report to evaluate you." When we were at lunch, I poured the rest of the laxative in the noodle, meat, and bean soup. Then came the moment of my triumph. If they had called me "dumb," they would call her worse. Martirio walked into my classroom with all her children and I welcomed them. Out of the corner of my eye, I saw that she was half pale, with an ash-white or olive-green color that already foreshadowed her fate. And right there, as if I were possessed, I delivered–on purpose–the longest lecture of my life about Artigas. I started with the colonial period and its characters, then I went on to talk about Artigas' grandparents, parents, siblings, and even his neighbors. I got to his baptism at Iglesia Matriz[20] and when I was reading the birth certificate, I saw–with a sideways glance–that Martirio was moving restlessly in her seat and that small drops of sweat appeared on her forehead…. Then I told and embellished–as much as I could–anecdotes of Artigas' life as a child in the countryside. She, Martirio, was fanning herself with one of the notebooks. By then she looked marble-white pale. And I, triumphant, glided like a dove among the lines of children, who were captivated by my master class. At the moment when I was lecturing about the time when José Gervasio entered the Blandengues infantry,[21] she made a move as if trying to leave. I jumped like a beast and stood between the door and her. Smiling, I looked at her. As she looked back, I knew that Martirio had lost it. Now she was trembling, afraid even of opening her mouth. Not to mention getting up. She clutched her fists and legs tightly. She whispered, "Teacher… I think… I think that's enough. I already have an opi…." She could not go on. The rumble of her contained intestines, the smell, and that yellowish liquid that began to overflow through her legs filled the whole room. And now it was not just Pedrito's voice… the entire school in chorus, as if it had been rehearsed, repeated, "The principal has

---

[20]   TN: Perla is referring to the Matriz Church (In Spanish, Iglesia Matriz), located in the neighborhood of Ciudad Vieja or "Old City" in Montevideo, Uruguay. It dates from colonial times and is the oldest public building in Montevideo. The church was consecrated in 1804 before construction was completed. It is dedicated to the Immaculate Conception and to the patron saints of Montevideo, Philip (Felipe) and James (Santiago). This church is also the Montevideo Metropolitan Cathedral, the main Roman Catholic Church in Montevideo, and the seat of its archdiocese.

[21]   TN: Blandengues is the name of a Uruguayan mounted infantry unit that dates back to the colonial period.

the shits." After that embarrassment, her only option was to ask for a leave of such length that I remained the only teacher until the end of the year. That was my first big battle won. It was my personal Battle of Las Piedras.[22] I got all the children to pass to the next grade, including Pedrito, and I was even congratulated by the zone inspector. And it was then that my legend began, the one of Perla the teacher, in whose classes all students were successfully promoted to the next school year. Parents fought for their children to be in my classes. That was until Sebastián Cuenca appeared. *(Urgently.)* No, I do not want to carry his negative karma. He will call me. He is going to come and will not allow me to remember these forty years of work. He's going to steal my memories and I'm not going to bear that. He is like those of the medical board: "She is too old to keep working. She was too exalted and vehement during the interview. We advise that she retires." He… he is like the private schools. The same people who used to fight to have me among their ranks now left me behind because I did not meet the target that the company wanted. *(She goes back to the boxes. She touches them.)* Ah… the years from '73 to '85. What years were those! The best of my life. How admired were my operational goals! Others would ask me to use them. My speeches, on every patriotic date…. And my wonderful regulation that made no male teacher…–well… real male teachers, there were very few–that no male teacher would be allowed to have a beard. It was predominantly a hygienic measure. They also had to wear a tie to school. And as for women, no miniskirts or pants: just skirts. The number of tramps whom I denounced and who were fired. The fools spoke casually at recess and what was one to do? I had to report them. Democracy is like this. If they don't like it, let them go to Cuba, right? Oh… and that colonel who came to school and courted me…. The times I went out with him…. Although he was a bit strange: he would ask me to tie him up and slap him while I read aloud those wonderful books of Moral and Civic Education. Those with hard covers. There was never again a book of that level…. Well… the colonel was useful until it was all over. *(Another tone.)*

---

22   TN: The Battle of Las Piedras (in Spanish, la batalla de Las Piedras) was fought on May 18, 1811 as part of the Uruguayan struggle for independence from Spain. Artigas was the commander and leader. The battle resulted in a total victory for Artigas and the revolutionaries.

Ha! The only things that did not change in dictatorship or in democracy were the gifts for the teachers. Every little flower vase, ashtray, and ceramic dove that existed was for the teachers. If I open each box and take out my ornaments, I could open a corny bazaar. *(More urgency.)* I don't want him to call yet; I don't want him to come yet. I have so much to remember…. *(She closes her eyes and, jumping like a girl, she touches the boxes and hums.)* "Eeny, meeny, miny, moe. Catch a tiger by the toe. If he hollers, let him go. Eeny, meeny, miny, moe." *(Her hand rests on one of the boxes, the year is not seen; she lowers it to the floor, a new light enters through a hollow space, and she shakes a little.)* It had to be this one. Oh, well, it must be fate. *(Takes out a list.)* Here he is. Sebastián Cuenca. The only one, but the only one, who repeated the school year in my long career. He is my Chinese ink smear, my lethal virus. Sebastián Cuenca. And he had to be the bearer of that last name. During forty years of service there was never another Cuenca to redeem myself. I checked entries, transfers, other teachers' lists. The only Cuenca was him. The loser who tarnished my career, my record, my work history, and my reports. *(She gets the cell phone, dials in distress. SEBASTIÁN's voice can be heard.)*

SEBASTIÁN: Hello….

PERLA: I am your teacher.

SEBASTIÁN: Miss Perla, I was about to….

PERLA: Cuenca, do not go on. You know that you have to wait for me to call the roll first. *(Reading.)* "Arana, Norberto; Araújo, Lourdes; Beltrame, Karina; Cuenca, Sebastián…."

SEBASTIÁN: Present, Señorita.

PERLA: Sebastián, how many times did you repeat the school year?

SEBASTIÁN: You know it well. You were my teacher.

PERLA: I know it. Unfortunately, I know it and the whole national magisterium knows it. But today I want you to say it.

SEBASTIÁN: *(Frightened.)* What do you want me to do?

PERLA: *(Upset.)* To say it out loud.

SEBASTIÁN: Ah…. Is it necessary?

PERLA: Yes, it is.

SEBASTIÁN: And… well, I repeated three times the first school year, I was in second grade for two years, two in third, two in fourth. In fourth A and fourth B. *(With pride.)* And only once in fifth grade….

PERLA: Very funny. Once, because at that point of your life you were already fifteen, had a beard, hair on your legs, and you were transferred to night school. And what happened? What happened?

SEBASTIÁN: You were the teacher.

PERLA: *(Out of control.)* Yes, I was. And there you were, Sebastián Cuenca. And again I failed with you. You did not learn, you did not learn, and you did not learn.

SEBASTIÁN: Well, one is the way one is.

PERLA: And that terrible phrase of yours rumbling inside Artigas' Mausoleum? Breaking the sacred respectful silence imposed by that place.

SEBASTIÁN: Which one? I went to the Mausoleum every year. It was a must. Poor the child who missed that day. You were relentless.

PERLA: Of course I was.

SEBASTIÁN: I saw classmates trembling with fever, wheezing asthmatics… and having measles, chicken pox, or mumps was no excuse.

PERLA: Do not try to distract me, Sebastián Cuenca. Since you like to repeat so much, repeat now that unfortunate phrase.

SEBASTIÁN: No, miss.

PERLA: Yes, student. It's an order.

SEBASTIÁN: I do not want to, Miss Perla.

PERLA: Are you embarrassed?

SEBASTIÁN: Well… a little.

PERLA: *(When she hears that, she loses it.)* A little… just a little. Mr. Cuenca feels only a little embarrassed.

SEBASTIÁN: It's not such a big deal.

PERLA: What do you mean, "It's not such a big deal"? For me it is. Nothing surprises me, but that phrase was like a big blow. Twelve words that were twelve stab wounds, twelve axe blows. *(She imitates him.)* "What a pain in the ass, always bugging about Artigas, Miss Perla." You already had the thick voice you have now. And the echo of the place kept repeating your phrase… over and over. Even the soldiers at the place lost their composure.

SEBASTIÁN: You remember such things….

PERLA: I have good memory, I'm fair, and I'm generous. Didn't I prepare you conscientiously so that–at least–you would get into the police force? And you didn't pass the entrance exam. OK. That's it. Are you coming?

SEBASTIÁN: I'm three blocks away from your house. I'm bringing an apple as usual.

PERLA: When you arrive, before walking in, wait for me to call the roll.

SEBASTIÁN: Look for one where my name comes first.

PERLA: Your name always came first when you repeated a school year.

SEBASTIÁN: *(Happy.)* Yes, yes.

PERLA: *(Roars.)* You really like being a repeat student…. *(She hangs up the cell phone. Back to the audience, she looks at the boxes, violently takes some out as she says,)* Repeat student…. Sebastián Cuenca, repeat student…. Cuenca, repeater…. Repeater. Repeater. Repeater…. *(Ends exhausted, the light sneaks through the holes left by the boxes.*

She starts to dress like Melchora Cuenca.) I, the teacher with 100 points. I, who managed to promote hundreds and hundreds of children, I could not deal with him. I didn't have the wits. Now that, retired, I can look back and weigh everything positive and negative, I have left as negative one single thing: Sebastián Cuenca, the repeater. And as positive: knowing that I defended tooth and nail the teaching profession for forty years. I have kept out of my way bad teachers, the bad citizens. Those... anonymous... so many... informing the authorities of any irregularities. The long calls–to the National Central Education Board–dropping comments on cleaners, cooks, teachers, principals, and even inspectors who were not worthy heirs of the holy father of our nation: Artigas. Oh... my José Gervasio. The man whom I loved as a young woman and who I love, today, more than ever. (*Starts to turn off the lights.*) Now I'm going to do what's right. I'm not mean, I'm fair. (*Brandishes the spear.*) I, Artigas' Melchora. I, Artigas' Perla, must set the record straight. I'm your lancer, Pepe. You, Pepe, you said, "Let the *Orientales* be as enlightened as they are brave." And there is one, there is one who did not want to be enlightened and who has to pay for that. (*Long bell. She pulls the spear pointing to the place where the sound came from. The musical theme* Disculpe[23] *starts being heard. It starts to get louder until it gets very loud.*) It's open.... Just come in, Sebastián Cuenca.... (*A beam of light indicates that the door opened.*) That apple smell.... Do not move. I have to call the roll. (*She starts to repeat by heart the names of the students; she remains in the shadows, her body cut out by the lights, her strong breath resembles that of a mad animal, ready to kill.*) Arroyo, María del Carmen... Añón, Pablo... Bentos, Alberto... Cuenca, Sebastián....

SEBASTIÁN: Present, Señorita.

---

[23]   TN: Disculpe (literally: "Pardon me") is a tango with the original French title Pardon Madame (literally, "Pardon me, Mrs."); it was made famous by Reda Caire, who was a popular singer in Paris from the 1930s to the 1950s.

(*An apple rolls up to PERLA's feet; she grabs it, has a big nibble and throws it to the side; a long shadow of the man approaches the spear, which PERLA brandishes tightly. Musical theme blasting and lights out.*)

THE END

Sacred Education

Álvaro Loureiro

To Perla's credit, despite being a retired school teacher and spinster and without any likely suitor in sight, it must be stated that none of her pupils–with just one single exception–had to repeat a grade. So she declares throughout this monologue in which, all of a sudden, intrudes the voice of General José Artigas'[1] wife, the lancer Melchora Cuenca, with whom Perla identifies; the two women are bound by their irrepressible love towards the Uruguayan national hero. The educator is capable of wielding a spear–like the ferocious Melchora–at the same time that she pronounces the scant expressions she knows in native South-American languages. Both would be willing to fight for Artigas to the end, but most of the remaining features that Dino Armas chose to depict Perla could be classified as extremely negative.

These touches of exaggeration, far from being gratuitous, are the satirical resources the playwright employs in order to assemble a text which demonstrates that not all educators in the world could be described as true models of generosity, abnegation, or self-sacrifice. More than anything, Perla is mortified that one of her pupils (whose last name is Cuenca, to top it off) became a repeat student, a detail that the reader or spectator must understand as detrimental, not to the weary Sebastián (who, what is more, made mistakes even when attempting to sing the national anthem) but to the very selfish Perla, who feels having a repeat student looks like a failure among her very long list of promoted students. Therefore, instead of experiencing satisfaction regarding the other former students under her belt, the teacher is besieged by the memory of the repeat student for whose improvement (one gets the impression) she did not do anything special. Consequently, like a recurring ghost from her past, Sebastián fuels the nightmares of an educator who, as Armas shows, is far from exemplary.

The characteristic sarcastic humor of many of the author's texts crackles in this monologue and allows us to assess that, besides, Perla has not been a good friend to Amanda, apparently the only person who phones her and offers her company

---

[1] Translator's Note: General José Gervasio Artigas (1764-1850) is considered the main Uruguayan national hero due to his role in the fight for independence against the Spaniards.

to go to the movies. With a patronizing attitude, Perla makes fun not only of Amanda's tastes and concerns but also of the very same virginal spinsterhood of the poor woman, whom she pejoratively calls "Amandita."[2]

Perla, who leaves much to be desired as a friend, is also guilty of not knowing how to be a proper daughter. Admittedly, tenderness was not the prevailing emotion between her parents. Almost constantly they yelled at each other in a climate of physical and psychological violence, which Perla inherited and now practices without a glimpse of goodwill–not even towards her surviving mother. The cruelty she nurtured from childhood surfaced again in her first years as a teacher in a rural area, when fits of jealousy or intimations of envy would make her lose her composure in the presence of an arrogant and reticent school principal whom she should have respected regardless. For Perla in this case, the only fitting response is to fulfill a ruthless desire for revenge that belies her dedication to teaching.

The viciousness of a very unprofessional Perla–an indecent docent, if you forgive the pun–is revealed with fervent precision by Dino Armas. It can only be matched by her lack of camaraderie or solidarity, which compelled her on several occasions to inform the teaching authorities against offending colleagues and employees, precisely during the dangerous times of a dictatorship. Perla does not think of this as a disagreeable period since, for such an undemocratic person as this "Señorita" that Armas presents us with, the absence of democracy allows her to reach the height of her splendour.[3]

---

[2] TN: Literally: "little Amanda."
[3] Essay translated by Álex Omar Bratkievich.

Present, Señorita in Buenos Aires

Susana Mosciaro

Awoman appears on stage with a characteristic outfit and begins telling her story and the love she felt and feels for one of the independence heroes. Then she sheds her costume and there another person appears: yes! The retired teacher, who lives and narrates such a rich life history to act, to watch, to read…. I've been told, "When the play began, I wondered who that woman was, and later the story made me go through all these emotions and moods." The same happened to me when I read the author's play; only a great text can provoke so many emotions.

In this version,[1] my first great challenge was to look for an independence hero of the importance and magnitude of General José Gervasio Artigas[2] in Uruguay; that's why I thought about General José de San Martín.[3] Melchora Cuenca was General Artigas' partner; therefore, I researched and chose María Josefa Morales de los Ríos, a beautiful Mexican woman who accompanied and hosted General San Martín in the Mendoza province. Among the historical candidates, I had no doubts about choosing this lady–it must have been intuition; right away I was imagining her outfit and how she was, in every sense, the opposite of our retired teacher, "Miss Perla." "Outstanding!" I thought, "Melchora with her spear and Josefa Morales de los Ríos with the curved saber that the General used in his campaigns and left for her to watch over."

Convinced of my historical version, in the remainder of the play I only tried to adapt words, given the uses and customs, places, and phrases of our country. I won't deny that, while this adaptation was born, I couldn't get away from the actress in me; then, as a performer, I conceived situations and sayings with my future performance in mind. Imagination, text, illusion, all within me.

---

[1] Date and place of the premiere: 3 August 2013, Centro Cultural Eureka! (Av. Corrientes 4269, City of Buenos Aires, Argentina).

[2] Translator's Note: General José Gervasio Artigas (1764-1850) is considered the main Uruguayan national hero due to his role in the fight for independence against the Spaniards.

[3] TN: General José de San Martín (1778-1850) is one of the main heroes of the fight for independence against the Spaniards in South America. His involvement contributed to the independence of Argentina, Chile, and Peru.

I suggested to Laura Pommerenck that she should do the direction and staging, since she's Uruguayan, so author and director are both from our dear neighboring country.

Time to rehearse…. We worked for months, in solitude and intimacy, talking about Perla and her first appearances. Something magical began to happen. There were many findings: this teacher had a complicated, mistreated childhood, and still suffers its consequences. As a spectator later said, "I recommend this play to have fun, to remember our experiences from primary school, but also to think about the consequences of child abuse; that subject is rarely talked about; you really have to see it."

In the adaptation, I took into account when this character lived; not only did she experience dictatorial governments as a teacher but, in my version, she was also born towards the end of 1945, when there was a military government in Argentina. Then, in the construction of the character, it would all add up: she was born during a dictatorship, her mother would mistreat her…. In her remembrances, this is depicted in the way her mother treated her hair: she would pull it when combing Perla, and, if wetting it, "the water was too cold or burning hot" (110). Her father would pamper her… but to what degree? If she witnessed her father hitting her mother, she is a symbol of the victims' victims within a family household (a family "home"?). Besides, all this evokes the years of dictatorship we endured. Obviously they had aftereffects; for the person who lived through a dictatorship, the effects are there, even if they're minimal. "Should I join a political party? No. What if the bad guys return and see my information and persecute me?" This happens to all of us who have lived through those terrible times.

Perla survived all that. In what way? She decided to be "the strongest" (110), but being the strongest comes, no doubt, with a hefty price; it's like putting on an iron mask, behind which there's the pain, the fragility, the desire to scream "please, take care of me." Perla forced herself to become the best teacher in the world, and I think she was happy with it. Her school uniforms shine. After all the punishment she had to endure, she shone when she ruled her school choirs to perfection. Surely she applied strict rules when working as a teacher. She's vengeful and capable of anything; she even gave a very hard time to a school principal who underestimated her (a moment of irony, grotesque, and roaring laughter in this one-woman show). The only person she couldn't deal with was

Sebastián, her former pupil; she found him, she's waiting for him, and he's about to come. Perla's wait and her anxiety get communicated and transferred onto the audience. At the end, he arrives!!! And Perla, before receiving him with her saber and fulfilling her mission, invokes General San Martín, addresses the audience, and says (in my version), "My saber will never be unsheathed due to political differences; on the contrary, this saber is only for justice, and there's someone who is not illustrious and has to pay for it."[4] I ask, from my writing, my acting, and my person, "To have political differences and not to unsheathe our own sabers... isn't that actually to live in a democracy?"

As an actress, I dare say, each time I am Perla, I go through all the existing emotions. On one hand, I am the sensual and brazen Mexican. It's not a coincidence that Perla dresses up as her: she wears a plunging neckline, she has had a lover and has experienced orgasms that have not been cut short; she's the opposite of Perla, with her covered-up neck and her lack of sexual pleasure, emasculated by her mother when, as a child, she was caught discovering her sexuality under a fig tree. The moment when Perla remembers this, together with a melody that takes me back and turns me into a child... it's incredible for me as an actress... actress and character, acting and writing–the two of us become one.

It was decided that I would be accompanied on stage by the puppets requested by the author: the dad, the mom, and Perla as a child. Two things happen with them: on one hand, they're there with me and we interact, and truly I don't feel alone; on the other hand, their perfection gives me joy and happiness. The puppeteer who supplied them[5] read the play before making them and captured in their faces and clothing every detail of these major or minor characters. It was a great challenge to learn to handle them.

Despair, joy, thirst for revenge, justice, and rancor: all this is felt by the character and also by the actress when she goes through the play. From within the acting, I've worked with voice changes, different body expressions, sarcasm, irony, humor, tears. Nothing in the play, no action or word, lacks justification; everything is carefully arranged by the direction for a purpose.

Perla gets desperate and phones Sebastián (another unique moment); he's her only stain, her lethal virus, bad pupil, and repeat student. He stained her

---

teaching career. She speaks, interrupts him, scolds him; he knows perfectly well that, before speaking, he has to wait for the teacher to take attendance.

I had the idea of writing down the first and last names of some of the spectators present during each performance (since the theater's management would provide me the names under the reservations) for the moment when the character begins to take attendance. There began the "present, Señorita" of my dear audience, from the first performance to the last… until I got to Morales/Sebastián's voice-in-off speaking his "present." A spectator said, "I didn't know whether Sebastián Morales existed, whether he would come or was simply a part of that poor woman's madness; it creates a lot of curiosity that there is so much talk about him without him appearing on stage."

What would have happened to Perla if she, as so many people, had emigrated from her country in times of dictatorship? Would she have been the same teacher? I think the idea never even occurred to her. She was a part of the system; she's looking for revenge, justice!!! The only difference between her and the spectators, my work team, and me is that we know, we realize, and we understand why this woman is like this and, in the end, she's pitiful. Minutes before the end and before fulfilling her mission, she turns around, looks at the audience, and, overcome with emotion, says, "I'm not mean; I'm fair!" (120).

After watching this version, a spectator asked me after the performance, "Did this teacher exist? Did she really kill her former student?" What will Perla's life be like after killing Sebastián? Surely for her it'll change colors so the musical theme at the end of the play, and at full volume, is *La vie en rose* from the great Edith Piaf.

I am grateful to life for allowing me to live this character because… HISTORY DOESN'T BECOME A SPECTACLE; HISTORY IS SPECTACULAR!!![6]

---

[6] Essay translated by Álex Omar Bratkievich.

A Brief Literary Analysis of a Great Monologue

María del Carmen Montañés Tejera

Presente, Señorita Maestra[1]

The title of the play took me back to my first years as teacher, when the pupils, respectful and attentive, would reply in a natural way to their young teacher's roll call, without feeling weighed down by the daily routine. If the title captivated me, the content did even more so, since the monologue has the precise ingredients to engross our attention: concise ideas, clear concepts, and a lack of decorative embellishments (which would only divert the spectator's interest). Armas has set a zigzagging path for his protagonist to unfold in this monologue where reality and fantasy, past and present, love and hate, merge or alternate in such a way that the listener's interest does not wane at any moment.

Even though *Present, Señorita* is a monologue in a single act and a single scene, a subdivision in moments can be suggested, based on the facets of Perla (the protagonist) that they reveal.

First Moment: Perla as Melchora Cuenca

At the beginning of the play, before a monochromatic background, a single light frames a still figure, not outlined but only suggested by a heap of clothes and hair. The austerity of resources focuses all the attention and interest in that figure which, in the stillness, the silence, and the almost ethereal set design, immediately awakens the spectator's curiosity.

Armas uses a dramatic effect to make an impression in the audience: slowly, that shapeless figure comes to life and it becomes clear it is the protagonist, crouched almost touching the floor, with peasant clothing and braids, accompanying with her rhythmic clapping a flow of Native South American words which, in a hoarse voice, she repeats almost with devotion until she is practically screaming.

---

[1] Translator's Note: Literally, "Present, Miss Teacher."

The character sits up and introduces herself without hesitation as Melchora Cuenca, General Artigas'[2] wife. From then on and with a surprising fluidity, she makes her ethopoeia with such fervor that the spectator will undoubtedly be able to recreate in her imagination Melchora's visits to the *pulperías*.[3]

A contrast can be observed between the concision of the sentences and the passion gathered from them. The phrases brim with spontaneity and their impact is direct, as when Melchora rounds off Artigas' alleged words with a resounding "Eat your heart out!" (104).

Melchora is exultant, gesticulates, and feels triumphant because she is the only of Artigas' wives that History remembers with "full name and last names"... (104)[4] until the sound of a telephone breaks the spell of that extreme elation. Upset, Melchora takes a cell phone from her skirt (modern item that might catch the spectator off guard), revealing that "Melchora" is a fiction within the fiction and introducing–without giving her name yet–the "true" Perla.

Second Moment: Perla, Amanda's "Friend"

As if with a smack and only with the sound of a cell phone, there occurs in the monologue an unexpected apparent temporal jump (not an actual jump since Melchora, a character from the nineteenth century, is here only a performance by Perla) that begins the second moment, in which Armas uses as a literary resource the flat character (that is, a character without psychological depth) of Amanda, who does not even get to the status of being a true "flat silhouette" of a character because we never see her–she is only a whisper on the other side of the line. The unexpected chat between the teachers (Amanda was a kindergarten teacher and, like Perla, is retired) will allow the author to gradually expose some of the many negative facets of Perla's personality.

The conversation is dynamic and conveys credibility, as when Perla tells her friend she cannot go to the movies as agreed: the unintelligible murmur on the other side makes Perla move the cell phone away from her ear. Those details provide the realism the playwright needs to give believability to the interaction

---

2   TN: General José Gervasio Artigas (1764-1850) is considered the main Uruguayan national hero due to his role in the fight for independence against the Spaniards.

3   TN: From the sixteenth century to the beginning of the twentieth century, pulperías were a typical commercial establishment in rural areas of South America. They combined the goods and services of a general store, a bar, and a place for social gathering.

4   Her full name was Melchora Cuenca Pañera de Artigas.

and, by extension, to the psychological profile of Perla that is being delineated.

In this apparent dialogue (we only deduce or imagine Amanda's interventions through Perla's comments and replies), perfect in form and content, Dino Armas, with the ability of a philosopher, allows us to gradually discover the meanness of humans of all times.

Perla knows her words hurt Amanda, who seems to be a lonely woman, without former pupils visiting her, nor a partner, nor children, only with this sharp retired colleague who does not miss an occasion to demonstrate her superiority. Perla's malice is even greater, however: immediately after a presumably benevolent act (encouraging Amanda to go to the movies and enjoy the film), her sarcasm appears by adding that "it lasts about three hours," highlighting that it is "really slow" (105) and even telling her the ending. In a swing of her twisted personality, Perla insincerely apologizes for her "involuntary" slip. Then, in a false duality of good and bad character, she alerts her colleague of the dangers on the street. Persuasive and mordant, she finishes off her comments warning Amanda to take an umbrella because heavy rains have been announced. Without a doubt, Perla, who smiles contentedly, knew how to rain on Amanda's parade.

Thus, the playwright gradually outlines the protagonist's most prominent aspect, her vindictiveness, which gripped her person since childhood and which she never shed. Amanda interrupted her evocation of Melchora Cuenca, and Perla, who had merged with the historical character, does not forgive her, hence her need for revenge.

Third Moment: Perla, the Director of the Children's Choir

When Perla briefly incarnates Melchora again, her tone changes to one of resigned longing, in which the Paraguayan woman is no longer Artigas' courageous and fiery lancer, but the nostalgic woman who returned to the Eastern Strip[5] "[c]arrying the pain with [her]" (106) and, alone, devoted herself to survive. This part of the monologue is serene and passionate at the same time, especially when Melchora gets rid of her peasant clothing and transforms into

---

5   TN: "Banda Oriental" ("Eastern Strip" or "Eastern Bank") was the name given to the land east of the Uruguay River and north of the La Plata River, comprising most of the modern Uruguayan nation as well as the modern Brazilian state of Rio Grande do Sul. It was the easternmost territory of the Viceroyalty of the Río de la Plata. In 1813, under the name of "Provincia Oriental" ("Eastern Province"), it became a separate administrative unit of the "Provincias Unidas del Río de la Plata" ("United Provinces of the Río de la Plata"), first named for the independent nation of Argentina.

the teacher who sings *A Don José*.[6]

In what I consider the third moment of the lengthy monologue, Perla's character apparently calms down when remembering her pupils and the children's choirs. The teacher stresses the homogeneity in the students' response to her teaching through the reiteration of the word "everyone" at the beginning of three consecutive sentences until, as if in a mental flash she remembered something upsetting, she completes her thought with an energetic and also repetitive, "Not everyone…. Not everyone" (106-107).

The monologue focuses momentarily on Sebastián, the only pupil that caused her—according to her standards—frustration in her teaching, primarily because of his limitations for singing, which "provoked laughter, mockery, sarcasm" from parents, colleagues, and the authorities, who blamed Perla for what she describes as the pupil's braying (107).

Furthermore, later we will find out that his learning problems made him repeat a grade each year, and for Perla that meant a stain in her teaching files. Her self-esteem was wounded, but her arrogant identity as a praiseworthy teacher does not allow her to perceive that maybe Sebastián also suffered. In Perla's mean-spirited interior world, the rancor and ill-will towards this student (the repeat student, the braying one) started to build up, feelings which, instead of slowing down with time, were revived by Sebastián's phone call, hence her anxiety, which is undoubtedly transmitted to the listener.

Fourth Moment: Perla, the Lecher

Again, the sound of the telephone interrupts her. Thus a brief fourth moment is opened within the dynamic monologue, marked by another apparent dialogue with Amanda, which excludes all traces of sincerity on Perla's part and is instead charged with the irony contained in the diminutive phrases "little darling," "little question," "little inquiry," "little movie" (108). When Perla pronounces them, those diminutives are not evaluative but derogatory, since they parody the speech of the former kindergarten teacher with her children. Upset by this second interruption, Perla says goodbye, hangs up, and—in a different tone of voice—makes an obscene call to Amanda. The fourth moment ends with a new call from

---

6   TN: "To Don José." Song composed in 1961 in honor of General "Don" José Gervasio Artigas by Rubén Lena, a rural teacher and principal. It was declared a Uruguayan popular and cultural hymn in 2003. It is still sung in Uruguayan schools.

the latter, who evidently has not perceived her "friend's" wickedness.

Fifth Moment: Perla, the Daughter

In the fifth moment of the monologue, Perla outlines a moral self-portrait based on her family relationships. In a brutal filial retrospective, she slowly broadcasts the hates and rancor focused on her mother. These molded her essence to such a degree that she brags of having provoked fights between her parents, coldly claims her mother deserved her husband's brutal abuse, and is even pleased that it was the mother and not the father who received a serious blow that caused her a head injury.

Dino Armas is an author of multifaceted vision, who dramatizes the teacher's character in different ways: the impersonation of Melchora, the conversations with Amanda, Perla's personal diary. In this fifth moment, he does it through an intense soliloquy that employs resources such as free association, a chain of events and actions, temporal breaks, and different images of the same situation (for example, Perla performs with puppets the family scenes she narrates) as an aid to effectively reproduce the character's experiences.

Suddenly, the flash of a memory transforms Perla's soliloquy into something even more intimate, when she remembers the only beating she received from her father and the reason for it. In a natural way, Perla takes her story back to her sensual awakening and the exploration of her body, a magical moment that the shrill voice of her mother interrupted. The words "nasty" and "degeneration" (111) were the coup de grace to the illusion of discovery that for a moment filled Perla with happiness. Then came the blows on her hands, getting locked naked in her room, and the beating received from her father—the only time and at the request of her mother.

The experience made her meaner. Finally, Perla comes out of the soliloquy to return to the direct monologue of the cold, calculating, hypocrite, cynical, and vengeful Perla, who describes as "family therapy" (111) the little blows she gives to her mother's bony body (now in a nursing home) with the same tool that once caused her head injury.

Sixth Moment: Perla, the Teacher

As Perla points out several boxes on the floor and integrates the audience into the theatrical event, we enter into a sixth moment, in which she makes a cold and harsh ethopoeia of herself by remembering her teaching years. At the beginning of this moment, Armas slows down the monologue and with pauses (represented graphically through ellipses), softens the emotional impact that Perla's intimate confession must have produced on the spectator.

Her tone of gentle longing and the difficulties to get to the first school where she worked (journeys by train, long walks, flooded streams) inspire sympathy towards this as of yet unknown Perla. But Armas subtly brings back the same old scathing and ironic Perla when the protagonist focuses on her relationship with the school's principal, with "false smile" and a "name […] bigger than her intelligence": Martirio (what a name for a teacher!)[7] Martínez Borda de Palazzo (112).

As she looks over old photos and remembers the school, Perla's tones, gestures, and expressive ability to evoke past events keep the spectator's attention. Perla gets excited by the memory of past vicissitudes and once again harangues the audience to join her, this time intoning the march *Mi bandera*.[8] With this, the monologue resumes a natural and emotional dynamism with patriotic themes, which create a moral commitment in the spectator–eluding them would be unpatriotic–and revive the yearning for country and childhood. Consciously or unconsciously, then, Perla manipulates the audience members so as to recruit them into her ranks; she integrates them into her world and positions them in the role of children, whom she knows how, and is able, to control.

Four characters marked Perla with their humiliations: her mother, Sebastián Cuenca (who she will deal with later), her pupil Pedrito, and Martirio, who interrupted her lesson, interfered with her pedagogy, exposed her in front of her pupils, and–what is worse–caused Pedrito to call her "dumb" and receive a pat from the principal as reward. At this point of the monologue, Perla's vindictive treatment towards her mother is already known; now her revenge against Pedrito and the principal are revealed: colder, more calculated and more intense than the first. To deal with Pedrito, Perla encouraged his father to punish him for an offense invented by her, which led to a beating so severe that the boy missed three

---

7   TN: Literally, "Martyrdom" or "Agony."

8   TN: "My Flag," a Uruguayan patriotic march which is sung at schools on every national holiday celebration.

days of school and, after that, "[t]here were still some bruises on his face" (114). The anecdote of her revenge against Martirio, unlike the others, alternates nimbly and naturally between serious and funny (her revenge includes a laxative) to such a degree that it skillfully leads the spectator to look forward to the intestinal outcome and, inadvertently for him, turns him into an accomplice of the maybe-deserved-yet-cruel retaliation.

Then, with heartfelt nostalgia, as she traces with her hands the boxes of her tangible memories, Perla points to a specific time: the years '73 to '85. According to her, they were the best years of her life, among other reasons because her operational goals were admired and her speeches requested.

Self-assured, she discloses her support of the dictatorial regime at the time by praising the rigid and authoritarian regulations imposed, her reports to the police, the dismissals, and the arbitrary rulings, and by boasting of the "number of tramps" (116) she reported and who were dismissed simply for not thinking as prescribed.

The coldness of Perla's account unavoidably takes me back to the same years, when I worked as a literature teacher and assistant to the principal in my hometown's high school. I cannot avoid getting emotionally involved since I witnessed events similar to the ones narrated with pride and arrogance by Perla. Unlike her, however, I am sorry to say I was silent witness to despotism and injustice, reports, senseless dismissals, the forced emigration of excellent teaching colleagues, the absurd rigidity of many of the adopted measures (the principal even admonished me for allowing a student who did not have the shoes required by high school regulations–because his father could not buy them–to wear sneakers one day). I have many experiences of those inflexible and authoritarian times that I lived through as a docent and I applaud the playwright, who, through the memories of the play's protagonist, insinuates almost carelessly a criticism of those years we would rather forget.

Back to the monologue, here is the first time Perla discusses her sentimental life, when she mentions a colonel "a bit strange" (116), who she used until she did not need him anymore. His strangeness consisted of asking her to tie him up and beat him while reading aloud a book on Civics and Moral Education. Maybe Armas imagined a colonel whose conscience or subconscious led him to want to be punished because of the moral and civic violations perpetrated by the military. Alternatively, it can be interpreted as a manifestation of the double standards of the official government, which allegedly protected the legal institutions while it actually infringed upon them.

Perla continues to recollect her life experiences and the urgency is noticeable: she awaits the visit of her former pupil Sebastián Cuenca but she does not want him to arrive before she finishes with her memories. The scene is composed of much more than Perla's lines: it is dynamism, movement, gesture, haste. From one of the boxes she takes out a list and finds Sebastián's name, the only student who smeared her teaching history, the only one who repeated grade after grade while everyone else moved on (the only one whose last name is, ironically, Cuenca).

Annoyed, she picks up the cell phone and dials. Once again Armas employs the same technique of voice recordings for the dialogues with Amanda, which provides dynamism to the situation, now with Sebastián as interlocutor. A blunt and cold dialogue ensues but, unlike the one with Amanda, Sebastián's replies are audible and clear, highlighting the different relevance that the two characters have for Perla and within the plot.

Perla, taking on her former role of teacher, takes roll call and, when she gets to "Cuenca, Sebastián…," the former student replies, "Present, Señorita" (120). Thus the play's title is explained to the members of the audience, who, taking into account the negative aspects of Perla's personality, may intuit that the teacher plots to do something in retaliation for the loss of teaching credence she had to endure on account of Sebastián.

The emotions intensify almost to an extreme. Vindictive, mordant, and resentful, Perla demands the ex-student repeat (maybe to shame and humiliate him) "that terrible phrase" of his which resounded within Artigas' mausoleum and, for Perla, was "like a big blow," "seven stabs, seven axe blows." Once Sebastián refuses, Perla becomes enraged and beside herself. Imitating his voice and out of control, she mimics the phrase of the former child ("What a pain in the ass, always bugging about Artigas, Miss Perla" [119]). Authoritarian or mad, Perla indicates that, when he gets to her place, he must wait for her to take roll call. She violently takes the lists out of the boxes…. At this point, Perla is all hate, rancor, and derangement.

Seventh Moment: The (Dis)Integration

Once again, in the last moment of the monologue, Armas takes us back to a former time through the teacher's remembrances. With passionate hubris, Perla boasts of having removed from her way "the bad teachers, the bad citizens" (120),[9] direct allusion to the arbitrary dismissals in public education in the first phrase, and to Artigas' thought in the second.[10]

Skillfully, the playwright has merged Perla, the frustrated teacher–dictatorial and resentful–with Melchora, Artigas' passionate lancer, who speaks to the man she loved and loves more than ever, and who fervently repeats the General's precept, "Let the *Orientales* be as enlightened as they are brave" (120).

In the back-and-forth of situations narrated in the monologue by Perla as Melchora and by Perla as the retired teacher, we suddenly understand that both have been a single thought, a single idea, a single feeling: to take revenge against someone who did not want to be educated, contrary to the General's ideals.

We can deduce, therefore, that the author has subtly united in a single character two different emotions felt for Artigas by two different women: Melchora's sensual and passionate feelings and Perla's almost religious admiration.

The final unification is revealed by the protagonist of the monologue, who, dressed as the Independence hero's wife, substitutes the name "Artigas' Melchora" with her own "Artigas' Perla" (120). The fusion is complete and, for the first time, both women emerge simultaneously.

The end is near, but the author delays its arrival: the sound of the doorbell, Melchora pointing the lance towards the front door, the command to come in since the door is ajar, the allusion to the smell of apples, and the "Do not move. I have to call the roll" (120) are more than enough elements to create an atmosphere of suspense that keeps the spectator engrossed.

The play concludes with an open ending presented through sensations: the

---

9   TN: In Spanish, "a los malos docentes, a los malos orientales." The official name of Uruguay is "República Oriental del Uruguay" ("Oriental" or "Eastern Republic of Uruguay"). "Oriental" is due to the country being located East of the Uruguay River. "Orientales" (literally, "Easterners") is a common term used by Uruguayans to refer to themselves.

10 TN: The phrase "a los malos orientales" (rendered in English as "the bad citizens") alludes to Artigas' famous precept "Sean los orientales tan ilustrados como valientes" ("Let Easterners, i.e. Uruguayans be as learned as they are brave").

semi-darkness of the stage, the noise of the rolling apple, Sebastián's long shadow when he approaches, the loud music, and the sudden lights out. Definitely, the surprising and unexpected ending of *Present, Señorita* is the cherry with which Dino Armas tops his fascinating monologue, the corollary of a mystery that goes on intriguing, and the back-and-forth of conflicting sensations and emotions provoked by the play.

Conclusion: The Multiple Facets of a Protagonist

The relative scenic sobriety of *Present, Señorita* (a single scene, one actor, a frugal set design) turns out to be the ideal form to get to know the protagonist, given that, almost without exception, her point of view is the only one represented. In the case of such a multifaceted character, this sobriety does not constrict the play but quite the opposite: it strengthens it. By being limited to Perla's perspective, everything is tainted with ambiguity and multiple interpretations arise.

For example, the open ending allows the spectator to give free rein to his imagination in speculating about who might have taken revenge against whom…. On the face of it, everything seems to suggest it is Perla who finally decides to make Sebastián pay for ruining her legend (the teacher that "got all the children to pass to the next grade" [116]). The dialogue with Sebastián, however, suggests possible resentments, both collective ("You were relentless. […] I saw classmates trembling with fever, wheezing asthmatics… and having measles, chicken pox, or mumps was no excuse" [118]) and individual (even now, years after no longer being his teacher, Perla humiliates him by forcing him to count the number of times he repeated grades). Why would an ex-student want to visit a "relentless" teacher who does not miss a chance to humiliate him? From this perspective, the apple that Sebastián brings to her "as usual" (119) is linked in this occasion not so much to the typical present from pupils to their teachers but with the poisoned apples of fairy tales (in a reversal of the typical story, the witch would be the one receiving it). In the final moment, the "*apple rolls up to* PERLA'*s feet*" (121) as if it were a bomb about to explode. Without a doubt, Sebastián's suffering on account of Perla would explain a desire for revenge.

There are also more disturbing readings. Details throughout the play allow us to question Perla's sanity: her "contact with the Holy Father of [the] nation Artigas" (107), the "*typically childish pose*" (108) she adopts to write in her diary, her obsession with Sebastián that combines contempt with an overwhelming need to meet with him, the progressive mimetization with the character of Melchora Cuenca. This interpretation is reinforced by the following stage direction from Armas:

(The background changes. Boxes can be seen. From the ground up to the ceiling, the boxes have numbers of years ranging from 1966 to 2006. In some of the boxes the numbers appear complete, in others only the beginning or the end of the numbers can be seen. These boxes form a labyrinth through which PERLA *will move. Each box she takes out will let a light go through that will make the environment feel more unreal. At regular intervals there are white tunics that she has worn throughout her teaching career and that are hanging like white shadows.)* (109)

If we are walking through the labyrinth of Perla's mind, nothing can assure us that what we find are anything other than ghosts (*"white shadows"*).

In addition, the manuscript of *Present, Señorita* originally had the following stage direction: "In order to maintain the structure of a monologue, the actress will also record the characters who appear on the telephone calls."[11] In those performances in which Sebastián's voice is recorded by the same actress who performs the role of Perla, it would be understandable to believe that the calls and Sebastián's visit might not exist outside of Perla's mind.

Another likely interpretation of the play, one which would take it far from realism and into an allegorical realm, is based on the equivalence Perla establishes between Sebastián, who did not want to be learned or enlightened (did not adjust to the status quo), and "the bad citizens" (those who protested) that Perla (the "lancer" [103]) reported to the authorities. In the context of a military dictatorship, references to "admired [...] operational goals" (116) and having "kept out of [her] way" (120) acquire sinister connotations.

If Sebastián is someone who did not learn and who faced again and again a relentless authoritarian figure, his "Present, Señorita" brings to mind the lists with the names of the ones who are absent, those who did not survive the encounter with the "*mad animal, ready to kill*" (120) of the dictatorial government, those who only are—as Sebastián's figure—nothing more than a shadow.[12]

---

[11] Note of the editors of the original Spanish version: This direction was taken off the version corrected by Dino Armas for this publication. (Email to the editors of the Spanish version. January 19, 2017.)

[12] Essay translated by Álex Omar Bratkievich.

CHAPTER FIVE
Social Turbulence, Oppression, and Indoctrination

The Media's Clutches

Sea Murmur

Dino Armas

Translation by Gabriela Christie Toletti

Characters:

> AMALIA
> AVELINO
> INÉS
> SANTIAGO
> LAURA
> PABLO

(AMALIA and AVELINO sitting in front of the television. She is watching very carefully. As he yawns every once in a while, he is partially paying attention. INÉS nervously looking out the window. Sounds of sirens, explosions, horns, distant confused noises. Suddenly, a different sound–like that of a tense wire that breaks–overpowers the other sounds. The three actors break character for an instant. They look at each other puzzled. The sound of the television comes back (now a voice in Italian) and the sounds outside (until now muted), and the actors return to their characters.)

AMALIA: *(Anxious. Pointing at the television.)* Look, Avelino, look….

AVELINO: Oh…? What…?

AMALIA: Floods. Now they are happening in Venice. Look. Look at the water marks on the walls. We are lucky to have grass. It must be so hard to live like that: with water everywhere, all around. I don't know how those old buildings can stay standing. There is even moss on the walls. *(Her face closer to the television.)* Because that green there by the channel must be moss… I think. *(She distances herself from the television. With a different tone. Talking to him.)* Italians have always had the reputation of being unkempt and careless. Because, I say…. I think…. Without land, all the waste has to end up in the water. And with so many Venetians needing to go to the bathroom

143

at the same time, that has to leave a mark.... Although the color wouldn't be green, right?

AVELINO: *(Showing no interest.)* I don't know....

AMALIA: How wonderful it is to be connected to the cable. I've learned more from cable than from all the teachers I had from kindergarten through sixth grade.

AVELINO: Well, yes! It looks as if you have been taking an intensive course. You haven't slept a wink in days, right?

AMALIA: Five, man. I have been hanging around for five days. And, God willing, I will endure five more days. But you cannot say the same. You have taken some good old naps....

AVELINO: I would sleep better in bed and not lying here, next to the television.

AMALIA: Avelino, we already talked about it. We agreed that you have to keep me company. Besides, just think about this, reason with me. We are already old, we have little time left to learn more....

AVELINO: With what I know I have enough to spare.

AMALIA: Yes, right! You are an ignoramus! We never even traveled anywhere....

AVELINO: Of course we have: we went to Punta Colorada;[1] spent a week in Concordia....[2]

AMALIA: And that means knowing stuff? I mean to know about the world, people, things.... Remember everything our sixth grade teacher Amabilia Rosa taught us. Keep her in mind.

AVELINO: Yes, of course I remember *"Chancha Colorada".*[3] She was fat and red-haired....

---

[1] Translator's Note: Punta Colorada (literally: "Red Point") is a small peninsula and resort in the department of Maldonado, Uruguay. It is very close to the resort of Piriápolis.

[2] TN: Concordia is a city in the north-east of the province of Entre Ríos in Argentina. The city's full name is San Antonio de Padua de la Concordia.

[3] TN: Chancha Colorada (literally: "Red Pig" or "Miss Red Piggie") is the nickname these characters use to refer to their teacher, who was overweight and had red hair.

AMALIA: She made us accurately memorize the names of the countries in Europe, Asia, and Africa, with all their capital cities! She was relentless. You could not forget even one. Poor *"Chancha"*! If she were resurrected right now and sat in front of cable television like we do, she would die again. The countries that she taught about no longer exist. What the... excuse the expression.... What the fuck! Always bugging us with the Belgian Congo and its rivers and capital. *(Gets louder.)* Indochina... Yugoslavia... the Soviet Union became Russia and the Russians stopped being Soviets and Communists. The same with Czechoslovakia. Czechoslovakia, the name of *"Chancha"*'s school.... A school cannot have the name of a country that is no longer on the map. Or can it? What do you think?

AVELINO: And, what do I know?

AMALIA: Why do I waste my time asking you? *(Triumphant.)* "School Amabilia Iturralde Rosa Fuentes." That's it! Instead of Czechoslovakia that does not exist anymore, the school should be named after the one who was first an exemplary teacher and then the school principal....

AVELINO: *"Chancha Colorada"* doesn't exist anymore either.

AMALIA: *(Looking at him angrily.)* True, she doesn't exist anymore. To think that so many good people die and others are still alive and well. *(Looks at the time. Changes the channel.)*

AVELINO: What are you doing?

AMALIA: Changing. I want to see what is happening in the Holy Land....

AVELINO: Don't tell me now that you're going to start praying next to the television?

AMALIA: Last night, in Palestine, when you were in the middle of one of your dreams, there was a clash between Jews and Muslims and they showed a close-up of the death of a Palestinian. I'm sure they will show it again. Blood ran across his face, chest... and he did not die. He screamed and moved....

145

AVELINO: What was he screaming?

AMALIA: I don't know. It did not have subtitles like in the movies. Do you think if they shot you in the face like they shot the Muslim, rather than screaming in Uruguayan, you would start to scream in other languages?

AVELINO: The cry of someone dying is the same here and everywhere.

AMALIA: *(Looks surprised.)* Suddenly you are wound up! You were able to say all that at once?

AVELINO: Sometimes I do not feel like talking.

AMALIA: Sometimes? Always.

AVELINO: Maybe.

AMALIA: *(Facing the television.)* I cannot find the death of the Muslim. Ah, but I like this one. *(Looks interested. More noise outside. INÉS stifles a scream.)*

AVELINO: What's wrong?

INÉS: Outside…. Things are worse. Don't you hear?

AVELINO: How is it possible to hear anything with the noise of your grandmother's television? Would you believe that she is watching a Chinese dance now…?

AMALIA: *(Stands up.)* Nippon, you are such a dumb-ass. The fact that they are all yellow, with stretched eyes, does not mean they are all the same.

AVELINO: Do not say anything else: another lesson of *"Chancha Colorada"*.

AMALIA: No. The difference between a Chinese and a Japanese I learned thanks to my son's gift. *(Caresses or points at the device.)* The Discovery Channel and CNN opened my eyes to the world….

AVELINO: Another difference. And that one is not one that cable taught me. I live it permanently. Santiago is your child when you associate him

146

with cable television, but when he argues and screams like crazy with his wife, then he is my son.

AMALIA: Again making speeches.

AVELINO: Speeches?

AMALIA: Yes, you said at least four consecutive sentences…. *(She changes the channel.)*

AVELINO: Amalia… since you changed the channel… by the way, why don't you turn the volume down a bit? Inés wants to know what's happening outside….

AMALIA: Oh, no… no way… I won't turn down the volume now that channel 37 is showing an earthquake live. Avelino, if one cannot hear the noises well, no earthquake is worth watching. Let's do a test. You cover your eyes and listen.

AVELINO: But….

AMALIA: *(Ordering soft but firm.)* Do it Avelino.

AVELINO: OK…. I'll do it. *(He closes his eyes. She lowers the volume.)*

AMALIA: So, tell me, always without opening your eyes, OK? What do you hear?

AVELINO: And… something like when you step on an egg… but a large egg…. *(She turns up the volume a little more.)*

AMALIA: And now?

AVELINO: Now as if there were many eggshells trodden by many people.

AMALIA: *(Sounding very self-sufficient.)* Sure… you heard that because I changed the volume. *(She positions herself behind him. She covers his eyes with one hand.)* With the volume so soft, an earthquake is not an earthquake. It's a soft tremor…. It's nothing. *(Turns up the volume, very loud. He jumps. The sound is annoying. She screams.)* Listen now. *(Happy.)* Isn't this better? You see that now the outside noises don't bother us?

147

INÉS:	*(Yelling.)* Grandpa, tell her to turn it down.
AMALIA:	Look…. Look how that house crushes those poor horses…. How it rips open their guts….
AVELINO:	*(Yelling.)* Darling, turn down the volume. The television is going to drive us crazy.
AMALIA:	*(Also yelling.)* What? *(AVELINO with signals, repeats his previous lines. She, almost disgusted, turns down the volume a little bit.)*
AVELINO:	Isn't there anything else to watch?
AMALIA:	At this time? You have horror movies, kung fu…. *(In a different tone.)* You wouldn't want to watch a soap opera, right?
AVELINO:	No. I want something quieter. May I…? *(He makes a signal to ask for the remote control. She hands it to him after doubting for a second. He turns down the volume.)*
AMALIA:	Don't turn it down so much, animal. *(He turns it up a little.)* So, Mister, you want something quieter? I'll have to look at a magazine…. *(Looks for a magazine. INÉS gets closer to her.)*
INÉS:	Grandma, can't we watch a local channel? Maybe they are showing what is going on out there….
AMALIA:	*(With the television guide in her hands, not looking at her.)* Upstairs you have two televisions. There's one in every room….
INÉS:	Mine is not working well and the other one… the other one broke last night.
AMALIA:	Your parents' television?
INÉS:	Yes.
AVELINO:	Ah, now it makes sense. See. Amalia, there were no street noises. Those were from the television. How can a television break? If it's not because of a short, it has to be pushed by someone… or you have to throw it at someone else… I do not know.

AMALIA: *(Talking to INÉS. Very cold attitude. Without looking at her.)* Yours is not working. Your parents' television broke. So no one touches my television.

INÉS: Grandma, here on the corner, they are mounting barricades, burning tires. I'm sure they are showing it on some local channel.

AMALIA: Burning tires.... They are burning tires.... It's what I always say. Uruguayan television cannot compete with any other. Burning tires when television channels around the world are showing people lighting themselves on fire. To the point that Argentineans are opening their eyes and–without showing people burning alive–are showing men and women, and–hear what I'm saying–even children chained to whatever. Trees, fences, even in their workplace. And here we are content with burning tires.... And just think how bad black smoke looks on television....

INÉS: But, grandmother, what's going on there in the corner is true....

AMALIA: And what I see here is also true. And it is happening at the same time in New York, in Australia, or in the most remote village in Africa....

INÉS: But what's happening outside is happening to our neighbors, to my friends, to people who have been living for years in the neighborhood. Or you two are going to say that you don't know Doña Rosa, Don Martín, their children...? It is for them that they are barricading. It is because of them that there is that black smoke that you find so ugly....

AMALIA: It is better to lose sight of those people than to find them. If something happens to Doña Rosa or her husband or her children, there must be a reason for it. Things do not come alone: they were looking for it. We are not erecting barricades and we are not burning tires. This is a quiet home. Here the police are not going to come for no reason.... And if you want to find out what is happening outside, you have the radio. Or are you going to tell me that the radio does not work either? Otherwise just go outside. Watch what is happening next door. *(Holding the TV guide. To*

149

her husband.) Here I found something very calm. The medical channel. It's 89.

INÉS: I'll talk to Dad. *(Fakes a movement.)*

AMALIA: *(Soft but with intention.)* Are you sure?

INÉS: Mom will understand me.

AVELINO: Do you think it would be wise? They are still locked in their room. I just walked by and strange noises could still be heard. *(To AMALIA.)* Do you think they are fixing the television? Does the boy know how to fix appliances? Maybe he learned it in the private school we sent him to. It was only for a few months... but who knows....

AMALIA: Maybe they are looking at the neighborhood troubles from the balcony. *(To INÉS.)* See? You can go to watch it there with them.

INÉS: Grandma... how can you be like that...?

AMALIA: They might not open because they are always locking their door. *(Turns her back to INÉS. To AVELINO.)* Read what's on television at this time. *(INÉS walks out.)*

AVELINO: *(Reading.)* "Heart surgery. New techniques...." *(Gasps.)* But....

AMALIA: Didn't you want something quiet? Well: these programs are the quietest. Almost without any text. They say stuff like, "tweezers," "scalpel," "more plasma," "what's the blood pressure?" And then nothing. You have to see the brightness of the scalpel when it opens the flesh; how cotton changes colors when the blood dries up. How well the laser sutures look. The text does not matter; the enjoyable part is in the picture, in focus of the lens. Close-ups of the gloved hands, the boxes with the instruments, the devices. It's amazing how much you can learn. A week watching this medical channel and I can leave the hospital's doctor open-mouthed. And you, you should do like me. Do not stick to Band-Aids and hydrogen peroxide. Try to learn, to assimilate. Look at the magazine... there is a program about the prostate....

AVELINO: Come on, woman; there is nothing wrong with my prostate.

AMALIA: For now. Watching this channel you can prevent it....

INÉS: *(With intent.)* And to prevent tongue cancer, is there anything yet?

AMALIA: *(Also with intent.)* And you want to know that because of a particular problem of yours? Sometimes I don't know who you take after. *(AVELINO looks horrified as he watches a surgery on television.)* You are the only strange one in this family. You don't take after me. That's for sure.

INÉS: Maybe I take after my grandfather.

AMALIA: Yes, it could be. Look. He looks green. He already put himself in the place of the patient being operated on. You two are always the defenders of lost causes. Instead of feeling like the doctor, no, he thinks of the sick. And you, in Doña Rosa's mess, you side with her. You always side with the losers. Yes, you definitely don't take after me, or after Laura, and even less after Santiago....

INÉS: *(Between irony and anger.)* Maybe I'm not their daughter or your granddaughter.

AMALIA: Inesita.... That is stuff out of soap operas and not real life. To your own chagrin, you are not the daughter or granddaughter of some *desaparecido*[4] or some gypsy woman who left you at the doorsteps of this house. You are—whether you like it or not—blood of our blood. Oh, speaking of blood, look, Avelino, that person is bleeding a lot. Is it a man or a woman? Covered like that, you cannot tell what they are. That's why you have to watch these programs from the beginning. Otherwise, you cannot tell who is acting as the patient....

AVELINO: *(Hopeful.)* Oh, they are acting as patients? So the program is really fiction?

---

[4]   TN: Desaparecido or desaparecida (literally: "missing" or "vanished") are those who vanished during the military dictatorships in the Southern Cone in the 1970s and 1980s. Most of them were political dissidents, militants, left-wing activists, students, journalists, and other private citizens who were arrested by the government just for thinking differently and who then vanished without a trace. The term desaparecido is most commonly associated with those who vanished during the Argentine Military Dictatorship known as the Dirty War (1976-1983).

AMALIA: No. These are actual operations. All real. *(He diverts—as before—his eyesight from the television.)* But look at the television, man. Do not look down. You're missing the best. That looks like a silver scalpel. Look how it shines.

AVELINO: You just said that they were acting as patients....

AMALIA: It's a way of talking. At the end of the day, don't we all act? You, her, me, Laura, Santiago.... *(Louder.)* Doña Rosa and her children....

INÉS: And what is your role, grandmother Amalia?

AMALIA: If you had lived the hardships that I had to go through as a girl, you'd know what my role is.

INÉS: *(Something like a litany, like something that has been repeated over and over.)* Oh yeah.... Hunger.... Having to eat rats.... Without shoes or decent clothes....

AMALIA: *(With a different tone.)* And the humiliation... the looks of disgust and pity poorly combined.... One had to survive despite everything....

INÉS: Grandfather Avelino, is that just a story of hers? Did you live through things like that? Is it true? Part of the truth? Or is everything a big lie?

AMALIA: Avelino, you don't have to answer.

INÉS: If you endured so many hardships, how come the family has all this now?

AMALIA: You mean, house, food, work, and an education for you?

INÉS: How did you make money to pay for those things?

AMALIA: *(Smiles.)* How? Oh, girl, God asks less and yet forgives. *(Loud noise outside. Siren. Inés goes to look out the window.)*

AVELINO: *(Watching television.)* Are those firemen?

AMALIA: It seems like a police siren....

INÉS: Grandfather, come here. Look.

AVELINO: *(From his place and position.)* You tell me. Tell me what you see.

INÉS: More and more cars, more people. They run through the smoke…
              some are dressed like us, others in uniform….

AVELINO: *(They look slightly startled. AMALIA and AVELINO may look at
              each other or not.)* Uniforms…? What type of uniforms…?

INÉS: Blue, green, gray, orange….

AVELINO: And white uniforms?

INÉS: No. I don't see any…. I don't think….

AMALIA: How can you be so sure? Being able to tell every color….

INÉS: Because it is so bright. There are many lights focusing on Doña
              Rosa's house. If you'd come here, you would also see it….

AMALIA: And miss this aphrodisiac recipe? No, thanks.

AVELINO: What recipe? Weren't we watching an operation?

AMALIA: I changed the channel.

AVELINO: I did not realize.

AMALIA: You are getting worse. And then you say I'm making it up. I even
              think that you're unable to differentiate between a ripe avocado
              and a kidney, a walnut and a brain…. Do not look at me like that.
              Since you're not doing anything better, just write the recipe because
              I want to have it. *(Gives him a note pad.)*

INÉS: *(Soft.)* They are surrounding the house. They seem to have
              weapons….

AMALIA: *(To the husband.)* Ginger. He added ginger, right?

AVELINO: *(Taking notes.)* Yes….

INÉS: There are so many people…. Why? In Doña Rosa's family there are only three... four. Her, her husband, two children...

AVELINO: What is the name of the youngest son?

INÉS: You don't know?

AVELINO: I have it on the tip of my tongue but it's not coming out. Marcos is the oldest....

INÉS: Pablo is the youngest....

AMALIA: Pablo is more or less your age, right?

INÉS: Yes....

AMALIA: He looks like an angel, like he could not kill a fly. But he is the worst of them all. I swear. The uniformed people must be there for him. First for him and then for the rest of the family. They are all in the middle of a big mess. They are in the middle of something they should not be. Something dangerous. (*Short pause. Looks at INÉS.*) You don't know anything, right?

INÉS: Me...?

AMALIA: You seem so interested.... Besides, you socialize with them. He has come here. I know. He has sometimes left things for you: packages, papers....

AVELINO: (*Loud. Changes the tone. Because of the recipe.*) I got lost. The cook is going so fast that I didn't have time to write the last part....

AMALIA: It's OK, stop doing that.

AVELINO: But didn't you want the recipe?

AMALIA: Yes... a tropical aphrodisiac recipe.... Take a look at yourself. Look at me. More than a recipe, we need a miracle. If the Pope was giving the recipe instead of that frog cook, then yes, I would make you write it down word for word.

AVELINO: Look, Amalia. I'm still a man. (*She looks at him fast and sideways.*)

AMALIA: Change the channel, put on *Chronicle*, and let's see if they show

154

some assault or a crime of passion, as I finish the conversation with Inés. (*He changes channels. Music of the* Chronicle *television program is heard.*)

AVELINO: You were right. (*Reads from the screen.*) "Tremendous crash on the road. There are three dead." (*Amalia has been slowly approaching Inés.*)

AMALIA: What were we talking about? Oh, I remember. I remember perfectly. We were talking about Pablo, the youngest son of Doña Rosa, the strange son who does not work... the one who disappears for weeks.... That one turned out to be a good friend of yours. Would you say that? Or should I use other words? Partners? Associates.... Yes, I like that better. Associates in... now I'll let you complete the sentence. Inés and Pablo are associates in...?

AVELINO: (*Loud.*) Amalia.... A children's rapist....

AMALIA: (*Runs to him and to the television.*) Where...?

AVELINO: In Brazil I think....

AMALIA: In Brazil.... Aha: did he rape black or white children?

AVELINO: I don't know. And what's the difference?

AMALIA: Of course there are differences. Someone white is not the same as someone black. Avelino, if you were black... you would have never laid a hand on me.

INÉS: (*Calm.*) Grandma....

AMALIA: (*Without looking at her.*) What...?

INÉS: We have some unfinished business....

AMALIA: What? (*Still not looking at her.*)

INÉS: You wanted to know....

AMALIA: Afterwards. Not now. (*To the husband.*) Did you see? It's like I thought. He raped more blacks than whites. That means something.

155

I bet that then he killed and buried them.

AVELINO: How do you know?

AMALIA: Years of watching television. *(Noise outside.)*

INÉS: They are using gas. But nobody is going to do anything? No neighbor is going to help out? I…. *(Starts to move.)*

AVELINO: *(Serious. Different tone.)* Stay out of this. *(INÉS is facing away from him. Stays still. Deep silence.)*

INÉS: And now? What's going on? You can't hear anything. No noise….

AMALIA: *(Hitting the television, tries to fix it.)* It's brand new. It cannot be broken. *(To AVELINO.)* Did you touch something you shouldn't have? It cannot just suddenly lose the sound.

INÉS: *(Monotone.)* Nothing can be heard outside either….

(Noise of broken/snapped wire startles all three. They break character.)

AVELINO: Already…?

AMALIA: It cannot be right….

INÉS: It's too early….

(The outside noises reappear loudly, but not the sounds of the television. Somewhat distorted at first, then they normalize. SANTIAGO and LAURA enter.)

LAURA: Excuse me. Is it too late?

SANTIAGO: There were no noises….

AMALIA: Your father must have hooks instead of fingers. Can you believe that he broke the television…?

LAURA: It did not last long. Like the one in our bedroom, Santiago. *(To AVELINO.)* Did yours also fall, inadvertently, like it happened with my husband?

SANTIAGO: Laura…. *(Serious. Threatening tone.)*

LAURA: *(Ironic.)* Excuse me: I must always think the worst. But there are so many coincidences. Could your son have bought it in one of those giant supermarket sales? *(To AMALIA.)* Just in case, mother, did you keep the warranty?

AMALIA: Santiaguito, tell your wife to stop throwing those insinuations around.

INÉS: Dad…. Out there….

SANTIAGO: Now we are not talking about outside, we are talking about my mother's television.

INÉS: But, Dad….

LAURA: Do not insist, Inés. Your father said the three holy words: "Mom" and "broken television." After that, there cannot be anything else. *(SANTIAGO, AVELINO, and AMALIA gather around the television and test different ways to fix it.)*

INÉS: But outside there….

LAURA: I won't ask you for the bill, Santi; you didn't use my card, right?

AMALIA: Make her shut up, boy.

SANTIAGO: Laura… stop it once and for all.

INÉS: Out there horrible things are happening and you….

AMALIA: *(Fierce.)* That comment about shutting up was intended for you too.

SANTIAGO: You heard what your grandmother said. You'd better stay out of all that.

INÉS: But you are not going to do anything?

SANTIAGO: No. Nothing. Neither you nor us. The problems of those people outside are theirs and theirs alone. Neither yours nor mine.

AMALIA: Your father and I have been telling her the same thing all day. But she didn't care to listen. Fortunately, you also told her the same thing.

INÉS: And you, Mom…. Do you think like them?

LAURA: I have enough with my stuff. I don't want to add one more problem. We will talk later, baby….

INÉS: When is later, Mom?

LAURA: Later, Inés.

INÉS: But I….

AMALIA: It seems as if we were speaking different languages. Then is then, and later is later. Is that so difficult for you to understand? The television broke and you don't seem to care. You care about other things. About strangers. *(Different tone. To SANTIAGO.)* Oh, baby, do you think I should call the service?

SANTIAGO: Not yet! Let me try something. I have a knack with televisions. Have faith in me.

LAURA: Don Avelino, don't get distracted. Try to help my husband. What if the television falls like ours? *(Laughs softly.)* This must be the Night of the Broken Televisions. Amalia *(Giving no importance to the previous comment.)* Do you know what I like about the cable, Santi?

SANTIAGO: No. Maybe cooking programs…?

AMALIA: That there are no commercials. Because, tell me, apart from going to the bathroom or quickly preparing something to eat, what can be done during commercials?

INÉS: People can talk to each other, grandmother….

AMALIA: About what? About how prices go up? About the weather? About diseases? About the latest politician in the spotlight? Or about families persecuted for what they do? *(Wire noise again. Louder and more prolonged.)*

158

AVELINO: We have little time left.

AMALIA: We have to speed everything up.

SANTIAGO: Should I begin or do you want to do it?

LAURA: I'll do it. *(He moves something on the television and sound comes out. Exclamations from AMALIA, AVELINO, and SANTIAGO.)* At least the television is fixed. Isn't that right, mother-in-law? Let's see how long it lasts….

INÉS: *(Distressed.)* No, let's not talk about the television. We need to talk about what is happening outside….

LAURA: I told you we'll speak later. *(Then to AMALIA.)* Since you know so much about cable television, tell me, are there any programs about battered women?

SANTIAGO: How far are you going to go?

AMALIA: Just drop it, boy! Let me tell you, Laurita, yes, there are many programs about battered women. I would say that of all races and colors….

LAURA: I'm relieved to hear that, Amalia.

AMALIA: Why?

LAURA: Because I thought it was just my problem.

AMALIA: There are Spanish, Argentinean, North American problems. Isn't that right, Avelino? Oh, he already fell asleep.

SANTIAGO: Should I wake him up?

AMALIA: No. What for? Leave him alone. But take the magazine and the remote control from him. He could break it. *(SANTIAGO keeps those two things. He reads or changes channels.)*

LAURA: And are there programs about Uruguayan battered women?

AMALIA: The official channel has one. But it lacks glamor. The ones that really get to me are the ones made in Miami. Do you want me to tell you about the last one I watched? Last night at dawn?

SANTIAGO: If we say no, you are still going to tell us. So, come on. We are listening.

AMALIA: Good, it turns out that a Cuban woman who now lives in Miami… kind of brown, she was… with furiously blond dyed hair and a red mouth, as red as it could be, and dressed in clothes that can only be found in Miami and nowhere else….

LAURA: Inés, get closer. Your grandmother is interested in fashion….

AMALIA: *(Pretends not to hear LAURA's comment.)* The Cuban was called María Fátima de Todos los Santos…. At a certain moment, she showed part of her body and you could see it was full of pimples….

SANTIAGO: Pimples…?

AMALIA: Of all sizes. A psychological reaction, she said. A product of the beatings that her concubine gave her. Oh, guess the man's name?

SANTIAGO: No idea.

AMALIA: Oh, baby, if he is Cuban, what could he be called? Fidel Ernesto. That's the only option. Well, it turns out that Fidel Ernesto, between sugar beet harvest and sugar cane harvest, would beat the hell out of her. And with so much beating and anguish, María Fátima got pimples everywhere. Until one day she was fed up, so she got on a raft and went to Miami. And there she found a gringo with money and all….

LAURA: Then, I will probably get pimples too. What becomes clear as I hear your story is that I have to get a raft and jump into the Río de la Plata.[5] Maybe I'll have the same fate as María Fátima and find myself a man from Buenos Aires, a Porteño[6] with dough! And to

---

[5]   TN: Río de la Plata (literally: "River of Silver") is translated as "River Plate" in British English and the Commonwealth and "La Plata River" (Occasionally "Plata River") in other English-speaking countries. It is formed by the confluence of the Uruguay and Panamá rivers and empties into the Atlantic Ocean. Depending on the geographer, the Río de la Plata may be considered a river, an estuary, or a marginal sea. In Uruguay and Argentina it is usually considered a river and, therefore, the widest river in the world with a maximum width of 140 miles.

[6]   TN: In Spanish, porteño (literally: "from the port") refers to people who live in a port city. The largest city to which the term is applied is Buenos Aires, Argentina. Since the end of the nineteenth century, Porteño

make everything fit perfectly, your son, my husband, would have to be named... Santiago Fidel, isn't that right?

SANTIAGO: *(Biting his lips.)* It seems that what you got a while ago was not enough....

LAURA: Let me see. You want me to think about the blows you gave me or what happened before that? Do you want me to remember that you tried to have sex with me, and again you couldn't? It's either that or the hitting? Say it out loud so that you clear that up for anyone who had a doubt, including me....

AMALIA: Laura, please. The girl is here. Why don't you talk about that stuff when you are by yourselves? (*With gestures to INÉS.*) We are in the middle of family television hour.

LAURA: Of course you had to come up with something like that. You know what I think? That the cable television guide is your little bible. No, not your bible. It's your self-help book. You can manage with a little magazine like that, but I need another type of self-help....

INÉS: Mom.... It's better to just drop it. You know how all this ends....

LAURA: Weren't you the one who asked me to speak? Now you want me to shut up?

SANTIAGO: You like to appear the victim in front of everyone. Too bad no one knows what you really are like when you are locked up with me in the bedroom. You are quite different.

LAURA: I'm the worst, right? Say it. Say it. Do not leave it up in the air.

SANTIAGO: You appear to be one thing but you are something quite different.

LAURA: I'm like you made me to be.

SANTIAGO: Do not blame me for your stuff. Deal with your madness like I deal with mine.

AMALIA: If you are going to argue, don't be so loud; otherwise, one cannot appreciate the news show.

has become a name or demonym for the people of Buenos Aires.

LAURA: I've had enough. You know what you can do with the wonderful television that your son gave you as a gift?

AMALIA: No, I do not know. I'm hoping you will tell me. I liked the word "gift." At least, Santi was kind enough and had the delicacy to remember Mother's day…. And you, what did your daughter give you for Mother's day?

LAURA: Nothing.

AMALIA: See? Then you cannot talk.

INÉS: Setting a date to give gifts is a commercial stupidity.

AMALIA: *(Taunting the other women with her tone and attitude.)* Good, then; thanks to that commercial stupidity, as you call it, I have cable television.

LAURA: *(Slow, without any emphasis, not screaming.)* That cable, along with the TV that you are permanently bragging about… you can just stick it up your ass.

AMALIA: *(To SANTIAGO.)* Son, just hit her! She well deserves it!

SANTIAGO: Mom, you didn't even have to ask me. To say "ass" to you…. *(Approaching LAURA with threatening attitude.)*

LAURA: Finally! This is the party I wanted to attend. Do not tell me, Santiago, that at last we will do it in front of everyone? Inés, now you will be able to participate in the only thing that your father and I do, almost every other day, while we are locked up in the room. *(To him.)* Tell me, are you going to cover my mouth so that I don't scream? Or can I scream today?

AMALIA: *(Very soft.)* Santiaguito… baby… if you're going to be very violent, better to take her upstairs. *(Elbowing AVELINO.)* And you, wake up, sloth!

AVELINO: What…? What…?

AMALIA: Do as I do. We have to stay awake. We can't miss anything.

162

SANTIAGO: *(Breathing heavily. LAURA, too. The two go on screaming and looking at each other.)* Finally you've shown your true colors in front of everyone. We will not go upstairs. I want them to see how you enjoy every stroke, how your eyes shine when I give it to you over and over....

LAURA: *(Taking SANTIAGO's tone.)* Santiago.... Do you want me to insult you? Or should I just let myself be hit? Should I scratch you? *(Cutting noise of the tense wire. Outside a very loud noise. Inés runs to look. Then she steps back slowly.)*

INÉS: It's Pablo.... He is in the middle of the street.... *(Inside noises get louder: noises of the television, insults, and the fight among the parents.)* Do something.... Do something! Don't leave him alone.... *(Everyone continues doing their own things. She approaches AVELINO.)* Grandpa... help me.... *(She pulls him. AVELINO distances himself and stands still, watching television or looking away.)* Grandmother Amalia.... You are in charge here. They do what you say.... *(AMALIA, as if she were not listening, turns up the television volume.)* You can. You can do something. Help me.... *(AMALIA, rabid, turns up the volume even louder. INÉS has to scream her words.)* But don't you see that he will be killed out there...? Don't leave me like this.... We must do something, Grandmother.... Grandmother Amalia. For goodness sake. Oh my God....

AMALIA: *(Ferocious, slams the television. The television sound stops working.)* This is my god. My only god. *(Stays standing wide-eyed. AVELINO repeats something very softly that cannot be understood. SANTIAGO and LAURA, in different corners, breathing agitated. Outside, silence also. INÉS looks at everyone.)*

PABLO: *(Outside.)* Inééééés.... *(Dry sound that interrupts his cry. INÉS, after slightly doubting, runs away. Exits.)*

AVELINO: *(Starts low and then raises his voice.)* By banging on the television, the channel got changed.... This one is local.... Look. She is the one running.... It's Inés. Look. It's Inés on TV....

AMALIA: *(Changes tone and attitude.)* On TV...? Inés...?

AVELINO: Yes, it's her. She is running.... She is running, but... but it looks like they won't let her through....

AMALIA: Our Inés on TV...? *(Approaching the television.)*

AVELINO: Yes, take a look. *(LAURA and SANTIAGO, after looking at each other, get close to the television.)*

AMALIA: My granddaughter on TV.... With what grace she runs.... What is that thing lying in the middle of the street...?

AVELINO: It looks like Pablo, doesn't it?

AMALIA: It's great that they are showing a close-up of her.... Inés looks cuter on TV than she really is. Must be because of the filters they are using... the lights....

AVELINO: They won't let her keep going....

INÉS: *(Outside, heard from far away.)* Pablo....

SANTIAGO: What did the girl say?

LAURA: Turn up the volume so we can hear better. *(AMALIA does it.)*

INÉS: *(Outside, live. Also recorded but not well-timed.)* Pablo.... Pa.... *(Sharp sounds that interrupt their words.)*

AMALIA: Pablo, she said Pablo....

(Sound of the tense wire that breaks and becomes a very long ringing sound. The actors start taking off some items of clothing and leaving them in an orderly manner inside a box. Now we can see that they wear a kind of uniform that homogenizes them. They also turn the television towards the audience and it is noticeable that it is hollow, that it is just a prop. They turn off the light bulb that provided the light.)

LAURA: We should finish....

AVELINO: Let's continue tomorrow.

164

AMALIA: If we can....

LAURA: If they let us.... (*PABLO comes in with a tape recorder and stands still for a moment. INÉS comes in and stays behind him.*)

PABLO: Today the sound did not come out very well. Good thing that all of you kept it going anyway. There was a time when I did not know what to do....

SANTIAGO: I'm not coming tomorrow. I have visits....

LAURA: And what do I do...?

AMALIA: (*To INÉS.*) Are you coming? (*AMALIA is no longer the character but quite the opposite. The same happens with the other characters. They are others.*)

INÉS: Yes. No one is coming to see me.

AMALIA: No one is coming to see me either. They used to come.... Elsa used to come with.... Not anymore. They no longer come. I might not have anyone left. I'll ask. But they might not answer.... (*Exits.*)

AVELINO: Oh, don't count me in for tomorrow. There's a very important soccer match. I want to listen to the game. (*Walks. Doubts. He looks at the others.*) Is the game tomorrow? Or the day after tomorrow? (*SANTIAGO shrugs his shoulders. AVELINO exits.*)

SANTIAGO: (*Asks everyone but no one in particular.*) Tomorrow is Saturday, right? (*No one answers. He exits. The doorbell rings.*)

LAURA: Last call.... (*Smiles shyly to the others.*) I'm leaving.... (*Walks away. Turns back.*) Why don't we change countries tomorrow? Instead of Uruguay, can we pretend we are in France? In Paris... under the Eiffel Tower or in Notre-Dame, beside the Seine River.... I have never been in Paris. I will like it. I used to know a French song... before.... (*She leaves, softly humming a French waltz. INÉS starts to walk away and exits.*)

PABLO: Are you leaving?

INÉS: You are not?

165

PABLO: They can come get me if they want.... I don't care.

INÉS: They sometimes mistreat people....

PABLO: Yes....

INÉS: I'm leaving....

PABLO: *(She walks. He tries to get her attention.)* I have a new sound for tomorrow.

INÉS: *(From her place.)* More shots? A new siren?

PABLO: Do you want to hear it?

INÉS: OK.... *(Shows insecurity or hurries. He turns on the tape recorder. A sea murmur sound can be heard.)*

PABLO: Waves... a beach....

INÉS: A sea... running water.... *(Turns away to leave.)*

PABLO: Wait. Do you like it?

INÉS: Yes....

PABLO: Today you used my name for my character....

INÉS: Yes....

PABLO: My real name. Tomorrow, whether we are in Paris or here, can you call me by the same name?

INÉS: Yes. *(Soft voice. Walks fast and exits.)*

PABLO: Wait. Can you say it again? *(She looks at him with an inquiring attitude.)* The name, I mean....

INÉS: *(Smiles.)* Pablo.... *(She rushes out. The doorbell rings insistently. PABLO sits on the floor. The tape recorder next to him, with the sound of the sea. He hugs himself and begins a back-and-forth movement.)*

PABLO: Pablo.... I am Pablo.... I am Pablo.... I am Pablo....

(The light dims on him. Darkness and only the sound, or murmur, of the sea.)

THE END

Dramatic Multiplicity in *Sea Murmur*

Dolores Rangel

Sea Murmur is a play that tackles a broad range of issues related to the dictatorship through metadrama as a starting point. This technique suggests the playwright is interested in detailing the nature and reach of theater itself and not only of what could be considered as the set of issues or thematic nucleus of the play.[1] In the case of *Sea Murmur*, the thematic content gets projected onto the suffocating and dehumanizing environment derived from a repressive political system, as well as onto the psychological behaviors, both collective and individual, that result from such a system.

The metadramatic structure disguises, with apparent simplicity, a dramatic complexity that translates into a questioning of theater's very ability of communicating. This communicative ability is exacerbated in the drama within the drama. Self-referentiality is indicative of the insufficiency of a single access plane to effectively add everything the playwright wishes to put forth on stage. Thus, the overlapped layers–or inserted dynamics–give the play a multidimensionality that becomes evident in the interpretation(s) given by the spectator.

The beginning and the end of *Sea Murmur* are the moments which show that the characters are, precisely, actors who are going to put on a theatrical performance. In this first plane, their intervention is brief and subtle. It could be said that the playwright intentionally minimizes the beginning so that the spectator might be able to disregard the fact that the substantial part of the play is an instance of role playing within the role and not a "direct" performance. This purpose crystallizes towards the end, since the senselessness and distancing obtained by returning to the first dramatic plane strike the spectator's awareness and make the final assimilation of the play difficult.

---

[1] Richard Hornby identifies five varieties of metadrama, which must be seen as instrumental. Two of these varieties are significant in Sea Murmur. One of them is the play within the play and the other is the role playing within the role. The first refers to the performance of a theatrical play framed within another, which generates questions of an existential kind about fiction and reality. Regarding the second type, for Hornby, a character's performance of another character suggests quandaries related to the human identity (Drama, Metadrama, and Perception. Cranbury, NJ: Associated UP, 1986).

The initial stage direction makes reference to three actors sitting in front of a TV and a series of noises, one of which takes precedence: that of "*a tense wire that breaks*" and causes them to react. Faced with it, the three actors break character for an instant and, a moment later, return to them (143). The play flows on immediately, without any additional reference to this jump to the other performance these actors are engaged in. The transition is smooth and consistent.

The movement out of this meta-referentiality comes at the end, with another stage direction about the "*[s]ound of the tense wire that breaks.*" At this moment, the actors change clothes and let the spectators see a "*kind of uniform that homogenizes them*" (164). It is also pointed out that the stage TV is a prop. The dialogue between the characters indicates that they have finished acting and will continue tomorrow. There are several comments regarding the possibility of certain changes, such as setting the plot in France instead of Uruguay. The last dialogue exchange occurs between Pablo and Inés, two youngsters who are apparently attracted to each other; he is happy because he has a new sound for the play, which explains the play's title and is, precisely, the sound of the sea.

The play performed by these actors, with certain regularity–apparently–and with occasional modifications–as mentioned before–revolves around a simple anecdote which displays elements of uncommunicativeness, estrangement, and domestic violence within a Uruguayan family affected at various levels by the repercussions of dictatorial repression. In this dramatic plane we see antagonistic nuclear groups, composed of an elderly couple, a younger couple (the male is the former's son), and the young daughter of the latter couple. The series of emotional and psychological tensions happens around and because of the television set, a prominent symbol of mass media. The television appears as a "subject/character" external to the family nucleus, yet internal and intrusive at the same time. It is a passive object but eminently active since it fosters certain family dynamics.

At this dramatic level the action is carried out in two spaces that entail two dynamics: the internal–the home of this Uruguayan family, and the external–the street and the houses of the neighbors across the street, where Inés' friend Pablo lives. Inés, daughter and granddaughter, acts as a bridge between the external dynamics of what could be called "real life" and the internal family dynamics, disturbed and out of touch with reality even though they are intimately connected to the "real facts" presented by the media.

The two spaces are highly significant since they circumscribe the possibilities of acting within these dynamics. The Uruguayan family nucleus that develops inside the house shows a complex relation of antagonistic forces linked to the coercive and violent dynamics derived from a dictatorial system. The characters can be "read" as forces of power in action.

The mother, Amalia, is an authoritarian, emasculating matriarch and the personification of the dictatorial system. Avelino, the husband, represents the series of subordinated elements in the system who obey without questioning, alienated, weak, without judgment or opinion or–even more so–personal decision. The couple's son is Santiago, an abusive man who beats his wife. He is the one who exerts physical violence in order to discipline the detractor to the system, which in this case is Laura, his wife. She is the civilian citizen abused by the system, who is revealed at the same time as an unhealthy subject whose masochistic condition is the direct result of the continuous abuse she receives. Inés is the character that seeks to consolidate a psychological neutrality and a communication based on direct action towards the real world.

The television stands for the media which do not communicate reality but instead stage fiction and escapism from the immediate true reality. The reality they do communicate, even though it could be true and "stimulating," is sedative and dehumanizing. Amalia says, "The Discovery Channel and CNN opened my eyes to the world…" (146). The TV's presence is accentuated by the extremely loud volume. Avelino says, "*(Yelling.)* Darling, turn down the volume. The television is going to drive us crazy" (148). Uruguayan TV programming is criticized and scorned by the grandmother: "[…] Uruguayan television cannot compete with any other. Burning tires when television channels around the world are showing people lighting themselves on fire…" (149).

The family dynamics are charged with physical violence, psychological pressure, and verbal abuse. This is demonstrated by the references to the beatings Santiago gives Laura, or by the TV broken because of the violence between the two of them. The psychological pressure and verbal abuse occur in the tense and aggressive confrontation between the characters, especially between Amalia, Laura, and Santiago, as well as in the allusions to Laura and Santiago spending all their time shut in because he beats her. The sarcasm and irony in certain dialogues reflect this verbal and psychological violence. Laura cannot interact directly with her mother-in-law, father-in-law, or husband except through sarcasm and irony as means to protect her voice. The opinions as to what is important are switched, which exacerbates the problems. This is the case when Amalia reacts against her granddaughter because the latter wants to help the neighbors in trouble and does not seem to care that one of the TVs just broke down.

The play denounces, instead of criticizing, the complex individual and group psychological relationships which emerge distorted and strongly interwoven when there is a dictatorial regime. Society is undermined in one of its basic foundations, cooperation for mutual well-being, and in one of its fundamental institutions, the family. *Sea Murmur* exposes the problems and the consequences, but there is not a criticism that works out the causes or the ideas supporting certain stances in detail; it does not focus on criticizing the dictatorship, the injustices, the power abuse, or the violence itself.

The play starts from this state of affairs and exposes the results of the situation as a series of attitudes, reactions, and negative ideas. It neither seeks to present a direct analysis nor to prompt an immediate analysis by the spectator: the assimilation of the exposed dynamics is left for the spectator to carry out. It does not seek to offer solutions or rectifications either; the situation is given and the spectator reacts primarily at an emotional level. It could be said that the first emotional reaction experienced by the spectator is frustration towards dynamics in which the characters trample on each other without seeing or seeking anything else beyond those dynamics. The immediacy cuts short the possibilities of resolution or change. The only character that has a chance, as we have already mentioned, is Inés, the granddaughter, symbol of the new generation and the disinterested spirit. Since she is only acting in a play, however, her ability to have an impact is limited. Nevertheless, something remains since at the end she agrees to make some changes in her performance. The changes suggest that relationships can become more personal, as she uses the real name of her fellow actor, Pablo, and as she displays emotion listening to the sound of the sea.

These two elements, even though apparently minor, perform an enormous contribution, since they reveal the presence of two vertices of human nature that are undermined by dictatorship. One is the ability to call things by name (in this case, Inés calls Pablo by his real name). The other is the ability to feel emotion in a way that is consistent with reality (even though briefly, Inés and Pablo react with some emotion and pleasure to the sound of the sea coming from the recorder). The effects of the dictatorship are revealed throughout the play in the inability of the characters to state the truth and to experience emotions in relation to and consistent with the nature of events.

Sea Murmur presents what Lola Proaño Gómez, in her study of the new theatrical poetics, calls "aesthetics of uncertainty." The author points to a difference in Latin American theater from the '90s on, when new theatrical poetics bring the political onto the stage and are characterized by being "rather a painful denunciation of concealed immorality and repression" and "demand[ing] that the spectator finds the unifying thread of the proposal. The aesthetics of uncertainty is this "lack of affirmations or definitive proposals."[2] Even though *Sea Murmur* ends with a degree of uncertainty about what will happen the following day, this uncertainty is presented with hopeful hints. No definitive proposals are expressed. The spectator does not know to where change will lead, but the mere possibility of change is encouraging. The sound of the sea and Pablo's display of affection towards himself, when he embraces himself, are the preamble to a better future. In this apparent absence of assertions, Dino Armas' play contains the seed of future projects.[3]

---

[2]   Proaño Gómez, Lola. "Lo político en el teatro latinoamericano [The political in Latin American theater]." Dramateatro: Revista Digital 14 Sep. 2008. 22 Sep. 2013 <http://www.dramateatro.com>.
[3]   Essay translated by Álex Omar Bratkievich.

Mass Media in *Sea Murmur*'s Conflictive Environment

Gabriela Christie Toletti

In *Sea Murmur*, Dino Armas provides commentary on the role of mass media in contemporary life and alerts us about the risks of abuse. In this essay, I demonstrate how the play magnificently illustrates the following points:

1) Mass media can contribute to the dehumanization, desensitization, and emotional numbness of contemporary societies, and, therefore, to the propagation of social and political wrongs.

2) The political system, often in conjunction with mass media, tends to look for ways to control its citizens and silence dissenting voices.

3) Mass media can become instruments of escapism from distressing political, social, personal, or family-related realities.

4) Mass media often contributes to the progressive blurring of the boundaries between reality and fiction.

5) The errors and tragedies of the past could be repeated if we do not adopt a reflexive, analytical spirit, and a more humane lifestyle.

The play begins with an elderly couple, Amalia and Avelino, sitting in front of the TV at their home in Uruguay, while their young granddaughter Inés nervously observes disturbing scenes of unrest in the neighborhood: "Grandma, here on the corner, they are mounting barricades, burning tires" (149). The grandparents refuse to acknowledge what is happening outside. Amalia takes this attitude to an extreme by immersing herself in her TV's world as a form of escapism in order to deny the turbulence, violence, and repression happening in her own neighborhood.

This play, like others by Armas, shows three generations of a single family: grandparents, children, and grandchildren. For most of the play only Amalia, Avelino, and Inés are present on stage. And even though Pablo (a young neighbor and Inés' friend) is mentioned, he does not appear until the last moments. Santiago and Laura (Amalia and Avelino's son and daughter-in-law) also enter late in the play.

Although *Sea Murmur* is set in Uruguay, the conflicts it shows seem universal and atemporal. It could be thought that this play is set during the Uruguayan dictatorship period (1973-1985); however, some details evoke pre-dictatorship events (for example, the confrontations between the Armed Forces and the members of the Movimiento de Liberación Nacional[1] or other activists from 1971 on). In that regard, the historian Marcelo de León Montañés wrote, in an informal correspondence:

> Even though it is clear that *Sea Murmur*'s characters are Uruguayan, the description of what is happening is ambiguous enough to allow us to think the play is set in another place and at another time. In fact, it reminded me more of the unrest before the military dictatorship than of the actual dictatorship. I also related it to a time of possible future unrest and found it ingenious that the play cautions against the dangers of indifference towards social wrongs and, in order to do that, recreates the violence of repression before the actual coup d'état.[2]

We agree with the historian that in this play Armas seems to use pre-dictatorship Uruguay as a frame of reference at the same time that he evokes a violent future in an indeterminate place and a timeless space.

The constant mention of cable TV indicates that *Sea Murmur* cannot take place strictly during or before the Uruguayan military dictatorship. Cable TV first appeared in Uruguay in the '90s, satellite TV in 2001, and multinational DirecTV in 2003. The play, however, evokes events such as those that happened before the dictatorship in order to warn us of the possibility of their recurrence.

In this way, Dino Armas may be alerting us that political repression, exacerbated violence, and social indifference can arise anywhere in the world in turbulent times, e.g., before a dictatorial regime. This reminds us of a famous Cicero phrase whose timeless content is universally valid (to such an extent that

---

[1] Translator's Note: "National Liberation Movement," or Tupamaros, was a Uruguayan guerrilla group whose activities in the early '70s were used as an excuse by the Armed Forces to depose the democratically-elected government and establish a military dictatorship.

[2] De León Montañés, Marcelo. E-mail to the author. 26 Oct. 2016.

it has been repeated in countless variations and attributed to different authors throughout time): "Those who cannot remember the past are condemned to repeat it." Ironically, this same phrase was also used by the Uruguayan dictatorial regime to warn that the guerrilla could return and thus to justify their repressive actions.

In *Sea Murmur*, Armas includes various sounds coming from "outside," maybe as a way to "awaken" the audience by drawing their attention to the social and political conflicts the playwright is trying to denounce. On one hand, there are outside neighborhood noises which correspond to a reality of political and social unrest: "*Sounds of sirens, explosions, horns, distant confused noises*" (143). On the other, inside the house the TV is always on. The audience does not see the images but learns about the programming topics through the characters' dialogue. Television, with its diverse programming, creates a constant noise or symbolic rumor (very different from the outside noises) which often dominates this family's conversation topics and interferes with their ability to communicate or to open their eyes to what is happening in their environment.

Of all the characters, Amalia is the most obsessed with everything TV-related. She insists on watching it constantly as a way to learn about the world, but her avidity to "learn" actually constitutes an attempt to escape from her surroundings so as not to face the sociopolitical problems around them. If the world is seen through the filter of a screen, it is then perceived more distant, less real and, therefore, less threatening. Through Amalia, the author is alerting us of the risks of mass media abuse in today's world. In fact, in our contemporary reality, TV and—by extension—all communication media constitute instruments of escapism from distressing political, social, personal, and family-related realities. This type of escapism can provoke a break with reality, which leads to the consequent inability of a human being to become an agent of dialogue, analysis, and authentic change.

Observing reality through a filter causes a certain degree of dissociation as a defense mechanism that allows us to regard ourselves and our reality from another perspective while avoiding any feelings. It is as if television and mass media have become some sort of desensitizing tool or psychological anesthesia. In fact, after being bombarded with multiple and constant stimuli, the contemporary human being becomes used to seeing the suffering of others without being emotionally affected in any significant way. Throughout the play, Amalia makes comments completely devoid of emotion or compassion about tragedies and misfortunes such as floods, earthquakes, explosions, deaths, murders, racism, gender violence, etc.

While Amalia and her husband Avelino watch TV, their granddaughter Inés looks through the window at what is happening outside and tries to draw her grandparents' attention to the turbulent situation and danger befalling their neighbors (for example, Pablo and other relatives of Doña Rosa). There seems to be a parallelism between the window and the TV screen. The TV is like an "illusion screen" that distorts, changes, rewrites, exaggerates, or deemphasizes reality, while the window symbolizes a screen or transparent wall that allows us to see what is happening outside, yet keeps us at a safe distance from the events in this outside world. Both are filters that guarantee different levels of distancing from reality.

During the play, Amalia repeatedly changes the channel and skips from one subject to another quickly and without discernment. The topics she watches on each channel are completely different and, generally, do not relate to each other (floods in Venice, the death of a Muslim, explosions, Chinese dance, earthquake, surgery, an aphrodisiac recipe, a documentary on domestic violence, etc.). The need to continuously change channels and, therefore, topics, perhaps alludes to the fragmentation of Amalia's internal world and her lack of judgment. At the same time, this information overload suggests an external reality which is also fractured and chaotic. We live in a world steamrolled by non-stop avalanches of information, images, noises, and interference coming from different channels and sources.

Amalia seems to focus on violence and disasters in remote places as a way to place what is bad/violent/distressing far away and to deny the presence of violence in her own community. It could be said that she rejoices in talking about the murder of a Palestinian, natural disasters (for example, earthquakes), the gender violence experienced by a Cuban woman, etc.

Amalia's thirst for information and knowledge does not seem to reveal an authentic desire to learn or be informed but rather seems an attempt to fill an existential void and to escape from reality through noises, images, and words. Television, which is on 24/7 (thanks to the "holy" cable), constitutes some sort of noise/companion that provides neither content nor knowledge but hinders the ability to think and observe reality. Amalia's exacerbated verbosity also contributes to limit her abilities of introspection and analysis. Avelino, on the contrary, allows himself moments of silence and reflection that lead him to think, reason, and analyze. For example, his introspective attitude lets him recognize that television interferes with the ability of listening to the outside events and, ultimately, with the possibility of perceiving external reality:

> AMALIA: *(Facing the television.)* I cannot find the death of the Muslim. Ah, but I like this one. *(Looks interested. More noise outside. INÉS stifles a scream.)*
>
> AVELINO: What's wrong?
>
> INÉS: Outside…. Things are worse. Don't you hear?
>
> AVELINO: How is it possible to hear anything with the noise of your grandmother's television? Would you believe that she is watching a Chinese dance now…? (146)

For Amalia, the news of social and political tragedies is mere entertainment. When referring to the death of a Palestinian man, for example, she says that she could not understand what he was shouting because the program "did not have subtitles like in the movies" (146). She equates world events to movies/ entertainment. At no moment does Amalia allow herself to feel distress due to the tragedies she sees on TV. She shows no compassion or empathy towards the "actors" in these human dramas. Everything for her is reduced to fun, entertainment, and escapism. We can see, then, mass media portrayed symbolically as a psychological anesthesia of the people, used when faced with a world too problematic and distressing.

Apparently, Amalia does not watch natural disasters out of empathy towards the afflicted nor to be informed about current events, but because of the adrenaline rush the sounds and images of destruction provoke in her. The earthquake noises are experienced as sound effects that contribute to the fun and sensationalism, similar to going to the movies to watch an action film. It would seem that in our contemporary world, the boundaries between real (such as current news) and fiction (such as action films) are getting blurred. The popularity of reality TV and the emergence of virtual reality are some of the obvious symptoms of the progressive disappearance of the distinction between reality and fantasy in today's world.

The fascination with sensationalism and the blurring of the boundary between reality and fiction can be clearly observed in this exchange between Amalia and Inés:

> INÉS: Grandma, here on the corner, they are mounting barricades, burning tires. I'm sure they are showing it on some local channel.
>
> AMALIA: Burning tires…. They are burning tires…. It's what I always say. Uruguayan television cannot compete with any other. Burning tires when television channels around the world are showing people lighting themselves on fire. To the point that Argentineans are opening their eyes and—without showing people burning alive—are showing men and women, and—hear what I'm saying—even children chained to whatever. Trees, fences, even in their workplace. And here we are content with burning tires…. And just think how bad black smoke looks on television….
>
> INÉS: But, grandmother, what's going on there in the corner is true….
>
> AMALIA: And what I see here is also true. […] (149)

Throughout the play, Inés proves to have a stronger character and be more analytical than Amalia, since she allows herself to take into account what happens outside her house and to develop her ability of introspection. She insists that her grandmother lower the TV volume in order to listen to the incidents on the street and also to be able to communicate with her family. However, the prospect of feeling, thinking, communicating, and becoming aware of the events outside is too frightening for the other family members who prefer escapism in the TV. No wonder there are so many TVs in this house!

Inés symbolizes the idealism and activism of the younger generations who try to familiarize themselves with the world around them in order to have a positive and progressive effect, potentially provoking social and political change, whereas her grandmother represents the older generations who have abandoned their ideals and prefer to live in the limbo offered by the sedative that is television. Furthermore, Amalia not only attempts to forget the outside occurrences but also criticizes and repudiates her acquaintances, her neighbors and, possibly, her former friends. She refers to them with coldness, as if they were complete strangers. For example, she mentions that if Doña Rosa and her family are in trouble, "there must be a reason" (147).

Avelino also proves to have a certain degree of introspection, sensitivity, and analytical abilities, although less than Inés. The following observation by Avelino, aside from being humane, points to the universality of the conflicts and tragic suffering tackled in Armas' plays: "The cry of someone dying is the same here and everywhere" (146).

When sleeping, we give free rein to unconscious free associations and let ourselves feel and process conflicts. Avelino allows himself to sleep; Amalia, on the contrary, stays awake and focused on the TV and its constant noise/rumors in order to avoid facing her emotional conflicts, unconscious sources of distress, and the authentic noises of external reality.

This family's group dynamics show that, before and during periods of dictatorship—be it in Uruguay or other countries—it is often the case that families are not monolithic in their ideology. For example, there are idealists and activists against the repressive institutions (such as Inés and, to a lesser degree, Avelino), but there are also unengaged people (such as Amalia, Laura, and Santiago), who do not want anything to do with the events around them.

One of the TV programs Amanda watches is about doctors and surgeries. There is something sinister, cold, and sadistic in the way she describes these surgeries (for example, when she talks about the gleam of the scalpel opening the skin). This sadism invokes the memory of the torture techniques used by the Fuerzas Conjuntas[3] (the Armed Forces and the Police) before and during the Uruguayan dictatorship. Amalia even subtly links the doctors with the authorities in power, and the patient with the losers/the neighbors persecuted for political reasons:

> AMALIA: [...] Look. He looks green. He already put himself in the place of the patient being operated on. You two are always the defenders of lost causes. Instead of feeling like the doctor, no, he thinks of the sick. And you, in Doña Rosa's mess, you side with her. You always side with the losers. Yes, you definitely don't take after me, or after Laura, and even less after Santiago... (151)

Amalia criticizes Avelino because, instead of identifying with the doctor (powerful/torturer/authority), he puts himself in the shoes of the patient (victim/

---

[3] TN: "Conjoined Forces."

tortured/subjects). Once more, we notice how human drama does not seem to move people like Amalia: what she always focuses on are the sensationalist images. In a world of beings anesthetized by an overdose of visual and auditory stimuli, context does not matter; we are merely attracted to entertaining images.

> AMALIA: [...] The text does not matter; the enjoyable part is in the picture, in the focus of the lens. Close-ups of the gloved hands, the boxes with the instruments, the devices. It's amazing how much you can learn. [...] (150)

Interestingly, while watching this program on doctors and surgeries, Amalia tells Inés that she (her granddaughter) is not the daughter of a "*desaparecido*"[4] or some gypsy, but blood of her own blood. Immediately afterwards, as if free associating, she refers to the blood oozing from the patient and how s/he is completely covered. For Amalia, doctors, surgeries, scalpels, covered and bloodied bodies and "*desaparecidos*" seem to be linked. This alludes to the crimes against humanity and the human rights violations perpetrated in the Southern Cone during the military dictatorships and even before them:

> AMALIA: Inesita.... That is stuff out of soap operas and not real life. To your own chagrin, you are not the daughter or granddaughter of some desaparecido or of some gypsy woman who left you at the doorsteps of this house. You are–whether you like it or not–blood of our blood. Oh, speaking of blood, look, Avelino, that person is bleeding a lot. Is it a man or a woman? Covered like that, you cannot tell what they are. That's why you have to watch these programs from the beginning. Otherwise, you cannot tell who is acting as the patient....

> AVELINO: *(Hopeful.)* Oh, they are acting as patients? So the program is really fiction?

> AMALIA: No. These are actual operations. All real. *(He diverts–as before–his eyesight from the television.)* But look at the television, man. Do not look down. You're missing the best. That looks like a silver

---

4 Desaparecido(s) or desaparecida(s) (literally: "missing" or "vanished") are those who vanished during the military dictatorships in the Southern Cone in the 1970s and 1980s. Most of them were political dissidents, militants, left-wing activists, students, journalists, and other private citizens who were arrested by the government just for thinking differently and who then vanished without a trace. The term desaparecido is most commonly associated with those who vanished during the Argentine Military Dictatorship known as the Dirty War (1976-1983).

scalpel. Look how it shines.

AVELINO: You just said that they were acting as patients....

AMALIA: It's a way of talking. At the end of the day, don't we all act? You, her, me, Laura, Santiago.... *(Louder.)* Doña Rosa and her children....

INÉS: And what is your role, grandmother Amalia?

AMALIA: If you had lived the hardships that I had to go through as a girl, you'd know what my role is. (151-152)

Amalia's comment that we cannot know if a covered patient is a man or a woman—since they all look alike—seems to point to the dehumanization of the people being tortured. It is easier to torture when the victims' faces are not seen, when there are no characteristics that identify them as human beings with individual features.

Another way to avoid experiencing feelings is to liken everything to a big play, as Amalia does in the lines above. Amalia suggests that we are all actors: her, her family, her neighbors, those who appear on the other side of the TV screen and, ultimately, all of us. If life is a great play or fiction, it is easier for Amalia (and for the "spectators") not to feel anything for the "actors," who would not be suffering since they are only acting their roles of "patients/victims of torture."

Cruelty also appears in this play in the form of domestic violence. We find out that Santiago abuses Laura daily and a television program about gender violence is mentioned. A parallelism can be perceived between the outside violence, the violence seen on TV (in several manifestations), and the violence in the bosom of this family. Perhaps Armas is alerting us of how the spirit of violence, once present, can propagate like a cancer to all society's organs or institutions.

As Inés mentions with more and more emphasis the violence occurring in her own neighborhood, Amalia keeps changing the channel (for example, she jumps from a heart surgery to a tropical aphrodisiac recipe). Besides talking about the incidents outside, Inés questions the origins of the family's secure economic standing. Along with Inés, the readers and spectators also wonder what Amalia and Avelino might have done to reach the standard of living they enjoy, given that they come from very humble origins. It is insinuated here that, even though Amalia and—to a lesser degree—Avelino escape from their surroundings through the TV and adopt an attitude of lack of social and political commitment, at some point in the past they might have betrayed or informed on their neighbors/friends/comrades, not necessarily out of conviction, but in order to receive economic favors or perhaps to avoid their own political persecution. In sum, everything points to Amanda being motivated by personal gain. She would rather escape, close her eyes to the circumstances outside and maybe even inform on her friends or neighbors in an effort to achieve economic stability and "relief."

Television, as it has already been mentioned, constitutes some sort of "desensitization tool," "psychological anesthesia," or "alienating drug" that provides oblivion to Amalia and allows her to become immune to human misfortunes and social wrongs. But in *Sea Murmur* it symbolizes much more. In fact, there are several allusions to TV (and everything related to it: cable, the TV guide, etc.) as a sacred and revered object. TV is so important that we might even say it plays the role of a character: a king, a demigod, or a deity who from a "virtual heaven" occupies a place of authority (the screen is the throne) to provide knowledge or pseudo-knowledge and indoctrinate without interacting with the followers, believers, devotees, or subjects. These are some of the references to TV, cable, and the TV guide as sacred:

AVELINO: Don't tell me now that you're going to start praying next to the television? (145)

[...]

LAURA: Do not insist, Inés. Your father said the three holy words: "Mom" and "broken television." After that, there cannot be anything else. (*SANTIAGO, AVELINO, and AMALIA gather around the television and test different ways to fix it.*) (157)

[...]

LAURA: Of course you had to come up with something like that. You know what I think? That the cable guide is your little bible. No, not your bible. It's your self-help book. You can manage with a little magazine like that, but I need another type of self-help... (161)

[...]

AMALIA: (*Ferocious, slams the television. The television sound stops working.*) This is my god. My only god. (*Stays standing wide-eyed.* [...])
(163)

Even when not working, the TV retains the main focus of attention and dialogue that drowns out the noises outside. The family members surround it, talk about the need to fix it, and try several ways to do so. Therefore, the TV represents some sort of modern totem which they gather around and venerate. The word *totem* comes from the Ojibwe language, spoken by the eponymous North American native group, and it refers to a spirit, sacred object, or symbol that officiates as emblem to a group of people. It is also used to refer to the carving which represents it. In this play, TV seems to combine both senses and represents some sort of totem for contemporary society, which is given quasi-sacred qualities and characteristics by the congregation of addicts. However, in spite of the great importance of television in *Sea Murmur*, Inés' descriptions of the tumultuous events in the neighborhood and the conversations about the outside happenings slowly start to acquire importance. It is as if reality were penetrating the dialogues' interstices up to a moment in which the world outside and what is being seen inside on TV coincide. This happens when Inés leaves the house and appears on a local TV channel:

> AVELINO: *(Starts low and then raises his voice.)* By banging on the television, the channel got changed…. This one is local…. Look. She is the one running…. It's Inés. Look. It's Inés on TV….
>
> AMALIA: *(Changes tone and attitude.)* On TV…? Inés…?
>
> AVELINO: Yes, it's her. She is running…. She is running, but… but it looks like they won't let her go through….
>
> AMALIA: Our Inés on TV…? *(Approaching the television.)*
>
> AVELINO: Yes, take a look. *(LAURA and SANTIAGO, after looking at each other, get close to the television.)* (163-164)

Amalia sees her granddaughter through TV's filter and for the first time seems to become interested in the outside incidents. Nevertheless, this interest is superficial and reveals mere curiosity and the novelty of seeing her granddaughter on the screen.

Sea Murmur's ending fully confronts us with a situation which might have gone unnoticed to the spectator, or may not have been given enough relevance previously since it happened only for a moment during the play's initial scene.

In fact, at the beginning the "actors" momentarily step out of their roles as "characters" and return to them later:

> *([...] Sounds of sirens, explosions, horns, distant confused noises. Suddenly, a different sound–like that of a tense wire that breaks–overpowers the other sounds. The three actors break character for an instant. They look at each other puzzled. The sound of the television comes back (now a voice in Italian) and the sounds outside (until now muted), and the actors return to their characters.)* (143)

Towards the end, the "actors" step out of their roles as "characters" once more but do not return to them again. We can clearly see how they completely leave their previous roles behind when they take off some pieces of clothing and remain wearing uniforms that homogenize them (of course, these "actors" are also actually characters in the play). Certainly, *Sea Murmur*–like *Beach Day*, another play by Armas also written in 2008–constitutes a magnificent example of metadrama or "theater within the theater."

Another element that also contributes to breaking the illusion of the preceding representation (what happened in the house and the neighborhood) is that, when the TV is turned around, it is revealed to be hollow, a prop. With this detail, Armas is perhaps suggesting that television–modern totem or contemporary demigod– is in fact a hollow farce, as is also frequently the case with the information imparted by it and, by extension, all mass media.

The "actors" seem to have created or portrayed a script/game, maybe as a way to process intense personal or family-related conflicts, or the sequels of sociopolitical violence perpetrated in the past against them, their relatives or their friends. By portraying these scenes, perhaps they immerse themselves in some sort of pseudo-group therapy that offers catharsis and helps them process their conflicts. They mention repeating these scenes or some variant of them daily or almost daily; we also find out that not all of the "actors" participate in these representations every day. The repetitive aspect of this kind of pseudo-group therapy can also be seen in *Beach Day*.

We do not know where the actors repeatedly interpreting these scenes are. Maybe they are in an institution, such as an asylum for mental patients, or a jail (the clothing that now homogenizes them would indicate something of the sort). It is possible they are part of an alternative group therapy, or actors, writers, and directors that create and rework a play with each presentation in order to denounce sociopolitical and family-related problems and bring to light the possible negative effects of communication media in contemporary society.

Geographically, even though the scenes allude to Uruguay (because of the Rioplatense Spanish[5] vocabulary and the references to the country), they could be from anywhere in the world. Here, as in other Dino Armas' plays, the human conflicts presented are universal and timeless beyond the local references. The actors emphasize this universality when they speak of pretending to be somewhere else the following time:

> LAURA: [...] Why don't we change countries tomorrow? Instead of Uruguay, can we pretend we are in France? In Paris... under the Eiffel Tower or in Notre-Dame, beside the Seine River.... I have never been in Paris. I will like it. I used to know a French song... before... [...] (165)

Towards the end of the play, there are some exchanges between the "actors" but we do not know much about them outside of their roles. Pablo may be the one we learn the most about. Pablo's earlier role as "character" was that of a young activist involved in the disturbances happening outside. When he steps out of this characterization (and he adopts the actor role), we find out he works the sound effects for the play and his real name (i.e. outside of the role he plays) is also Pablo.

> PABLO: Today you used my name for my character....
>
> INÉS: Yes....
>
> PABLO: My real name. Tomorrow, whether we are in Paris or here, can you call me by the same name?
>
> INÉS: Yes. (Soft voice. Walks fast and exits.)
>
> PABLO: Wait. Can you say it again? (She looks at him with an inquiring attitude.) The name, I mean....
>
> INÉS: (Smiles.) Pablo.... (She rushes out. The bell rings insistently. PABLO

---

5   TN: The Spanish dialect spoken in the areas in and around the La Plata River basin of Argentina and Uruguay.

sits on the floor. The tape recorder next to him, with the sound of the sea. He hugs himself and begins a back-and-forth movement.)

PABLO: Pablo…. I am Pablo…. I am Pablo…. I am Pablo… (166)

It seems Pablo wants to reaffirm his identity by keeping his own name in future representations. Maybe this reveals that the limits between "activist character" and "actor character" are beginning to blur for him. Pablo is in charge of the noises of unrest outside (shootings, sirens, stampedes, etc.), but the sound he introduces when he plays the tape at the end of the play is the sound of the sea:

PABLO: *(She walks. He tries to get her attention.)* I have a new sound for tomorrow.

INÉS: *(From her place.)* More shots? A new siren?

PABLO: Do you want to hear it?

INÉS: OK…. *(Shows insecurity or hurries. He turns on the tape recorder. A sea murmur sound can be heard.)*

PABLO: Waves… a beach… (166)

During the play there is a barrage of disturbing noises that aid our understanding of what is happening "outside," and there are also "inside" noises coming from the TV—which help Amalia escape her surroundings. But the sound of the "sea murmur" seems to fulfill a different function. Maybe the sea and its hypnotizing murmur symbolize the flow of the unconscious, which allows these actors to create or interpret scripts in order to immerse themselves in a pseudo-therapy or catharsis that helps them process personal, group, or family conflicts. Hence, perhaps, the play's title.

In conclusion, *Sea Murmur* evokes the unrest, the violence, and the repression before a coup-d'état or the instauration of a dictatorial government. Even though the play seems to be set in Uruguay before the last dictatorship, it is also ambiguous enough so as to suggest a violent future in an indeterminate place and a timeless space.

The play alerts us that the errors and tragedies of the past can be repeated if we do not adopt a reflexive, analytical spirit and a more humane lifestyle.

Furthermore, Dino Armas calls upon us to become aware of how mass media can contribute to dehumanization and desensitization in contemporary societies and, therefore, to the propagation of social and political harms. A desensitized people is more likely to be controlled and dismembered. The political system (government, dictatorship, Armed Forces, etc.), often in conjunction with communication media, makes a practice of attempting to develop and refine ways to anesthetize the people in order to cut, operate, and mold the social fabric or fiber while thwarting the screams or noises of protest.

It is befitting to consider the paradox observable in modern societies: we have more and more access to new and various mass media and social networks, yet this coincides with a decline in our ability to effectively communicate.

We surf in a highly technological world, connect instantly by Internet with people around the globe, and have immediate access to all kinds of information. We live in an era of great technological innovation and novel communication media: the advantages and opportunities are amazing and promising, but the risks and disadvantages can also be fatal and irreversible.

Through Amalia, *Sea Murmur*'s author seems to be alerting us to the risks of communication media abuse. In fact, television and, by extension, all communication media can easily become instruments of escapism from political, social, personal, or family-related problems. This kind of emotional escape can lead to a break with reality and the consequent inability of a human being to become an agent of dialogue, analysis, and change.

Maybe Dino Armas is, with this play, speaking or murmuring to the "Amalia" we all carry inside when we watch the news of tragedies on TV with a degree of emotional numbness. In the same way that it happens to Amalia (although expectedly to a lesser degree), many people tend to perceive current events as entertainment destined to fill a gap, rather than information. Gradually, it becomes more difficult to discriminate. The lines between reality and fiction get blurrier in a world riddled with reality TV, virtual reality, round-the-clock access to hundreds of channels, multiple social networks, graphic video games, etc. Even though all this seems to be characteristic of today's world, maybe the borders between reality and fiction have always been blurry, as it has been repeatedly suggested in countless literary plays throughout time. Is not reality itself like a great play?[6]

---

[6]   Essay translated by Álex Omar Bratkievich.

Rhetoric of Sounds in *Sea Murmur*

Aida L. Heredia

*S*ea Murmur, by Uruguayan playwright Dino Armas, is structured over a series of sounds and noises manipulated by the actors and employed as an instrument of criticism towards a contemporary world of violence, alienation, and indifference. The six actors that comprise this dramatic play adopt characters (Amalia, Avelino, Inés, Laura, Santiago, and Pablo) whose interactions and situations embody the expression of a psyche deformed by an entire set of social harms, among which stand out the implementation of the military dictatorships suffered by Uruguay, Argentina, and Chile in the '70s and '80s, racial discrimination, poverty, marginalization, sexual violence, and intrafamily violence. In particular, the noises of individuals being chased in the street, sirens, shots, a broken wire, and a very loud television bring to the reader's or spectator's mind auditory and visual images of the torture carried out by the aforementioned totalitarian regimes' machine. But the manipulation of the sounds that Dino Armas executes through the actors at the same time fulfills the rhetorical function of denouncing a social and political reality that transcends the geographical limits of the Southern Cone to echo the social injustice faced by peoples and communities in different parts of the modern world. The purpose of this essay is to analyze the rhetorical use of formal elements and the philosophical vision around which this dramatic play revolves.

Before fully getting into the analysis of the structural use of sounds and noises in the play and the multiple meanings they generate, it is necessary to point out another technique in *Sea Murmur* that operates as the nucleus of the auditory sensory moments. We refer to the fact that the action and the witnessed scenes are part of the social material that the six actors depict through the characters they adopt. In other words, the names "Amalia," "Avelino," "Inés," "Santiago," and "Laura" do not identify the actors themselves but the characters which each of them portrays in the dramatization of the social situations they create and stage daily. Only Pablo appears with his real name within the drama reproduced by the actors; this is highlighted by the play's final moment, when he seems to thank Inés for having called him by his own name (166). Such use of theatricality–the splitting of the actors into characters–confers an episodic nature to the play that connects in turn with the fragmented, violent, and ruinous world with which *Sea Murmur* confronts the reader and spectator.

Sea Murmur begins within a space saturated with auditory vibrations: "*Sounds of sirens, explosions, horns, distant confused noises. Suddenly, a different sound–like that of a tense wire that breaks–[…]*" (143). The sound of the breaking wire forces the actors to break character for an instant. This initial stage direction captures the theatricality of the actors as individuals playing the role of other characters. At the same time, the bewilderment in the actors caused by the wire's noise is a sign of the repression that they suffer in their "real" life, mentioned only in the final scenes. The wire's sound (which is part of the sounds mechanically generated by the actors but at the same time seems to originate from repression) is established as a leitmotif on which converge the multiple stories of dehumanization laid out in the play and the traumas these entail.

The sounds named in the stage direction evoke, without a doubt, the repression in Uruguay during the military dictatorship. In addition to those sounds, there are noises coming from the television that monopolizes the attention of the characters Amalia and Avelino, a married couple. Amalia insists on raising the TV's volume to the limit so as to drown out the noises of "*sirens, explosions, horns, distant whispers*" that can be heard on the street and that are encroaching onto the interior of the house. Amalia's absurd game of escalating the TV's volume is reinforced by her screams to Avelino, forcing him to remain in front of the TV with her. Her behavior, aside from having an exasperating effect on the reader/ spectator, is an indication of her attempt to suppress her awareness of the military persecution carried out outside of her house, in the streets of her neighborhood ("You see that now the outside noises don't bother us?" [147]).

That the emotional destabilization and the aggressiveness within the family is a survival mechanism, which can be seen in the almost animalistic relationship of this married couple, can also be surmised from the exclamations of the character called Inés, granddaughter of Amalia and Avelino. Inés is the conscience that Dino Armas uses to contrast with the indifference portrayed by the other actors. This girl cries out for her grandparents to stop watching TV and pay attention to the hunt occurring outside. Inés appears looking through the window, determined to find out what is happening, why there are men in uniform, why they are going after Mrs. Rosa's family and–especially–Pablo, the youngest son. Her dialogue mentions barricades, people burning tires, lights from the police forces besieging Rosa's house (149). The meaning of this scene is obvious: it highlights the psychological and emotional effects caused by the memory of the atrocities perpetrated by dictatorial regimes. From this point of view, Amalia's cynicism goes hand in hand with the contemporary world's authoritarianism that has destroyed the lives of people.

The insistence of Inés' character in becoming aware of what is happening outside emphasizes a central theme in Sea Murmur's humanistic rhetoric: the false division between "in" and "out," between the interior and the exterior worlds. The "house" where the characters portrayed by the actors live and the "street" towards which Inés' verbal and body language draws attention constitute the same space of interaction. Destabilizing the dichotomy, this fallacious way of conceiving the social disasters produced by human beings seems to be a fundamental goal of the structural use of sounds and noises by Dino Armas. These sensory elements confound the spaces occupied by the actors, disorient the reader/spectator, and fill with ambiguity the development of the scenes in the play.

Laura and Santiago, in the role of spouses and Inés' parents, show that the interior world of the house is made up of the same immorality that characterizes the outside world. With them, domestic violence is added to the dynamics of moral decline captured in Sea Murmur through countless allusions to oppression, racism, classism, death, indifference, cynicism. Both characters appear on stage widening the range of screams, insults, and intrafamily psychological violence. Intertwined with this situation, Inés can be heard pointing to what is happening outside (the military repression taking place in the neighborhood) and indicating her desire to help Pablo, whose house has been stormed by police agents: "They are using gas. But nobody is going to do anything? No neighbor is going to help out? [...] And now? What's going on? You can't hear anything. No noise..." (156). At that moment, the "[n]oise of broken/snapped wire" can be heard, which "startles all three. They break character" (156).

The bewilderment felt by the actors at the wire's sound leads to a dialogue which highlights more explicitly the themes of ambiguity, fragmentation, and dehumanization explored in the play. On this occasion, the sound of the broken wire is interpreted by the actors as a sign that they must conclude their dramatization for the day:

AVELINO: Already...?

AMALIA: It cannot be right....

INÉS: It's too early... (156)

193

We are faced with a dialogic theatrical technique that exacerbates the sense of an ambiguity which resides not only in the situations recreated by the actors but also in the space occupied by them as individuals who, outside of their characters, dwell in a real social world. Where are the actors–as individuals with a real dimension–within the play? Which are the real circumstances they live, amidst their theatrical performances? *Sea Murmur* does not offer a definitive answer to these questions. On the contrary, towards the end the noises and sounds intensify, highlighting the artificiality carried by the fragmented memory of deranged, traumatized beings. An illustration of this is the instant when the intrafamily violence and the resulting screams reach such an extreme that the only thing which overcomes everyone's degrading actions is another noise, a forceful punch to the television. That punch is the technique employed by Armas to introduce a change of awareness in the actors/characters and a change in perspective for the reader/spectator. Among such screams and punches, the reader/spectator is allowed to find out that the TV *"is just a prop"* (164).

The television, a device that molds and distorts the thought and the actions of the characters even more, fulfills–as a dramatic element–the obvious function of being a critique of the indifference towards the pain of fellow human beings that so characterizes contemporary society. This psychological, sociopolitical, and dramatic moment of the plot becomes complicated when the actors get rid of some of their clothing and show themselves in *"a kind of uniform that homogenizes them"* (164). The ambiguity and fragmentation that prevent univocal answers from the play are strengthened. The following comments, in which terror is implicit, have the same effect: "We should finish…," says Laura; "Tomorrow we continue," remarks Avelino; Amalia and Laura answer, respectively: "If we can…," "If they let us…." Amalia mentions that nobody comes to see her: "They used to come […] I might not have anyone left" (165). Further on, Santiago's and Avelino's comments suggest the dramatic action witnessed consists of a performance in a place where they can freely come and go: "I'm not coming tomorrow. I have visits…", announces Santiago; Avelino states that they should not count on him the following day since he wants to hear the soccer match on the radio (165).

The logical breakdown in the conversations and the use of faltering statements, together with the elliptical judgments strewn throughout, turn *Sea Murmur* into a play that aims to situate itself within the multiple and contradictory spaces that configure the individual and collective memory of certain events. With what objective? Maybe with the objective of understanding the roots of harms generated by the human being and, from such understanding, *acting* in search of the reintegration of the person with the true development of her humanity. As explained above, one of those spaces of the memory is composed by the atrocities committed during the dictatorship. According to this, the actors could be either at a reformatory or a psychiatric hospital where they are allowed acting games as a way to amuse themselves, or at a detention center for conscientious objectors, or at a school where they are kept under strict surveillance but with moments of "recreation."

Likewise, they could be at a place of their own (a house) where they gather as individuals to explore together–theatrically–various situations of human life as a way to process the afflictions caused by totalitarian regimes and, from a wider perspective, by a world full of oppression and destitution.

On the other hand, if the actors find themselves in a situation of state violence that deprives them of their freedom, how can we explain the entwining of the anxiety exhibited by the actors each time they hear the sound of the "*tense wire that breaks*"–which later becomes "*a very long ringing sound*"–and the reminder that they must finish soon (164)? For this mystery there is not a definitive answer either. This aspect of the play's ambiguity and fragmentation lays bare the torment suffered in the remembrance of political and social crimes against humanity. According to this interpretation, the reconstruction of such memory invites us to consider the frequently fruitless search for liberation and creation of a fair society.

In the disturbing spatio-temporal and sensory dynamics that define the interior space occupied by the characters, all the actors are present but Pablo. Where is he? What role does he perform in the play? Which situations does he embody from a dramatic point of view? In the plane of the situations reproduced by the actors, Pablo performs the role of the young dissident persecuted by agents of the Uruguayan dictatorship. Pablo, like Inés, is presented as a conscience that struggles against the apathy and alienation observed in the other characters ("Out there horrible things are happening and you…," Inés states, to which Santiago replies, "The problems of those people outside are theirs and theirs alone. Neither yours nor mine" [157].)

Pablo shouts Inés' name from outside; she runs out of the house towards him when she sees that he is alone in the street, exposed to the mistreatment of the police, and surrounded by overwhelming sounds, among which the wire's noise stands out ("*Outside, a very loud noise,*" "*Inside, noises get louder: the noises of the television, the insults, and the fight among the parents*" [163]). By way of a maneuver that resembles fantasy literature, the noises and punches cause the TV to switch channels and make the others become aware–through the TV–of Inés' presence next to Pablo in that alleged exterior world which her relatives are trying to repress. Thus Dino Armas brings the reader/spectator closer to the dénouement of the rhetoric we are examining, one that exposes the fact that Pablo is the one who has been producing the sounds and noises in the scenes with the help of a recorder. The final scene hints at this being a habitual practice by the actors in order to explore paths of freedom, ways of aligning themselves with the truly human.

In fact, in the final scene Armas discloses another fold of the play's dynamics by showing the actors out of their characters and leaving the physical space where they carry out their performance ("*They are others,*" states the stage direction [165]). The bell sound warns them they must leave (the play never points out where the sound comes from or its purpose). "Last call...," says Laura shyly (165). The bell is not a part of the repertoire of sounds Pablo handles, which gives rise to the interpretation that the bell sound is an "actual" foreboding element, an indication of the society of death inhabited by the denizens of planet Earth. Laura's proposal to the others of changing the country ("Instead of Uruguay, can we pretend we are in France?" [165]) seems to support this interpretation.

Another moment that alludes to the play's tenacity in denouncing such reality is the moment in the final scene when Pablo decides not to leave the place ("They can come get me.... It's the same for me.") in spite of the bell ringing again and Inés reminding him that they "sometimes mistreat people..." (166).

Before concluding the scene, Pablo invites Inés to listen to "a new sound for tomorrow"; he turns on the recorder, which plays the sound of the sea. "Waves... a beach...," he says. Inés listens to him in an automatic way as she leaves. Pablo holds her back with another question: "Today you used my name for my character [...] My real name. Tomorrow, whether we are in Paris or here, can you call me by the same name?" Inés replies that she will and runs out. "*The doorbell rings insistently. PABLO sits on the floor. The tape recorder next to him, with the sound of the sea. He hugs himself and begins a back-and-forth movement,*" as the stage direction points out (166). Holding to himself and enveloped by the sound of the sea, Pablo projects a double hope: on one hand, resistance to dehumanization;

on the other, commitment to the collective and individual search for a new awareness of justice. Pablo's reiterative statement and the integration of the word and the body with the sound of the sea seem to address this hope: "Pablo.... I am Pablo.... I am Pablo.... I am Pablo..." (166). Reclaiming the individual's humanity is the idea that supports the linguistic, auditory, and visual image with which the play concludes.

Even though the dialogues that accompany the ending refer specifically to Uruguayan society, Pablo's image can be interpreted as the metaphorical link that draws attention to the situations lived in other places of the world. Ironically, however, in this hopeful ending embodied by the image of Pablo embracing the sea and his experiment with different sounds, another conceptual image can be surmised that evokes the failure of human groups regarding actual practices of social transformation. From the interstices created by the fragmentation and ambiguity that configure the plot conceived by Dino Armas in *Sea Murmur* springs up a sea murmur sound (167) that insists on the utopian vision of attempting to create in the mind, in the soul, in the conscience of each individual a core that is not corrupted by authoritarian powers. The problem is that the same ambiguity of the play leads the reader/spectator to interpret that the *sound* of the possibility of creating ways for people to arrive at their own humanity, through the reintegration with the other's humanity, holds at its core the *murmur* of failure.[1]

---

[1]   Essay translated by Álex Omar Bratkievich.

Chapter Six
Sorrows of Exile

The Traces of Exile

Just Yesterday

Dino Armas

Translation by Gabriela Christie Toletti

Characters:

> ANTONIO
> EDUARDO
> MARISA
> AMALIA
> DANIEL

(The stage is dark. The tango Los mareados[1] *is heard softly in the background. Louder than the music, a radio broadcasts news of the day. Both sounds and music get increasingly louder. Two spotlights on EDUARDO and ANTONIO. EDUARDO stands facing away from the audience. ANTONIO stands facing the audience, with a letter in his hand. He begins to read it out loud.)*

ANTONIO: "Madrid. December 31, 1973. January 1, 1974. Dear all. Amidst this flurry I'm holding twelve grapes tightly in my hand at La Puerta del Sol,[2] pushed by people, dodging bottles of cider being thrown out from all the balconies, jumping because of the firecrackers–which sound louder here–looking at some African Americans who seem to be high from doing too many drugs and dancing among themselves, and at the same time trying not to miss the hands of the clock which seem to be procrastinating today more than other times in joining at the top… I'm thinking about all of you. Here, in this long minute and with all this around me, I feel

---

[1] Translator's Note: *Los mareados* (literally: "the dizzy ones" or the "tipsy ones") is a tango composed by Juan Carlos Cobián in 1920, with lyrics by Enrique Domingo Cadícamo added in 1942. *Los mareados* is about two lovers who are parting ways: "[…] Tonight, my friend, with alcohol we're getting drunk; I don't care if they laugh and call us 'the dizzy ones.' Everyone has their sorrows and we have ours. Tonight we will drink because we won't ever see each other again…. Today you're gonna enter in my past, in the past of my life. A wounded heart carries three sentiments: Love, Regret, Pain […] today we'll follow new paths. How great has been our love and, yet, alas, look what's left."

[2] TN: La Puerta del Sol (literally: "The Gate of the Sun") is a public square in Madrid, Spain. It is one of the best known and busiest places in the city. This is the center (Km 0) of the radial network of Spanish roads. The square also contains the famous clock whose bells mark the traditional eating of the Twelve Grapes and the beginning of a new year.

lonely…". *(EDUARDO repeats at the same time 'I feel lonely' or says it a little afterwards, like an echo of the other, and turns left to face the audience. ANTONIO makes the inverse move.)*

EDUARDO: … Alone, yes. Who must have invented such a short word for something as big and tremendous as this of being alone, of feeling lonely, of experiencing loneliness…? Here, next to me, it seems as if everyone knows each other. They sing, they dance, they walk with joy on shattered glass, and the murmur grows louder and louder. Nobody seems to feel the cold of this last night of December…. *(Soft laughter.)* Cold…. Can you see, Antonio? Even the cold separates me from you. Reassure Mom because I think I'm hearing her wonder if I'm wearing warm clothes. But I look like a bear. I put on everything I have. One layer on top of the other. I am here, feeling cold, and you, surely, will be in the backyard, under the vines already flourished at this time of the year. Or not yet? I write this and feel the heavy and sweet smell of those old vines. Grandfather planted them. I remember when he told me that he brought them to America because it was all he had in his town. Dad must continue taking care of the vines, leaf by leaf. You, surely, now must have finished the barbecue and you must be wearing those blue shorts that every year you promise to throw away. Mom barefoot, as her only concession to the summer, will grumble at Daniel for any little thing. Dad must be giving the last touch to his usual fruit salad. And in the middle of all this, the television, thanks to the complicated extension that the old man installed and of which he is so proud. The embroidered tablecloth and the tall goblets, the two things Mom brings out only for the holidays. The walnuts and hazelnuts, of course, from Manzanares,[3] because they have them at a better price and they are on sale…. And I am here, standing in the middle of these people, waiting for midnight to swallow all the grapes before the last bell strikes. This is how my three wishes can be fulfilled. Three things… too many. One is enough for me: to return. To return. To return, to return, to return.

---

[3]   TN: Manzanares was a supermarket chain that manufactured and/or processed several of the products it sold, such as cooking oil, dried pasta, honey, coffee, soap, candles, etc. It was founded by two brothers from Galicia, Spain: Manuel Manzanares, who immigrated to Uruguay around 1880, and Máximo Manzanares, who arrived in Uruguay in 1899. At one point the business had 89 branches. The number of branches decreased in the 1980s and the business closed in 2002.

To be there, with all of you, even with the withered forehead, as Gardel[4] said, he who knew it all. But I don't want to bring you down. And don't think I'm so down. Look at the plan I have for later: I have a lot of pesetas[5] in my pocket to get drunk, real drunk. One of those strong, serious intoxications. I know of a tavern where many Chileans, Porteños,[6] and Uruguayans go, which has a special wine, so good that I cannot even explain. One of those that make you dizzy little by little. I have it all well-organized. First, not to talk. Quickly have five glasses, one in honor of each of us; then I will softly sing a tango. I keep drinking and singing a little louder; and then, yes, stand up and sing it to the Spaniards and as a final number, the song farewell of *Los asaltantes*,[7] of course. For days I've been thinking about the tango I'm going to sing. Finally, I've decided. I'm going to sing *Los mareados*. Do you remember when we sang it as a duet? *(Sings softly.)* "Strange, as if on fire, I found you drinking, cute, and fatal. You were drinking and in the din of champagne, crazy you laughed, rather than cry...."

(He continues singing softer and softer, while ANTONIO continues reading the letter, walking towards the table, soft light on EDUARDO. ANTONIO remains in a semi-shadow until lights go out.)

ANTONIO: "I plan to write a story about it. The two of us singing, the old man looking at us, the grandfather's grapevine.... The idea has been going around my head for a long time. I'm going to start the year writing it. After the hangover, of course. A hug and a big kiss to all.

---

[4]   TN: Carlos Gardel (Dec. 11, 1890 - June 24, 1935), was a tango singer, songwriter, composer, actor, and the most prominent figure in the history of tango. There are three countries that claim him as their own: Uruguay, Argentina, and France. Some claim that he was born in France and that there was a French birth certificate in his name. That birth certificate is now considered to be false by many historians. Gardel had a Uruguayan passport that stated his birthplace as Tacuarembó, Uruguay. Historians have found evidence of Gardel indeed being Uruguayan by birth. Argentina claims him as its own because it was there that he was raised and rose to stardom. His name is most often associated with the long tradition of tango music and dance of Argentina and Uruguay.

[5]   TN: *Peseta(s)* was the basic monetary unit of Spain until replaced by the euro (monetary unit of the European Union) in 2002.

[6]   TN: *Porteño* (literally: "from the port") in Spanish refers to people who live in a port city. The largest city to which the term is applied is Buenos Aires, capital of Argentina. Since the end of the nineteenth century, *Porteño* has become a name or demonym for the people of Buenos Aires.

[7]   TN: *Los asaltantes* (literally: "the robbers" or "the assailants") is a Uruguayan carnival *murga* group (a band of street musicians) founded in 1928. It is one of the most traditional *murgas* of the Uruguayan Carnival. It participated in Carnival until 2013.

A January first without all of you, but still a wish for a Happy New Year. Eduardo."

(News show, soft music of the time, and superimposed, sound of a clock, which will be heard more clearly in the silence of the scene that follows. MARISA walks in.)

MARISA: *(Exclamation.)* You startled me…. What are you doing in the dark?

ANTONIO: Nothing….

MARISA: *(Turns on the light.)* I did not hear you when you got up.

ANTONIO: I could not sleep. I stayed awake.

MARISA: *(Pointing to the ashtray.)* Looks like you've been up for a while. *(Throws away the cigarette butts.)*

ANTONIO: Well, yes…. It is this heat that is keeping me awake. The sheets are sticking to my body. *(Lights a cigarette. Fidgets with the letter.)*

MARISA: Today, it's because of the heat; yesterday, it was the rich food. You can't go on like this, without sleeping every night.

ANTONIO: It's not every night. Then, in the afternoon, I lie down for a little bit.

MARISA: Look at the dark bags under your eyes. It's bad not to sleep….

ANTONIO: Do not exaggerate. I do sleep. What happens is that I have my schedules inverted. You are a little bit too fired up.

MARISA: You should continue to drink a glass of warm milk before going to bed. *(While looking for a glass, the coffee jar, etc.)*

ANTONIO: I do not like milk. I never liked it. As a kid, they had to slap me so I would have some. Besides, it doesn't do anything for me. And reading doesn't either. It makes me stay awake even longer.

MARISA: Can I make you some coffee?

ANTONIO: No. I just had *mate*.[8] That thermos turned out to be a good one,

---

[8]   TN: *Mate* is a traditional South American bitter infused drink, particularly in Uruguay, Argentina, Paraguay, and Brazil. It is made by an infusion of the dried leaves of the *yerba mate* plant. It contains mateine, which

huh? The water keeps the heat....

MARISA: They gave it as a present to your mom, right?

ANTONIO: How long ago did the other one break? We bought it from Doña Angelina. She brought it from Chuy.[9]

MARISA: I thought this one was the other one.

ANTONIO: Maybe because it is the same color.

MARISA: Could be.... Where's the sugar?

ANTONIO: There, behind you.

MARISA: Maybe drinking so much *mate* is what does not let you sleep.

ANTONIO: No, it's not that.

MARISA: The point is that you do not sleep. Is there something wrong with you that I do not know about?

ANTONIO: No, nothing is happening to me. Everything is the same.

MARISA: *(Looks at him, stirs her coffee, pauses.)* Your mom says that parsley tea is infallible....

ANTONIO: Neither parsley nor lettuce tea. I can write a fat manual of everything that doesn't help to sleep. Where did you put the ashtray?

MARISA: Up there. You smoke a lot.... *(He shrugs.)* I did not know the water was so hot.... *(Blows.)* If you were determined, you could smoke less.

ANTONIO: I was determined so many times.... But no. I can't quit.

MARISA: You don't want to quit. My boss's wife smoked two boxes a day. Two. One day she said, "I'm not smoking anymore." And since that day....

---

is an analog to caffeine. It is usually drunk with friends and served hot in a hollow calabash gourd with a special metallic drinking straw called *bombilla*.

[9] TN: Chuy is a duty free border town located in eastern Uruguay, in the Rocha Department. It shares its name with its sister city Chuí, Brazil. Both cities are separated by a shared avenue that acts as border.

ANTONIO: Some people can quit smoking. I cannot. *(Short pause.)*

MARISA: As for me, I sleep all night long like nothing. I think I don't even have dreams....

ANTONIO: Well, your case is different.

MARISA: Different.... How so?

ANTONIO: You go out, you work, you move, you do things. You get tired....

MARISA: Those things don't make me sleep more. You too, if you wanted....

ANTONIO: You see, in that we are different.

MARISA: In what way? You do not tell me anything.

ANTONIO: It must be something up here. *(He points at his head.)* I have a family history. You know it well.

MARISA: Come on, you can't be serious.

ANTONIO: I'm being serious.

MARISA: Antonio....

ANTONIO: Are you not going to eat anything? *(He gets up, brings a package.)* They are from yesterday. *(He opens it.)* They must be a little hard. Do you want me to put them in the oven for a little bit?

MARISA: No, that's OK. I don't have much time. *(He eats, with his arms crossed, behind her.)*

ANTONIO: Once I saw my grandmother in the asylum, but I do not forget.... I remember that Mom stood still. She cried and did not move. She just looked at her and cried silently. They had her tied up....

MARISA: You know that madness is not hereditary....

ANTONIO: You say it's not? Oh, yes, it is.

MARISA: No. It is ignorance to believe that.

ANTONIO: She was rolled up into a ball lying in a corner. There was a spoon beside her. The nurse had used it to open her mouth. They had broken a tooth and she still had dried blood on her face.... You know what? I do not remember what Grandma was like. If she was young or old, if she was cute or ugly.... To avoid looking at her or my mother, who was crying without saying anything, I stared at the spoon lying on the floor. The yellowish color, the shape of the handle, with some little spinning drawings that....

MARISA: Is that what you were thinking about before?

ANTONIO: No. I don't know why I'm telling you this now. It just came out.... *(Pause.)*

MARISA: Antonio, why don't you...?

ANTONIO: Why don't I do what?

MARISA: Nothing, nothing. You can't order someone not to think....

ANTONIO: No.... *(She looks at her watch.)* Is it getting late for you?

MARISA: Yes.... *(He sits opposite to her.)*

ANTONIO: Are the biscuits good?

MARISA: Yes.... *(Pause, she eats and lowers her head. Music and sound of the clock. She lifts her head. Staring at him.)*

ANTONIO: *(Touching his face.)* What do I have?

MARISA: What...?

ANTONIO: I'm asking what I have...

MARISA: Nothing.

ANTONIO: Since you were staring at me....

MARISA: I was not staring at you. I was thinking.

ANTONIO: I thought I had something on my face.

MARISA: *(He can play touching the glass with a spoon, he does not look at it.)*

They say that in order to sleep well there is nothing better than to have relations with your own woman....

ANTONIO: Come on, be serious.

MARISA: *(Looks at him.)* I am being serious.

ANTONIO: Anyone who overheard our conversations would not know if it's Monday, Tuesday, or Sunday....

MARISA: Do people speak differently on those days?

ANTONIO: No. But we always repeat the same things. Isn't it true what I say?

MARISA: Now you have to add that it is all my fault and then we definitely repeat what we do every day.

ANTONIO: I am not so closed up. Blame always goes both ways.

MARISA: Continue. The conversation is not complete yet.

ANTONIO: Or sometimes three....

MARISA: Well, now it is complete. We start the second chapter. *(Smiles with sarcasm.)* Let me continue. That if I compare you with Eduardo, if I was happier before than I am now, if etcetera, etcetera, etcetera....

ANTONIO: Did you notice how you said it? We do not even argue anymore.

MARISA: Do you want to argue? Do you need to argue?

ANTONIO: We talk, but just until this point. *(Points forward.)* But beyond that we can't. You don't allow it. You don't continue any further.

MARISA: Antonio, is it me who doesn't allow it? Or are you talking about yourself?

ANTONIO: We could talk about so many things. I don't know. You never tell me anything about your work....

MARISA: But... but what can I tell you about my work? If every day I fill out the same papers, I do the same paperwork, I have coffee at the same time. And also at the same time I put the cover on the typewriter and I greet my boss with the same professional smile. Or do you want me to lie to you? Do you want me to invent things so that you overthink stuff as you walk around enclosed here, in this kitchen? Do you want me to tell you that I go to Plaza Zabala [10] so that the guys flirt with me? Or that I sit on my boss's knees to play cards? We're old enough now, Antonio. Quite old. Nobody calls me "Miss" anymore. Everyone uses the "Ma'am". So, why this out-of-place teenage outburst?

ANTONIO: *(He sighs deeply.)* You're right.... I always have to end up telling you that you're right.

MARISA: And you're never going to rebel, are you? What for? You're never going to say, "Well, I want this to be like this or like that...."

ANTONIO: Who understands you, Marisa...?

MARISA: You do not. Or at least you do not try. *(Begins to pick things up.)* I'm quite late and I still haven't brushed my teeth.

ANTONIO: Let me pick everything up. *(He does, she starts to exit.)*

MARISA: *(From the inside, or not.)* Well, today is the morning of surprises. Did you fall off the bed? Don't just stay there. Come in. From the inside you can hear everything better.

ANTONIO: *(Half calling, half sure.)* Daniel?

DANIEL: *(Entering.)* Yes.

ANTONIO: Do not listen to her. She got up in a bad mood. She did not mean it.

DANIEL: She did not mean what?

ANTONIO: That you were eavesdropping.

DANIEL: She's right. I was eavesdropping. I was waiting to come in.

ANTONIO: *(Justifying himself.)* Well, besides we have nothing to hide....

---

10   TN: Plaza Zabala is a plaza in Montevideo, Uruguay. It is located in *Ciudad Vieja*, which is the oldest part of the city of Montevideo. It takes its name from Bruno Mauricio de Zabala, founder of the city. The Plaza was established in 1890 when an equestrian statue of Zabala was installed.

DANIEL: How's the day?

ANTONIO: Beautiful.

DANIEL: And the old woman?

ANTONIO: She went to the fair early. You know that if she is not the first one to arrive, she thinks it will be suspended.

DANIEL: I'll be back in a little bit.

ANTONIO: Where are you going?

DANIEL: *(He shrugs.)* Are you reading that letter again?

ANTONIO: Well… until another one arrives….

DANIEL: The old woman should light some candles to the Saint of Uruguay's Post Office to see if they hurry the delivery of letters or so they don't lose them.

ANTONIO: Yes; they arrive every once in a while.

DANIEL: Are you going to write to him?

ANTONIO: Yes, today. It feels heavy for me today….

DANIEL: Tell him about the price of the meat or ask him if it is a joke that he is always mentioning the barbecue in his letters. *(He starts to walk away.)*

ANTONIO: Mom will ask for you.

DANIEL: I'm going to the backyard for a while.

ANTONIO: Are you going to study? *(DANIEL exits without answering.)*

MARISA: *(Walks in, she has put on makeup, has her purse.)* I'm leaving.

ANTONIO: Are you coming back at the same time as always?

MARISA: *(Looking inside her purse.)* Yes….

ANTONIO: Should I call you later?

MARISA:	What for?
ANTONIO:	No, I was just saying….
MARISA:	Aren't you going to kiss me? Or at this point should we just shake hands? (*Stretching her hand.*)
ANTONIO:	Who is the teenager now? (*He kisses her on the face.*)
MARISA:	Just like that? Just today I changed toothpastes. You don't want to see how it tastes? (*He is going to kiss her; she prevents it because she starts to laugh.*)
ANTONIO:	What are you laughing about now? What's the matter?
MARISA:	This sounds like a television commercial. (*With a Central American accent.*) "I changed my toothpaste so he would kiss me." (*Still laughing. They separate. They don't kiss. She exits.*)
ANTONIO:	Marisa….
MARISA:	What?
ANTONIO:	The propane tank has to be refilled…. Can you leave some money?
MARISA:	It has to be refilled already? Didn't they recently take it to be refilled?
ANTONIO:	Well… a month ago or so…. And the price went up again.
MARISA:	(*Looking inside her purse.*) That's crazy. Is this enough?
ANTONIO:	Yes.
MARISA:	(*Leaving money on the table.*) Do you want to buy cigarettes?
ANTONIO:	Well… yes. I have only one left.
MARISA:	OK. Buy that too. (*AMALIA walks in, dressed in mourning.*)
AMALIA:	Are you still here? But… what time is it?
MARISA:	I don't know. I do not want to know. It must be very late. Bye. (*Exits.*)

211

AMALIA: See you later. *(ANTONIO watches her go, puts the money away slowly. AMALIA, putting down her bag.)* Oh, I'm worn out…. I thought I wasn't going to make it back. My legs are swollen again…. Look away; I'm going to lower my stockings. *(While doing so.)* The doctor told me not to wear the garters any more…, *(she lowers her stockings, he sighs)* but how do I hold my stockings? And at my age I will not wear those pantyhose tights.

ANTONIO: What's wrong? Can I turn around?

AMALIA: Yes.

ANTONIO: Ah, I know… pantyhose incite sin.

AMALIA: I don't feel comfortable with those. They are uncomfortable for everything. And do not laugh about sin. There is not a single tramp who does not wear them. They all go with the colored pantyhose tights, yes, but so transparent that you can see everything. I don't know what they wear them for. It must be to attract attention.

ANTONIO: It's a fashion. And, like every fashion, one day it will be outdated and in a few years it will reappear. It's the industry and everything that is hidden behind it.

AMALIA: It must be. But as far as I'm concerned, leave me alone with my thick stockings and my garters….

ANTONIO: Even though they are bad for your circulation.

AMALIA: At this point in my life I will not change my ways. *(With a sigh she gets up and takes things out of her bag.)* Besides, it must be because I walked the whole fair three times from end to end. *(Looks in her wallet and takes out three or four pieces of paper.)* Here, add everything up to see if it is correct. *(ANTONIO stands up, looks for a paper and a pen. He lights a cigarette, throws the box away and sits down.)* These people from the street fair have lost all shame. Imagine, from one block to another the prices of the same things increase so much that it is outrageous. They think that one is stupid, or that one likes to be robbed. What they do with the fruit is such an old trick that they don't fool anyone. In front they put the most beautiful, well-polished, and then when you buy a pound, that's it, they give you the fruit from behind, all bruised and stung and with insect bites…. Luckily they know me and know that they cannot fool me…. But still you have to stay alert to everything. With the scale, controlling the change they give you back…. Look at these zucchini. I got them cheap. But what a pain! You know that I always buy from the red-haired Italian guy, the one who comes from Lezica.[11] Well, I passed by and he shouted at me, "Ma'am, look at the zucchini I brought today. Especially for you. You will not find others like these in the whole fair." Yes, that's what he said. And hear this, a block down—just a block, yep—I found them at five pesos less per pound…. Of course I bought them there, but I had such indignation…. As I went by again, I acted like I was looking the other way, and can you believe that he yells at me with that loud voice of his, "And, customer, are you going to take the zucchini or not?" It was as if I had been propelled by a rocket. I turned around. I went towards him, I put the bag under his nose and told him clearly that he was a thief, that they were cheaper over there and that they were also better than his. Even worse, he was bagging three pounds of zucchini for a fat woman. When the woman heard me, she told him that she was not going to take them, and in front of the Italian she asked me where the other place was. The eyes of the Italian went from the woman to me and from me to the woman. I still told her where the other stand was, because we have to help other people, right? That's what we are in the world for, right? The fat woman left faster than running. You can't imagine! The Italian's face turned redder than his hair and he just started yelling at me all kinds of things, except that I was pretty. The first thing he told me was such a gross rudeness about your late grandmother that he must have been born out of a cabbage and not a woman. (Laughs at her own joke.) And it could be, because he is a produce vendor, right? Of course, everything that he said to me, came in one ear and went out the other. But deep down it hurt. So many years buying from the Italian. He shouldn't have done that to me. But well, someone said that God is everywhere and that he does not like dirty business. As soon as I left the Italian with the

---

[11]   TN: Lezica is a working class neighborhood in Montevideo, Uruguay. It borders San José Department to the west and Canelones Department to the north.

insults in his mouth, some of which I did not understand because he began to speak in Italian, I ran into an inspector. One I know from having seen him there before. I told him what had happened to me, that the Italian was overcharging and I also told him that he may want to check his scale. The inspector told me to stay calm, to rest assured he was going to give him a fine. Just in case, I stayed right there until I saw him giving him a fine…. I felt better after that. I don't know. I felt a weight had come off my shoulders. I had done a good deed…. Look at this piece of cheese. What do you think? A piece like this, which is a little over a quarter pound. I had it weighed three times. Well, do you know how much I had to pay? Look, I don't know why I ask you, because when it comes to prices you seem to live in the clouds. I don't know where we are going to end up with this situation of prices going up almost every day. What they will get out of this is that people are going to stop eating cheese if they continue charging so much. If it was up to me, I wouldn't get it. I buy it for you and your brother. *(She eats a piece, speaks with her mouth full.)* To think that in the time of your father we would buy a whole wheel. Hey, is there something wrong with you that you are not saying a word? *(From a drawer she takes out brown paper and wraps the cheese.)*

ANTONIO: You don't let me. You start with the fair and the prices and you forget everything else.

AMALIA: It's the only place I go out to. For me it's like going for a walk. *(Cuts out another piece.)* Do you want a little bit?

ANTONIO: No, not now….

AMALIA: The truth is that it is very good. But it hurts to have to pay so much.

ANTONIO: Did you fight over the price of the cheese, too?

AMALIA: Do you think I am a scandalmonger? That I just go to the fair to fight?

ANTONIO: What I think is that for you it is therapy. You vent there. I wish I had a fair for myself….

214

AMALIA: The fair belongs to everyone. You could just accompany me….

ANTONIO: I mean it figuratively.

AMALIA: You are already talking like that. But look, if you had to go shopping and monitor the scale as I have to do….

ANTONIO: … I would just go to a supermarket and that's it.

AMALIA: What for? To go in and leave buying something you hadn't even thought about. And in the supermarkets nobody helps you. Who do you ask for a discount? You have to pay what the sticky paper shows and that's it. Leave the fair for me.

ANTONIO: *(Giving her the receipts.)* Here. Everything is alright.

AMALIA: *(Soft, as if by chance, without meaning to.)* Your wife, if she continues arriving late to work, one of these days she will lose her job….

ANTONIO: You cannot call her "Marisa"?

AMALIA: What? Isn't she your wife? Or is it incorrect to call her that?

ANTONIO: No, it's fine. But, you could easily call her by her name.

AMALIA: You are always correcting me. Look, I got to middle school and….

ANTONIO: … and you were the standard bearer, I know.

AMALIA: If I were a dumb-ass, as you think, I could never have been the standard bearer, right?

ANTONIO: From a rural school where there were two students in middle school….

AMALIA: Are rural schools not schools?

ANTONIO: *(Giving up.)* You, if you don't win, you tie. The old man did earn his way to heaven with you. What endurance he had!

AMALIA: I do not like you laughing at those things. Your father was… special.

215

ANTONIO: If in marriages there were standard bearers, he would be one.

AMALIA: Your wife was late on Friday too. She did not hear the alarm....

ANTONIO: And you can't let it go. Nothing is going to happen for being late a day (*getting ahead of AMALIA,*) or two. She has been working there for years and is very well-regarded.

AMALIA: And you still believe in those things? In the years served and how well people are regarded? How long did you work in the publishing house? Longer, much longer than she has been working in this company. And did that help you? It did not help you at all, at all, Antonio. They fired you when they felt like it. And now you are... we are in the situation we are.

ANTONIO: It was not my fault that they fired me. And you know it well. Or did you forget? (*Short pause. Masked reproach.*) Not me.

AMALIA: She left you the money, didn't she?

ANTONIO: Why do you ask me if you saw it on the table?

AMALIA: Hey, what a way of talking. Did you wake up on the wrong side of the bed today?

ANTONIO: It's you, your "things" that make me talk like that.

AMALIA: My "things"? Now it turns out I'm the one to blame.

ANTONIO: Let's leave it there. (*Uncomfortable pause. He turns the volume of the radio louder and then turns it back down.*) Yes, Marisa left me money, but it is to refill the propane tank.

AMALIA: There is no more propane left?

ANTONIO: No.

AMALIA: Oh... at the fair I ran into Néstor's mother. She told me that he is now in Barcelona.... Your brother does not talk about him enough in the letters.

ANTONIO: And if one is in Barcelona and the other in Madrid.... Maybe it just slipped his mind.

AMALIA: That can happen in one letter. But in all the last ones, not a word about Néstor. He did not even tell us that he was in Barcelona. Look, on the other hand, it is better. I never liked him a whole lot.

ANTONIO: But you hardly knew him.

AMALIA: If your brother got into trouble with politics, it was because of him. There is no one in the neighborhood who speaks well of Néstor. Remember that his mother even had to move because of the shame....

ANTONIO: You, too?

AMALIA: Just stop it. You always defend the whole world. No one is bad according to you. But it was because of Néstor... and because of keeping bad company that your brother is not here, here, with us.

ANTONIO: It was not the bad company. It was everything. It was about those in power. It was about what couldn't be said or done anymore. Do not simplify things like that. You know it, and Eduardo knew it too. He was not a little boy who was cheated.

AMALIA: What I know is that they wrapped him up with those ideas, they filled his head.... And what did they want? What were they looking for? Deaths, disasters? I do not go on because we have already spoken about this more than a thousand times and it seems that when we get to this point you stop listening to me. Immediately you get... you get that look, those eyes. I know you, Antonio.

ANTONIO: And I feel I know you less and less. You're more convinced by a television newscast or a newspaper release than what Eduardo can tell you, what I lived, or the ideas that Dad had. Or are you going to tell me that the old man was not a socialist and that you didn't keep him company everywhere he went?

AMALIA: Do you remember that? Still...?

ANTONIO: It was the old man's pride. The woman he had chosen accompanied him, too, in his ideas.... He told this to Eduardo and me once and a

217

hundred times. He would leave the *mate* aside and watch you cook or water the plants and his eyes would shine in a different way. His voice even changed…. Which Amalia are you? That old man's? The one with a son in exile? The one who endured on her feet when we were raided? Or the Amalia who believes the television releases and who is afraid of what the neighbors will say?

AMALIA: *(Pause.)* Who am I? What a question…. Look at me…. I was all of those and none of those I am now…. I don't even know myself, Antonio…. If I look in the mirror or go to the dresser and look for the photos I have with your father, I see that I am no longer the Amalia of Francisco…. If you look at me now, this old and unkempt Amalia is not the same one that was thinking about wearing for the first time that cute white dress, with blue dots, at the holiday parties before your brother left…. That dress that I never wore…. Look at my legs. Swollen, with varicose veins. They are not the same ones that endured without trembling when they went through the house all night looking for those very compromising papers that they said Eduardo had hidden…. *(Choked with emotion.)*

ANTONIO: But, deep inside, Mom, what you believed, what you wanted….

AMALIA: What I wanted was to have a family…. To have us, all of us, here, together, or near…. Before I thought that with the force of an idea, of a behavior, I could take the world by storm…. And look, even in that I changed because of fear, because of resignation, so that nothing would happen to all of you…. Francisco is no longer here, your brother is far away, Daniel is getting more distant and every day I understand him less… your wife, a stranger who lives with us… I can only think of God… and, hear this, in the past I almost… I almost did not believe and now I do…. *(Noise, the two turn their heads startled, DANIEL advances towards them.)*

ANTONIO: Who…? Oh….

AMALIA: What are you doing there?

DANIEL: Nothing.

ANTONIO: Have you been there for a while?

DANIEL: More or less.

AMALIA: Have you had anything to eat?

DANIEL: No. And I do not feel like it.

AMALIA: Are you not going to have any breakfast?

DANIEL: I do not want to. I don't feel like it. I'm not going to die because of
            that, right?

AMALIA: But, baby....

DANIEL: I said no, Mom. *(All three look at each other. Pause.)*
            You don't keep on talking because I'm here, right?
            AMALIA: Are you silly? Why do you think that? *(Searching for
            another topic.)* Where did you put the paper for the propane tank?

ANTONIO: There, under the vase. Is it there?

AMALIA: Yes.

ANTONIO: We need to take it to the store before ten so that they can have
            it refilled by the afternoon. Otherwise, we have to wait until
            tomorrow....

AMALIA: *(To ANTONIO.)* Are you going to take it?

ANTONIO: Yes, in a little while.

DANIEL: Give me that. I can go now.

ANTONIO: Here's the money. By the way, can you bring me Kendall cigarettes?

DANIEL: OK. *(Takes the money, looks for the propane tank.)* Oh, Mom, wash
            my jeans. I left them on the bed. Will they dry for tomorrow?

AMALIA: Yes. If I lay them out on the terrace.

DANIEL: Don't iron them. It's not in style.

AMALIA: If I hang them with all the water dripping, they don't need to be
            ironed. *(DANIEL exits.)* He was listening.

ANTONIO: He is always listening.

AMALIA: You have to talk to him. He will probably pay more attention to you.

ANTONIO: I don't know....

AMALIA: Well, I'm going to wash the jeans. What are you going to do?

ANTONIO: I feel like writing to Eduardo.

AMALIA: Oh, good idea. *(Exits.)*

ANTONIO: *(He gets up, turns on the portable radio. Newscast. Organizes some papers, AMALIA returns with the jeans, sweatshirts, and stockings.)* You are not going to wash them in the bathroom?

AMALIA: No, I'd better wash these in the sink. These are large clothes. *(Partial exit.)* Write him a nice letter.... Make him write more often.... *(Walks, turns, and walks back.)* Oh... I did not finish telling you. Néstor's mother told me that he does not plan to return. That he is doing well there. That in these days he has changed his car and opened a local foods restaurant with a Spaniard who has lots of money.... Hear this, he is going to send his mother a plane ticket for her to go see him.... Write him a nice letter....

ANTONIO: Do you want to write something to him at the end?

AMALIA: No, I have horrible handwriting. Tell him that I am in good health and ask him if he still misses my pancakes with *dulce de leche*.[12] *(Exits.)*

ANTONIO: *(Looks for the pen. Turns the radio a little louder.)* Montevideo, January 15, 1980. Dear brother.... *(Pause, he is going to write, he changes his mind, crumples the piece of paper, looks for another one.)* Montevideo, January 15, 1980. Eduardo.... *(Very short pause.)* I have been wanting to write to you for days. Because of one thing or another I could not. Today, at this moment, alone, in the kitchen, in the place where you always sat down to read the newspaper and

---

[12] TN: *Dulce de leche* is a caramel spread made by boiling down milk and sugar. It is very popular in Uruguay and Argentina.

drink *mate*, I start this letter that I think will make you happy....

(His voice gets softer and becomes a murmur, while the newscast gets louder and is heard in its entirety. The light gets softer focused on ANTONIO until lights out. The light returns. ANTONIO is not there. DANIEL is reading. AMALIA, next to him, with a shoe box on her lap. Pause. One can hear when he turns the pages. AMALIA looks at him every so often, then looking forward, soft but cheerful, intense.)

AMALIA: A week ago already.... Today.

DANIEL: *(Without looking at her.)* Huh...?

AMALIA: That your brother came back a week ago. Early today I kept my promise with the Virgin. I brought her a bouquet of carnations and two candles.... Oh, you have to come with me tomorrow.

DANIEL: Where?

AMALIA: "Where?" I made the promise to go with you to seven o'clock mass.

DANIEL: Already you and your promises....

AMALIA: Hey, aren't you all not doing well in return? You see what happened with your brother. He came back, didn't he?

DANIEL: And why didn't you promise to go to mass with him?

AMALIA: Oh, yes, and if he refuses to go? It's been so long since we've seen him. What if he...?

DANIEL: What if he became a Mohammedan, a Buddhist, or a member of the Moon sect? Do you want me to ask him?

AMALIA: Give me a break. I'm not saying he would have changed so much. But people change. And besides, he has his commitments, he does not have a lot of time.... He doesn't slow down for a minute.

DANIEL: And my time does not matter? I want to end this.

AMALIA: All I want is for you to accompany me to church. Whoever heard you talking would think I'm asking you for a horrible thing.... *(Buzz.)* If this was something "anyone else" asked you to do, you

221

would run to do it. But, since your mother asks something that is for the good of all of us, no, Mr. Daniel feels annoyed....

DANIEL: *(Won over by fatigue.)* It's okay. Do not carry on anymore. I'll go. I'm going to go. But now let me finish this.

AMALIA: Are you telling me to leave?

DANIEL: *(Snaps his tongue.)* No, stay. As long as you let me read quietly.

AMALIA: Well.... *(Silence, she opens and closes the box, DANIEL turns a page, AMALIA begins to speak softly, more to herself than to DANIEL.)* I prayed so many times for it to happen that when Eduardo walked in the house I almost... like I could hardly believe it.... Did you see that I stood still? I could not move.... I did not have the strength to move. I just looked at him... until he, without saying anything, stretched his arms.... I hugged him so hard that he had to push me away.... Did you see that I did not cry? I don't know, I could not.... I wanted to, but I had a lump in my throat and my heart was beating so fast in my chest like it was going to explode.... I thought I was going to die right there; but I did not care because I had my son back again....

DANIEL: I had never seen you like that....

AMALIA: Now I have everything I wanted. When he walked in... when I heard he was calling me.... He was also moved.... His voice trembled.... Look, I remember and I get goose bumps.... Tell me, Daniel, at the airport, after those people delayed him with the interrogation and he saw you and Antonio, the first thing he did was ask for me, didn't he?

DANIEL: You're not going to make me tell you about the airport again, are you? Every other day you make me repeat it.

AMALIA: He is a little thinner, but in good spirits, his face looks good.... He looks cuter.... And Antonio is another person since his brother is here....

DANIEL: *(Looking at her.)* All of us are different now.

222

AMALIA: And when he saw you…? Is it true that he told you that he did not recognize you? That he did not imagine that you would look like this, so grown up?

DANIEL: Again. Don't you want me to tape it for you? So you have it all the time?

AMALIA: Give me a break. Don't be bad. I like to repeat things. I live them over and over. And the neighborhood… what a fuss, right?

DANIEL: *(Closing the book.)* Well, who stops you now.…

AMALIA: *(Looking desolated.)* And if I do not talk about this with you, who would I talk to? *(Fast.)* Do not tell me with the priest, because I will slap you. *(He gestures like he's not going to say anything and crosses his arms to listen to her.)* Huh, more than four were floored when they saw him. People, when they want, can be very bad. About Eduardo, about you, about me, they said all kinds of stuff. Remember. That he had stolen, that he had committed suicide, that I was the mother of a communist, that we protected a Tupamaro,[13] that all of us in this house were his accomplices, that the police came here every night, that we had always been strange.… What do I know…? All kinds of stuff was said. In the end, everyone knew more about Eduardo and about our life than me, his mother.… And to think that there were people–friendships of years–that, when all that happened, stopped saying hello. And people who used to spend so much time here, from one day to the next they stopped visiting.… It was as if everyone in this house were a leper, when all your brother had done was think differently.… And, of course, now that he came back, well-dressed, with money in his pocket, they have to swallow everything they said.… And what makes most people upset is that I always walked down the street with my head held high and not hiding or in shame as they would have wanted me to.… Do you know that many of those people have already started to greet me and to stop me in the street to

---

[13]   TN: *Tupamaros* was a left-wing urban guerrilla group in Uruguay in the 1960s and 1970s. It is also known as *Movimiento de Liberación Nacional Tupamaros* or Tupamaros National Liberation Movement. The Tupamaro movement was named after the indigenous revolutionary Túpac Amaru II, who in 1780 and 1781 led a large uprising against the Viceroyalty of Peru. The rebellion continued after his death in 1781 and into early 1783.

talk to me? I act as if nothing had happened.... I am not the one who gets humiliated. It's them. Oh, look.... *(Looks in the box.)* Eduardo wants to see old photos. I set some aside. Here in his first communion. Look how serious he looks. Here, with Antonio, at school. Maybe you have not seen these? I seldom take them out.

DANIEL: Yes, once, I think.... And that one?

AMALIA: *(With a smile.)* This is one of the picnics we had at the Granja Dominga....[14]

DANIEL: Which one is you?

AMALIA: This one. The face I have in that photo! I look like a fool looking at your father.... I had curled my hair.... And your father, with the wine boot in his hand.... It was all joy. That smile that was so wide... and the mustaches that were so fashionable.... People were closer before. The whole neighborhood took a truck from here. Women would put the food we had brought on a large table, and while men played soccer or cards, we would cut everything. We had such good times! Then we would eat and, for dessert, the stories. *(In reaction to his face.)* They were not as dirty as they are now, but they made us laugh so much.... And then the dance. There was always someone with an accordion. Those *paso dobles*.... Your father liked those so much! And how well he danced them! They would gather around us and we danced in the middle.... Until I could not continue because of how agitated I was.... But Francisco was tireless and took someone else out to dance, and then another.... All the women wanted to dance with him.... There was no other like Francisco.... I did not get tired of looking at him.... And although he did not tell me anything, I knew he liked it.... Francisco.... You know something? He was jealous. It did not seem like it, but he was... and how much! Wait.... *(Looks for a picture.)* Look at him here. Look at his face....

DANIEL: It's in the same place.

---

14   TN: Granja Dominga (literary: "Dominga Farm") was a farm in the Manga neighborhood of Montevideo. The Granja Dominga was well known for the parties, picnics, dances, banquets, and celebrations that were held on its grounds. Its heyday was in the 1950s. Several well-known tango singers, dancers, and orchestras performed at the Granja Dominga over the years. It had a family-oriented atmosphere and attracted neighbors and families for a variety of events. The farm also produced its own wines, ciders, and hams.

AMALIA: Yes, at the Dominga. It was the time we brought Gavioli[15] and his orchestra.

DANIEL: Whom?

AMALIA: *(Very natural.)* Romeo Gavioli. I do not remember who came up with the idea, but all the families chipped in some money to bring him. Francisco got in a bad mood. He had such a face. And it was understandable. What a handsome man Gavioli was. So soft, with that voice, and so charming…. We were all crazy about him. No woman wanted to dance that afternoon. We all wanted to hear him and look at him. I remember that I approached to ask him to sing *María del Carmen*, which I liked so much…. *(She can hum it or not.)* And… I began to say to him: "Mr. Gavioli, could you sing…?" And Francisco pulled me back so strong that I almost fell in front of Gavioli. And he grabbed my hand and did not let go of me all night. I was standing there, glancing at Gavioli, who, illuminated by those beautiful garlands that they had hung from the trees, seemed even more handsome…. A soft blue light was shining on one side of his face, and a pink light on the other side. Francisco did not speak to me for three days and three nights. And he never got completely over it. To say that every time Radio Artigas played one of Gavioli's records, he changed the station immediately…. How sad it was when I learned about his death…. What a horrible death! He threw himself into the port with the car all closed. They say he had cancer. After I found out, I had dreams about him, I do not know how many nights…. Look, hiding it from Francisco I cut out and kept everything that came out in the newspaper. *(She gives him the cut outs.)* They are yellowish now…. *(Looks for another photo.)* Here you have your father again…. He must be your age there. You have the same face, the same eyes…. *(She gets up.)* Do not put away those photos because they will get mixed in with the other ones. Leave them aside for Eduardo to take a look.

---

[15] TN: Romeo Alfredo Gavioli (1913-1957) was a Uruguayan musician, tango singer, candombe singer, and director of small traditional musical groups.

DANIEL: It's better if you take the box, so there's no confusion. Where are you going?

AMALIA: To the door, for everyone to see me waiting for my son.

(AMALIA walks out with the box, DANIEL looks at her, looks again at the photo of his father as if he wanted to discover something. He softly touches the picture and then his face, as if trying to recognize who he is. The light gets softer and a tango starts playing. Brief lights out. Bluish light. The same tango continues to play. Sitting in the dark, EDUARDO. Wine bottle, a glass, and the radio playing soft music, and he whistles along with the tango; he has the photos in his hand. He sits up straight when he hears something. Turns down the radio completely. MARISA walks in, takes a few steps in, he flickers the lighter and puts it against his face.)

EDUARDO: Welcome. Good evening or, rather, good morning…. *(She makes a gesture as if she is going to leave.)* Are you leaving because I'm here? I'm not the boogeyman, you know.

MARISA: I could not sleep….

EDUARDO: Then, there's two of us. *(She moves.)* Do not go….

MARISA: It's also hot here….

EDUARDO: And what are you going to do? Toss and turn in bed?

MARISA: I was sitting at the chair by the window all night.

EDUARDO: But it feels better here…. Stay…. Since I arrived I have been wanting to talk to you, like this, calm…. Do you hear?

MARISA: What? Did someone get up?

EDUARDO: No, nobody…. This silence. The silence of those who sleep in peace… of those who die in peace.

MARISA: Since you arrived, Antonio has begun to sleep well. He wasn't before.

EDUARDO: Nothing moves. You cannot hear anything. It's as if there were no one else but you and I.

MARISA: It seems like it, but they are all here just two or three steps away.

EDUARDO: But right now they are here and they are not.

MARISA: Like you: you are here and you are not. *(Walks.)*

EDUARDO: Stay....

MARISA: What for?

EDUARDO: To talk. To be here. To look at you.

MARISA: Right, I must look good at this time and being wide awake all night.... *(Mechanically she fixes her hair.)* I wanted to have a glass of water.

EDUARDO: This wine is nicely chilled. *(Fills the glass.)* Here....

MARISA: No, I came to get some water. My mouth is dry....

(Without speaking, he stretches his arm offering her the glass. They stay like that for a moment looking at each other. She runs her hand over her mouth, she gets closer very slowly. She takes the glass. She drinks slowly. He turns on the radio.)

EDUARDO: You drank from the same side as I did. Now I will know all your secrets. Look at me and I'll tell you what you're thinking. Are you excited or scared? *(She shrugs, he smiles.)* Let's see, let's see.... You are wondering if now I see you as beautiful as before....

MARISA: But how could you...?

EDUARDO: I have not finished yet. "Does he see me older? Does he notice that I have gained five pounds? That now I dye my hair? That before going to bed I put cream on my face, on my elbows, on my knees...?" Well, did I guess or not?

MARISA: *(Putting the glass down.)* See you tomorrow, Eduardo.

EDUARDO: Again?

MARISA: It does not make any sense for us to be talking at this time and whispering like two conspirators....

EDUARDO: I have no problem talking loudly or blasting the radio. *(He does.)*

MARISA: *(Quickly turns the radio down.)* You are crazy. You're going to wake everyone up.

EDUARDO: *(He takes her hand.)* We don't have anything to hide, do we? What evil can there be in a conversation between brother and sister-in-law...? You have the same skin. *(She pulls her hand away. He smells his.)* Admit that I was right about something: Pond's C cream, Seven Day Plan.

MARISA: Nivea cream. It's cheaper.

EDUARDO: You know something? You look prettier. The same eyes, the same mouth gesture, but everything better....

MARISA: You have definitely changed.

EDUARDO: For the worse?

MARISA: I don't know. You look different.

EDUARDO: Do you say it because of this? *(He shakes his hair with his hand.)*

MARISA: No, it suits you. It makes you look younger.

EDUARDO: What do you mean that it makes me look younger? I'm young. We are young. *(He runs his fingers through his hair again.)* I would not have dared to have it like this here. The people in the neighborhood would have called me all kinds of things. From "queer" to "faggot," anything.... But there, away, one sees things differently. I dared to do many things. Things I would have never done here because of pride, because of what people would say, because of... everything.

MARISA: See, in that you have changed. Now you have a "there." You name things, people, places.... A "there" that for us is very vague or is nothing at all, and that for you is something concrete, tangible: a color, a land, a smell.... It is as if you were here and at the same time there.... Divided. Separated....

EDUARDO: That's worth a drink. *(He pours a drink.)*

228

MARISA: What?

EDUARDO: *(After drinking and filling the glass for her.)* You trying to figure out who I am. They sound like phrases from some storyline of mine. Here.

MARISA: You are laughing at me.

EDUARDO: No, because you're partly right.

MARISA: You look serious.

EDUARDO: Me? No, I don't….

MARISA: Yes, you have that wrinkle on your forehead. *(Points.)* There. Whenever you would get serious about something, you had that wrinkle….

EDUARDO: Do you realize that this is the first time since I arrived that we are talking?

MARISA: Do not exaggerate. We have talked.

EDUARDO: Hardly. Two or three things as social graces… about the weather, about travel, things like that…. And you look at me as little as possible… or if you do it, it's when you think that I'm not looking at you…. You never wrote.

MARISA: Antonio wrote for the both of us.

EDUARDO: But you didn't. In each letter I asked about you. I would send comments for you….

MARISA: And why would I write to you? Why?

EDUARDO: Was it so hard for you to do that? Not even a secret postcard….

MARISA: To do something else in secret for you? No, I did not have to write to you. It did not make any sense.

EDUARDO: This is the second time you say that something does not make sense.

MARISA: It's the only expression that suits this.

EDUARDO: When Antonio wrote me that he was marrying you, I could not believe it. He wrote it as a postscript without any clarification or anything. "I will marry Marisa on Saturday." I read it, I do not know how many times. Until I tore the letter up and threw the pieces all along Gran Vía....[16] My Asiram was marrying Antonio....

MARISA: Marisa married Antonio. Asiram was an invention of yours.

EDUARDO: Of the two of us.

MARISA: The old idea of calling things by another name or saying them backwards.

EDUARDO: Before you used to like that I called you "Asiram...."

MARISA: Before…. Who remembers before?

EDUARDO: I do.

MARISA: Not me.

EDUARDO: What I lived with you was the best thing that could have ever happened to me.

MARISA: And you let it go.

EDUARDO: You did not want to follow me.

MARISA: I followed you in everything you did here, in Montevideo. And what could I expect with you? To endure hardship together?

EDUARDO: You never stopped being a bourgeois in disguise. And look how you ended up? In this situation? Here? Next to Antonio? You had little ambition or you did not have any luck…. So going to distribute flyers with me was just a pose? Was painting graffiti on the walls a game? Was it all just lip service? You didn't have any conviction, did you? Was it all just a game for you?

---

[16] TN: Gran Vía (literary: "Great Way") is an ornate and upscale shopping street located in central Madrid, Spain. Gran Vía and Paseo de la Castellana are the two most famous streets in Madrid; they are mentioned in Spanish operettas, books, and featured in films. Gran Vía is known as the Spanish Broadway, and it is one of the streets with the most nightlife in Europe.

MARISA: A game, you say? You well know that if back then you were caught with a flyer, you were putting yourself on the line. And I did it all the same. Not as a pose or to play. I did it for you. I wanted to share everything with you. The good and bad. I ignored everything else. I did not listen to anyone. My poor father trembled with rage not being able to do anything when he handed me the phone and he heard me talking to you and then saw me going out at a minute's notice, at any time of the day or night. And I... I went, did, and said.... I did not care about anything. So, where, why, and for what did I do it all? Because everything I did, I did with you. Only for you....

EDUARDO: You never said it like that....

MARISA: It is not a reproach.... I can say it now in hindsight. I see myself and you, helping faces that passed in front of us only once, blurred people that we took to places where we would never return.... How many hands we held just once, how many gray faces....

EDUARDO: Do you regret it?

MARISA: I don't know. What I do know is that I would not do it now. You were my engine. And we were so young.... We thought we would change the world....

EDUARDO: And when we had the chance to change it, you did not follow me. You could not bring yourself to do it. I had to leave alone.

MARISA: Everything happened so fast. I could not even think. How much time did you give me to react?

EDUARDO: But we had talked about it....

MARISA: Only as a possibility.... But you called me just like any other day. Your voice sounded almost the same. I went to meet you as usual and there you were pale as a ghost. How could I put my thoughts together, when you were completely out of control? You hugged me tightly and started to repeat, "We're leaving now, right now." And that was all. You did not explain anything. You just said, over and over again, "We're leaving now, right now."

231

EDUARDO: I do not remember what I said to you. I know it rained a lot, it poured. And that we surely looked like two crazy people, there, in that dark corner, crying, hugging, and tugging at each other.... Yes, two crazy people.... *(Long pause. They look at each other.)*

MARISA: And so the romance of the downtown upscale girl and the neighborhood boy, with fifty percent of political obsession and fifty percent of tango singer. *(Patting his back.)* Writer, there you have a theme. A topic that you would surely disregard, right? It is closer to Corín Tellado than to Shakespeare. At most it would give you the lyrics of a tango. One of those that you used to like singing to me when we were coming back from one of the jobs. Walking just for the pleasure of walking.... *Los mareados, Uno,*[17] *Amarras....*[18] Do you remember?

EDUARDO: You skipped the part that would make your trashy romance novel sell better.

MARISA: Our novel. If it is not the embrace in the rain and not the walks along the street singing old tangos.... It has to be the farewell of the young man to his city, boarding the plane as the last passenger and with no money in his pocket. Alone, without family, without his pure girlfriend.... *Volver,*[19] *El día que me quieras.*[20]

EDUARDO: You are making another mistake, Corín. The young girlfriend had ceased to be pure for quite some time and of her own free will.... Do you not remember?

MARISA: What do I have to remember?

---

[17]   TN: *Uno* (literally: "One") is a 1943 tango with lyrics by Enrique Santos Discépolo and music by Mariano Mores. It starts: "One searches full of hope for the path that dreams had promised to their longing.... One knows the struggle is cruel and it's great, but one fights and bleeds out...."

[18]   TN: *Amarras* (literally: "Moorings") is a 1944 tango with lyrics by Carmelo Santiago and music by Carlos Marchisio. It starts: "I'm roaming like a tormented shadow, under the gray covered corridor, I reflect upon myself and I am nothing...."

[19]   TN: *Volver* (literally: "To Return") is a tango created in 1934 by Carlos Gardel and Alfredo Le Pera. Gardel composed and performed the music, and Le Pera wrote the lyrics. This tango has been covered by multiple singers, including Julio Iglesias, Libertad Lamarque, Los Panchos, and Andrés Calamaro. This tango is about returning to the homeland and/or to an old love.

[20]   TN: *El día que me quieras* (literally: "The day that you love me") is a tango with music by Carlos Gardel and lyrics by Alfredo Le Pera. Originally featured in the 1935 film of the same name, it became a heavily recorded tango standard, even by artists outside of the realm of tango. The song was inducted into the Latin Grammy Hall of Fame in 2001.

EDUARDO: Asiram, it hurts me too. It is easier to forget everything, to think that it did not happen. But it all happened. Everything was real. The rain, the corner, explaining everything in a rush, walking around the block–I do not know how many times–just not to stand still, waiting for the truck that was coming to pick me up. The room where I had to wait for the passport and the directions.... That room, Asiram, that was like a storage of old things....

MARISA: The little lightbulb that was moving back and forth....

EDUARDO: The rain that made such a loud noise on the zinc roof that it did not let us hear what we were saying, what we were shouting at each other....

MARISA: On one side there was a broken glass and the wind came in, it was cold.

EDUARDO: The newspapers and the rags that I laid out on the ground so we could be together.

MARISA: The big headline of a newspaper read, "Brigitte Bardot defends the seals...."

EDUARDO: That moment with you.... I never felt with anyone what I felt with you there. I loved you the most! I would come in and out of you knowing that it was the last time.... I wanted to give you everything I had. My breath, my blood, my fears... I spoke to you, I caressed you, and I hugged you. And you too... you scratched me, you turned so much.... Then they came and the last thing I saw of you was that you were coiled.... I covered you with your raincoat.... It was plaid, I think....

MARISA: The lining was plaid... brown and light yellow....

EDUARDO: I left you there.... Your hair covered your face. You had one hand between your legs and the other one under your head.... You stayed there....

MARISA: I do not know how I got back to my house.... Then they told me that I took a few steps in the hallway and that I fell down.... I was

233

in bed for a week. I did not recognize anyone and they said I kept repeating your name. Only out of fear my parents didn't call the police…. I never wore that raincoat again…. Then, two or three times, someone called and hung up…. Once they stopped me in the street to ask me to continue doing your work and I couldn't. They insisted. But without you I couldn't…. I had done it for you….

EDUARDO: And how could you come to live here?

MARISA: I don't know…. Almost without thinking. One day your brother showed up at home…. He would stay next to me, looking at me…. He would wait…. He would talk to me…. I would just look at him. He looked so similar to you…. He had the same smell…. He seemed not to mind that I did not speak to him…. He still kept coming every day at the same time…. One day I discovered that I was waiting for him. We started to go out…. Then came the separation of my parents, the death of my Mom and in a year I was left with nothing, no one…. I only had Antonio….

EDUARDO: When he wrote that you were both getting married, I thought so many things….

MARISA: You were so far away…. He was here, next to me….EDUARDO: You were very important to me.

MARISA: And you too. You were. I'm not the same one now. We all change.

EDUARDO: (Serious.) Do you… do you love him like you loved me?

MARISA: (Trying to change the mood of the conversation.) Corín Tellado? Pascual Contursi? Or Troilo and Manzi?[21]

EDUARDO: No, "Eduardo." Your "Eduardo." Did you ever have a night like that with him? Do you enjoy it as you did with me? If I tell you that when I decided to return, what I wanted the most was to see you, to have you, not caring about Antonio or anyone else… when I see you around the house I have to restrain myself from holding you….

---

[21] TN: Pascual Contursi (1888-1932) and Aníbal Troilo (1914-1975) were famous Argentine tango musicians and composers. Homero Manzi (1907-1951) was an Argentine tango lyricist and author of various famous tangos.

MARISA: But Antonio does not deserve....

EDUARDO: I already told you that I don't care about him or anything. I returned for you, Asiram.... You are still my Asiram.... I want to do it again with you....

MARISA: You do not know what you're saying.

EDUARDO: We're going to do it.... I waited for you to leave work and you pretended like you did not see me and ran away.

MARISA: I cannot do that to Antonio....

EDUARDO: You are not happy with him.

MARISA: That's not a reason to....

EDUARDO: You want to do it too. You knew that I was here, waiting for you.... If it were not so, you would not be shaking as you are doing now.... *(He gets closer to her, she does not move.)*

MARISA: Not here.... Not in the house.

EDUARDO: Not what? Don't you see that you are thinking the same thing as me? You want the same as me? *(He grabs her by the shoulder, she screams, he covers her mouth with his hand. He caresses her gently.)* Do not say anything.... Let me look at you. Like this.... Do not think about anything, about anybody.... Now we are alone, you and I. You and I as before. Look at me like you did before... with that look... like when I read the books you said you did not understand well. The economic essays by Che,[22] do you remember? I would put down the book. I would hold you by the hand and, looking into your eyes, I would explain it to you with my own words. I would sink in your eyes until I would see that you had understood me. You are shaking. Now, there, there's my Asiram again.... You're back.... *(He starts kissing her eyes. He moves her hand away from her mouth. She breathes heavily. They look at each other. He gently caresses her lips. He grabs her hand. He takes her hand to his lips. She lets her arms hang down on each side of her body. Slowly he*

---

[22]   TN: *Che* is Ernesto Guevara's nickname. Ernesto *Che* Guevara was an Argentine Marxist revolutionary, physician, author, guerrilla leader, diplomat, military theorist, and a major figure of the Cuban Revolution.

caresses one of her breasts. He kisses her neck. He continues to kiss her down the neck until reaching her breasts. He kneels down and stays in that position hugging her waist. She slowly raises her hands and strokes his hair. They stay like this for a while. The radio begins to softly play the tango "Los mareados." He gets up, takes her by the hand and spins her. They walk. She stops. Without letting her go, he continues. Their arms are stretched.) Come… outside… come….

(He exits. MARISA, stays still, looking at him. Outside, he whistles the tango; she takes a few steps. DANIEL comes out of the shadows. MARISA turns around, looks around the inside of the house. EDUARDO's whistle and music get louder. DANIEL walks towards MARISA. They look at each other. Both still in the same place. She shakes her head, as though she were helpless. She's going to say something to DANIEL and the whistle gets louder. Suddenly she turns around and she exits running towards EDUARDO. DANIEL slowly follows her. The whistle stops. DANIEL stops. He looks at them. Then turns around. Goes to the table, sits with his back against the place where they are. He picks up the pictures. He looks at the pictures and slowly starts to tear one. The music gets louder. The light dims slowly until lights out. The music is changed for a newscast. Lights and we see AMALIA and MARISA making gnocchi. They move silently through the kitchen. Lightning and thunder.)

AMALIA: *(Makes the sign of the cross.)* Blessed Santa Barbara. Oh, my Goodness. *(Pause.)* Do you need much more time?

MARISA: *(Soft.)* No, I don't.

AMALIA: And those boys left the house without umbrellas…. What a long newscast. And always talking about the same. All day long, all you can hear is about the damn elections…. *(MARISA changes the station.)* I did not say it for you to change it. Maybe you are interested in knowing. As far as I'm concerned, listening to one is enough. They all repeat the same things in the statements. Well, they are politicians, are they not? First they promise you the moon and then, when they are in power, they do not remember us. And it seems as if people like that. And those who are in bad shape are the worst. They scream, they are fanatical, and end up voting for the same people from yesterday as if they did not know what they are

236

about. The tantrums that Francisco would have. His socialism did not even make a dent. It was always like this and it will continue to be the same way. The same political parties: white and red,[23] red and white…. Francisco always said that every country has the government that it deserves. Don't you think he was right about that?

MARISA: What…?

AMALIA: I was asking if you thought Francisco was right…. *(Looking at her face.)* You were not listening to me. And you are not paying attention to what you are doing either. Look at those gnocchi. They look like number eights. Give me that, I will continue. *(MARISA steps back. Thunder.)* Look, I told them to take something with them, that the weather was not good…. Is there something wrong?

MARISA: No. Why?

AMALIA: I don't know. You look strange.

MARISA: It must be your imagination. I am the same as always.

AMALIA: I notice you more serious. More quiet. Distracted. And you are not one of those who gets nervous about a summer storm. Is there something wrong that I do not know of?

MARISA: What could happen here without you knowing?

AMALIA: You talk as if I were a busybody…. Did you fight with Antonio?

MARISA: No. And if that were the case, you would know about it, would you not? Antonio has no secrets from you.

AMALIA: See? One speaks well and you act so jumpy….

MARISA: Could it be that you want to see things that are not there?

AMALIA: But look, I do not say it because of today. I've been noticing it for days.

---

[23] TN: There two traditional political parties in Uruguay; the *partido colorado* or red party and the *partido blanco* or white party. The colors refer to the color of their flags.

MARISA: Sometimes I do not feel like talking or being talked to.

AMALIA: Yes. I know that well. I do not need you to tell me. It was the first thing Antonio told me when he brought you to this house. You always talk very little to everyone. And with me even less.

MARISA: I speak just enough. Don't you think?

AMALIA: Look. Let's be frank. We both know that we do not love each other very much. Everyone in this house knows it. Or am I lying?

MARISA: You are incapable of lying…. *(AMALIA looks at her.)* I mean, because of your Christian background, right?

AMALIA: You are a girl whom I never understood. I did my best to understand you, to appreciate you….

MARISA: I do not deny it.

AMALIA: And you did little to help.

MARISA: Yes. I do not deny that either. And now we are like this… just putting up with each other, right?

AMALIA: Do not talk like that.

MARISA: You asked me to be frank. Let's say that we coexist well together. That we are not like those mothers-in-law and daughters-in-law in the soap operas who are always saying that they understand and love each other.

AMALIA: *(Fast.)* That's why I am the first one to tell everyone that you help us a lot. You provide so much without us asking for it; and sometimes, if it were not for what you….

MARISA: I do what I'm supposed to do. I live here, I eat here, and I sleep here.

AMALIA: I often think of what you had before. Family, money….

MARISA: I try to live in the now. I had all that. But everything I had before is now gone.

AMALIA: *(Looking at her for a long time.)* You have the same body and face as when you got here. We've all been changing during these years, but not you. You do not look the age you are. And you are older than Antonio. And older than Eduardo.

MARISA: Two years older than Antonio and only one year older than Eduardo. That's no difference.

AMALIA: For me, yes. I do not like women being older than men. Francisco was fourteen years older than I....

MARISA: And what a punishment for you, right? I was the woman of both your sons.

AMALIA: *(Disturbed.)* You have a way of saying things....

MARISA: A way of telling the truth. Wasn't it you who wanted to be frank? Well, today for the first time we're both here alone, talking. Want to continue? Or should we keep quiet as we do every day, keeping in what you want to tell me and what I want to say to you. Or, if not, we can do the usual: you tell me things through Antonio and I tell you things through Daniel. But today I want to continue. First I was Eduardo's woman and now I am Antonio's wife.

AMALIA: You have all three wrapped around your finger. Even Daniel.... He does not talk to me and he spends hours talking to you. My sons would not be in the situations they are now if it weren't because of you. If they got into politics, it was because of you. First Eduardo, then Antonio, and now who knows what things you are putting into Daniel's head.

MARISA: So powerful do you believe me to be?

AMALIA: I know my sons.

MARISA: But not me. And you are talking about knowing your sons.... I wouldn't say it with such confidence. It was actually the other way around. When I met Eduardo, he was already in trouble up to here. *(Points to the neck.)* And, according to him, he did no more than follow the example given to him by your husband. He wanted to fulfill the old man's dream. Or am I wrong? You cannot deny that.

AMALIA: Francisco was an idealist…. It was all talk…. He never got to…. *(She stops.)*

MARISA: He never got to what? Don't stop. Or were you going to say, "He never got to do what Eduardo did?" Wasn't it that you knew your sons? Or don't you want to admit that Eduardo stole, was a messenger, glued posters all over the place, and even had meetings here? Maybe in this kitchen. You didn't see that? You did not know it?

AMALIA: Whoever listens to you would think that Eduardo is a delinquent…. If he were like that, he would not be here again, among us.

MARISA: Nobody is listening to us. And be calm. He was not a delinquent, nor is he the hero you think he is. What happened to him also happened to too many others. And Eduardo didn't end up so badly. Some died. Others were tortured, ended up handicapped. Most of them spent years in jail. And everything that Eduardo did, everything he got around to doing, was not because of me. It came out of here, out of this house. He was raised, he grew up in front of your own eyes. Wasn't it so? Or do you think I'm making it up? *(MARISA reaches her highest pitch. The two of them look at each other. AMALIA turns her back on her. MARISA follows her. DANIEL walks in giving the impression that he had been around for a while.)* You are not answering.

AMALIA: Do not touch me.

MARISA: You have to answer.

AMALIA: I do not have to tell you anything else.

MARISA: If I am to blame, I am not the only one. You raised them, you saw them grow up. You gave birth to them.

AMALIA: Don't forget that you are in my house.

MARISA: In my husband's house too.

AMALIA: Your husband. Yes, your husband. I went crazy when he told me he was going to marry you. I would spend so much time crying. I talked to him. I told him all kinds of stuff. But nothing of what I did, of what I said, made any difference. It all seemed to make him fancy you more. Do you even know what I ended up doing? I went to a healer. I brought her some stockings and underwear so she would make the sign of the cross over them.

MARISA: You? You, such a believer?

AMALIA: Yes, me. And I would have done much more. But Antonio was blind. He did not believe anything, he did not see anything. And he doesn't see now either.

MARISA: What do you mean by that?

AMALIA: You understand me well. You and Eduardo in this house together....

MARISA: Everything with Eduardo is over.

AMALIA: Is it over? Are you sure? Is it over? One has to only look at the two of you. The only one who does not realize is poor Antonio. What are you seeking now? What do you want to do?

MARISA: Don't worry about what I want or what I seek. I already spoke with Antonio and he is the only one who I owe any explanation to.

AMALIA: You know how to control them all. First Eduardo and now Antonio. (*Lightning flashes. She turns around and sees DANIEL.*) Daniel.... What are you doing there?

DANIEL: I just walked in....

AMALIA: But you're soaked. Wait, I'll bring you a towel. And your brothers?

DANIEL: They stayed at the corner coffee shop with the boys.

AMALIA: Take off your shoes before you catch a cold. Look, I told them to take something, that there was bad weather, then they say that one is always.... (*Exits while talking, DANIEL takes off his shoes and sits down.*)

241

DANIEL: It seems that the storm is not only outside, eh? Did you make the old woman lose it?

MARISA: Give me the shirt. It is soaked and, if it dries on your body, I don't want to know how you feel tomorrow.

DANIEL: Hey, now you are taking it out on me.

MARISA: I do not take it out on anyone. I tell you this for your own sake. You do whatever you want.

DANIEL: Knowing you, I'd rather take my shirt off than have to put up with you later. *(Ironic.)* Besides, if it's for my sake that you tell me…. *(He takes off his shirt and leaves it rolled up.)*

MARISA: But Daniel, how are you going to leave the shirt like this? Give it to me that I will hang it. *(Puts it on the back of the chair.)* And it's the new shirt.

DANIEL: Yes, the one you gave me.

MARISA: And this is how you take care of the things one gives you? It will not last. Is it too hard for you to hang it? Was it a lot of work? *(Daniel does not answer, he just looks at her.)* If you only had one shirt, you would be…. Why are you looking at me like that?

DANIEL: *(Soft, serious.)* There is something wrong with you, right?

MARISA: *(Taking the same tone.)* Is it so noticeable?

DANIEL: I can tell…. And? What are you going to do?

MARISA: Do? With what?

DANIEL: With you. You know what I'm talking about.

MARISA: You are talking about the other night…?

DANIEL: Are you going to leave with him?

MARISA: But… the things you say… how can you think that…?

DANIEL: When Eduardo leaves, are you going to go with him?

MARISA: But, Daniel, you know that....

AMALIA: Here. Dry that hair well. Look at the shoes.... And they say that I exaggerate. But, of course, what one says in this house seems to go in one ear and out the other.... *(Drying the shoes with newspaper.)* Then they admit that I was right, yes, but after these things happen.... Are your brothers going to stay forever at the coffee shop? I'm waiting for them to come so I can put the gnocchi in the boiling water....

DANIEL: Why are you telling me this?

AMALIA: And who am I going to tell it to? I'm talking to you, right? They delay everything as long as they want, and then they are in a hurry. They think this is a restaurant. It's my fault, only mine. I'm the one who has spoiled them. They arrive at any time they want, they sit down and this Christ of a woman serves them food right away. But one day I'm going to get tired.... And then, if I do not eat, because I'm bored of waiting and seeing the food ready on the table, they get mad at me....

DANIEL: *(Conciliatory.)* If you want, I'll go get them....

AMALIA: So that you get wet again? No, stay right where you are.... *(Nervous, moves her feet. Hits her knee with her hand and gets up mumbling.)* Oh, no, no.... I won't stay like this. I will put the gnocchi in the water and if they get overdone, so be it. I'm not going to be at the disposal of those two.... *(She continues mumbling in a singsong tone as she continues doing her chores. DANIEL whistles and goes to put his shoes away. MARISA looks out the window. Laughs and loud voices can be heard. ANTONIO and EDUARDO walk in.)*

EDUARDO: Fuck it with the rain. Screw that shit, man. Huh? It looked like it was not going to rain heavily and....

AMALIA: There you have a towel.

ANTONIO: I'll dry myself first.

EDUARDO: Daniel, you disappeared suddenly. What happened?

DANIEL: I wanted to be here.

ANTONIO: He's always shutting himself up, hiding. He's getting more and more awkward with people. Here. *(Hands him the towel.)*

EDUARDO: You were not like that as a boy. What I remember most about you was your laughter…. You would fall or stumble on something and you would burst into laughter…. *Joder*,[24] you were such a happy lad….

ANTONIO: Watch out, you are talking like a Spaniard again. So you remember this one's laughter? And now, since you came back, have you heard him laugh? Or say more than ten words in a row?

DANIEL: *(To MARISA.)* Looks like I'm the target today. *(To them.)* Do you want me to leave so you can talk more comfortably about me?

AMALIA: People would stop me on the street and congratulate me because he was always being so witty and funny. Everyone liked that laugh. It seemed like he was going to be cheerful all his life…. Now, they wouldn't get a smile out of him even if they paid him.

ANTONIO: In that he has a lot in common with Marisa. They are two of a kind.

EDUARDO: You're right. Look at them now. Instead of our brother, he seems to be her brother.

ANTONIO: What a perfect pair for a funeral, right? *(They laugh among themselves.)*

MARISA: What a shame that we do not drink as much as you do to enjoy the jokes.

ANTONIO: That is easy. There has to be something to drink in this house.

EDUARDO: Come on, Antonio is right….

ANTONIO: Right on. *Vale*,[25] as you say, Spaniard. *(They laugh.)*

---

[24] TN: *Joder* is a vulgar expression used primarily in Spain. It can be translated as "fuck" but, like in English, *joder* is not limited to describing sexual activity but has a variety of other meanings and uses.

[25] TN: *Vale* is an expression used in Spain to express approval. It can be translated as "okay."

MARISA: How many *cañas*[26] did you have? Or maybe Grey Goose?

ANTONIO: Grey Goose? Us? I can swear on the Grey Goose of the old woman that we did not drink any grey hair. *(Laughs at his own reversal of words.)* Did you hear me? I said "Grey Goose" and "gray hair" instead of "gray hair" and….

EDUARDO: No, we only drank *grappas*.[27]

MARISA: And it seems you had a few, right?

ANTONIO: How many did we drink, Eduardo?

EDUARDO: The last ones, here with the boys, were two each….

ANTONIO: I had two. You had three.

EDUARDO: Three? I did not notice. Good. Let's say three. We started to drink at Bar Hispano, about six or so, then the other drinks we had at…. *(Stops.)* But how many bars have closed….

ANTONIO: *(Silently, counts with his fingers.)* Look, we'd better not count the bars we went to.

AMALIA: Because you don't have enough fingers to count them. From here I can smell the stink of alcohol.

EDUARDO: But old lady, one does not come back to the country every day. I go out and I always find a friend who wants to pay for a round of drinks. And it is not right to refuse. I was drinking, yes… we were drinking. But you're wrong if you think I'm drunk. Look, I can stand on one leg very well. *(He grabs her and spins her.)* Oh, look at that.

AMALIA: *(Pushing away.)* Let me go. Don't be annoying. There's nothing I like less than a drunk.

ANTONIO: And I can stand on one leg over and over again. *(Tries to dance with MARISA.)*

---

[26] TN: *Caña* is a hard liquor made from sugar cane.

[27] TN: *Grappa* is a grape-based hard liquor of Italian origin that contains 35 to 60 percent alcohol by volume (70 to 120 US proof). *Grappa* is made by distilling the skins, pulp, seeds, and stems (pomace) left over from winemaking after pressing the grapes.

MARISA: You'd better get out of those wet clothes.

ANTONIO: You see? That's what I'm telling you. They have no sense of humor.

EDUARDO: And the worst thing is that they do not let us prove that we are not drunk.

ANTONIO: They don't want to give in. The ladies believe that we are drunk and drunk we have to be.

EDUARDO: Let's show them. Come. *(With a gesture, he invites him to dance.)*

ANTONIO: Come on.

EDUARDO: I'll lead. *(ANTONIO whistles. They dance.)* Hey, do you not know how to dance without stepping on other people's toes?

ANTONIO: The problem is that you don't know how to lead. *(They change roles.)* Like this, see?

EDUARDO: Oh, what a klutz you are!

ANTONIO: It's you. You always had stiff feet. So, are you convinced or not?

MARISA: Antonio, stop making a fool of yourself. Take those clothes off.

EDUARDO: You see. In this world, women have the last word. *(ANTONIO takes off his shirt, EDUARDO does the same.)* Well, here we are in the open. *(MARISA takes ANTONIO's shirt. She walks.)* Hey, beautiful, and what about me? Am I chopped liver? *(Offers his shirt.)* My shirt….

AMALIA: Give it to me. *(The two women leave.)*

DANIEL: It is not raining anymore….

EDUARDO: Did you see the guys? When they were standing in a circle and said to me: "Sing, Sosita,[28] sing …." I don't know, something ran through my veins…. Sosita…. Only they could call me that. "The man." Now, on the twenty-fifth or the twenty-sixth, is the date of his death. I get confused by the dates. But before I used to know

---

[28]   TN: "Sosita" is a diminutive of Sosa and an affectionate way to refer to Julio Sosa (1926-1964), who was a famous Uruguayan tango singer.

everything about Julio Sosa. Do you remember when I would style my hair with gel and wear one of those big handkerchiefs to look more like Julio Sosa? "Sing, Sosita, another song...." And how they applauded me. More than one had teary eyes....

ANTONIO: (*Softly.*) Sing, Sosita, sing for us.... (*EDUARDO gets up, takes a chair to a corner, and sits astride. The women walk in.*) Sing, Sosita, that tango that we like so much.... (*EDUARDO begins to sing* Los mareados. *In the meantime, the women, in silence, set the table: tablecloth, plates, glasses, etc. EDUARDO finishes singing and only ANTONIO applauds.*)

AMALIA: Time for dinner.

(*They sit down, ANTONIO and EDUARDO walk embraced towards the table. The light begins to dim, and then AMALIA begins to serve dinner. Lights almost out. Only a dim light on the radio. Just the beginning of a newscast can be heard, to show that the date is different from the one in the previous scene. Lights on and they are seated in the same places, to give the feeling of a daily ritual and the passing of time.*)

AMALIA: Well, in light of the fact that no one offers to wash the dishes.... (*She stands up. MARISA, seeing her, does the same.*)

EDUARDO: (*Raising his hand.*) I'll wash tomorrow. (*They clear the table.*)

AMALIA: Yesterday you said the same thing.

ANTONIO: Are you going to make some tea?

MARISA: Don't we always make some tea?

ANTONIO: For me, with a lot of lemon.

MARISA: If you had eaten less.... (*Exits. AMALIA tries to take away a piece of bread that was left on the table.*)

EDUARDO: No, leave it.

AMALIA: Don't tell me that you are still hungry....

EDUARDO: No. It's just that I like to eat the heel. Leave it here....

AMALIA: Daniel, shake the tablecloth outside.

DANIEL: Why me?

AMALIA: Because…. *(Exits.)*

ANTONIO: I see gnocchi and cannot contain myself…. *(Patting his stomach.)* Look how I ended up….

DANIEL: *(Pushing the glasses out of the way.)* It's Eduardo's fault. The other day he praised them so much that now the old woman shoves us gnocchi every day, whether it's the 29[29] of the month or not. *(He leaves with the tablecloth in his hands; Antonio and EDUARDO are left by themselves, and they look at each other. EDUARDO stretches out his hand and gestures to the other one.)*

ANTONIO: *(Without understanding.)* What…?

EDUARDO: Give me your hand, man.

ANTONIO: What for?

EDUARDO: Give it to me, damn it. *(The other one stretches out his hand, EDUARDO caresses it.)* Brother….

(ANTONIO does not know what to do and puts his other hand on top of EDUARDO's. Then the two, nervous, to change the mood of the moment, continue to put one hand on top of the other, as though playing a children's game. In the end, they laugh. MARISA walks in to pick up the glasses and DANIEL returns with the tablecloth, which he begins to fold. They look at them and look at each other. Tango and lights out. Lights on now on EDUARDO and ANTONIO. Sitting, drinking wine. They wear different shirts or sweatshirts to indicate that some time has passed. MARISA and DANIEL are there too. She moves forward, picks up the bottle from the table as if wanting to take it away.)

ANTONIO: What are you doing? *(Taking her by the hand.)* Leave it there.

MARISA: Don't you think you have had enough?

---

[29]   TN: Eating gnocchi on the 29th of every month is a tradition in Uruguay and Argentina, brought to the Southern Cone by the Italians. The 29th is the day when the Italian saint—Saint Pantaleo—was canonized. Many miracles are attributed to him, and the original tradition is to honor him. Families and friends in Uruguay and Argentina gather on the 29th to eat gnocchi together for good luck.

ANTONIO: Do not say another word: you are the representative of Alcoholics Anonymous in this house.

MARISA: *(Severe.)* Antonio, I'm serious.

ANTONIO: And so am I. Leave the wine here. You take so much care of it that it seems as if you had paid for it. But not this one. This one and those in the fridge were bought by my brother. And he did not buy them for show.

MARISA: Antonio....

ANTONIO: Are you going to just stand there?

MARISA: You know. I already told you, didn't I?

ANTONIO: Ugh, yes, I know. You're always telling me something, warning me about something. But this wine stays here. *(Serves abundantly.)* Here. *(To EDUARDO.)* Cheers to us both.

MARISA: I'm going to bed.

ANTONIO: Fine.

EDUARDO: Until tomorrow. *(She leaves without answering.)*

ANTONIO: And how about you? Are you staying with us or are you going to sleep?

DANIEL: I'm not sleepy yet....

ANTONIO: Then, here. *(Pours him a drink.)* Come on, sit here.... Like this.... *(He is going to drink, stops.)* The three of us together.... Another day all us three together. I can hardly believe it.

EDUARDO: A drink is in order, is it not?

ANTONIO: Of course. For the three of us. *(They toast and they drink.)* To us. *(Looks at each of them. Starts laughing softly, then strong.)*

EDUARDO: What's wrong? Do we have something on our face?

ANTONIO: Sitting like this, the three of us, reminded me of a story that the

249

old man used to tell us…. I used to like it and at the same time it scared me…. But I asked him to repeat it every night. The old man used to say, "Again? Don't you want me to tell you another one?" And although I knew it by heart, I would tell him that I wanted that same story…. *(Points to EDUARDO.)* The big bear…. *(To DANIEL.)* The little bear…. *(To himself.)* The middle bear…. The three little bears….

EDUARDO: *(With deep voice.)* Who sat in my chair?

DANIEL: *(With soft voice.)* Who had my soup?

ANTONIO: *(With normal voice.)* Who slept in my bed? *(Laughs, repeats seriously.)* Who slept in my bed?

EDUARDO: Who is going to give us these ten years back?

ANTONIO: No one. They can give you money, medals, things; but time… who can give it back?

EDUARDO: Time…. *(To DANIEL.)* To think that I did not see you grow up. When I left, you were like this and now to speak to you I have to raise my head. I saw you grow up in spurts, by pictures they sent me. But that is not enough. You are not the Daniel I left here. I have to learn to erase the image that I had made of you and put in its place this one of who you are now….

DANIEL: You, on the other hand, haven't changed.

EDUARDO: But I've changed. I've changed, Daniel…. *(Smiles.)* You say it like everyone else, almost like an obligation or because it sounds good…. But look at me. These gray hairs, I did not have them before. These wrinkles here, either. And everything I could not write, who do I blame for that? Who can give that back to me? I would sit down to write and couldn't. I didn't have the air of this house, Mom's familiar noises, and the familiar noises of the street…. Here I had my characters, my corners, what I had lived. Not there. Ten years there, ten long years… they left me with no roots… they dried up…. I'm neither fish nor fowl…. I wrote and tore it up. I wrote and tore it up. Most of the time I fell asleep on top of the papers, overly tired. The great novel I wanted to write.... The desire to be another Galeano,[30] another Benedetti,[31] maybe an Onetti,[32] it remained that, a wish. I do not have my novel because I lost ten years of my life learning to live elsewhere, in other places, with other people.... It was a very high price that I had to pay. I lost my identity. There, at the beginning, I sang all the tangos I knew, smoked black cigarettes one after the other, spoke about the Rambla[33] and about the Conventillo Mediomundo[34] until the Spaniards would get tired of listening to me... and now, here, I stand in front of a window display and think *escaparate* rather than *vidriera*[35] and my suitcases are *maletas*, not *valijas*,[36] and you laugh because I say "vale".... I walk along 18 de Julio Avenue and I think of the Gran Vía.... I lost my codes, my subtexts, my implicit references.... I am a foreigner here and I am a foreigner there. I have lost my history. They stole it from me, they erased it ten years ago.... Even this.... *(Raises the glass.)* Drinking it, I miss the cognac of Plaza del Moro and there I miss the red wine of the Barrio Sur....[37] that's what I am now, what they made me become:

---

[30] TN: Eduardo Hughes Galeano (1940-2015) was a Uruguayan journalist, writer, and novelist. Galeano's best-known works are *Las venas abiertas de América Latina* (*Open Veins of Latin America*, 1971) and *Memoria del fuego* (*Memory of Fire Trilogy*, 1982–6).

[31] TN: Mario Benedetti (1920-2009) was a Uruguayan journalist, novelist, and poet. He published more than 80 books that were translated into twenty languages. In the Spanish-speaking world he is considered one of Latin America's most important writers of the latter half of the 20th century.

[32] TN: Juan Carlos Onetti (1909-1994) was a Uruguayan novelist and author of short stories. He became one of Latin America's most distinguished writers, earning the Uruguay National Literature Prize in 1962.

[33] TN: La Rambla de Montevideo is the avenue that goes all along the coastline of Montevideo, Uruguay, and also the longest continuous sidewalk in the world. At a length of over 13.7 uninterrupted miles (22.2 km), the promenade runs along the Río de la Plata (*La Plata River*) and continues down the entire coast of Montevideo, Uruguay. The Rambla is an integral part of Montevidean identity.

[34] TN: Conventillo Mediomundo (literary: "Half World Tenement House") was a tenement house in Barrio Sur, which is a neighborhood in Montevideo, Uruguay. The *Conventillo Mediomundo* became a symbol of Uruguayan candombe music and Afro-Uruguayan culture. (Candombe is a Uruguayan music and dance that derived from African slaves' culture. It is considered an important aspect of the culture of Uruguay and was recognized by UNESCO as a World Cultural Heritage of humanity.) Conventillo Mediomundo was inaugurated in 1885 and demolished by the Montevideo City Hall during the military dictatorship in 1978.

[35] TN: The words *"escaparate"* and *"vidriera"* both mean 'window display' or 'store window.' The word *escaparate* is more common in Spain while the word *vidriera* is used in Uruguay and other South American countries.

[36] TN: The words *"maleta(s)"* and *"valija(s)"* both mean 'suitcase(s).' The word *maleta(s)* is more commonly used in Spain while the word *valija(s)* is used in Uruguay and other South American countries.

[37] TN: Barrio Sur is a neighborhood in Montevideo, Uruguay. The history of Barrio Sur started around 1835 with the foundation of the Central Cemetery of Montevideo. With the end of slavery in Uruguay, it became predominantly inhabited by Afro-Uruguayans. To this day, Barrio Sur remains very connected with Afro-Uruguayan music and culture.

an old guy, too old already, who does not know where he's going
to or who he is....

ANTONIO: For us you will always be the same one.

EDUARDO: No. Because you did not share with me what I lived. You only
know what I put down in the letters. But you did not smell the
scents of El Rastro[38] in the summer, nor did you see the Guernica
painting; you did not see how choked up I was.... I cannot be the
same person for you, because you don't know everything I did,
everything I went through.... Hunger, cold, looking for comrades,
desperate, disoriented, with a piece of paper where I had written
down an address that was always the wrong one.... "Sing, Sosita,
sing".... Here I do it for pleasure. There I did it to eat. Dressed up
as a Latin American, along with some Chileans who were crying
for Allende and some Argentineans who were swearing at Videla.[39]
And there we were. Five of us, with a guitar and a drum. Freezing,
lit by the window display lights of the *escaparates* rather than the
vidrieras in the middle of the Plaza del Sol, surrounded by curious
people and tourists who laughed and took pictures of us.... "Sing,
Sosita, sing...." Yes, I sang until my throat felt like sandpaper and
the noise that came out resembled anything other than singing. And
then I changed fast to the guitar, before that group of people would
scatter and go listen to five other ones like us. And after counting
the coins and distributing them, each of us would split until the
next day. Thinking, in front of a pot of chestnuts, whether or not I
should spend the money.... I did all kinds of stuff. Things I would
have never done here. Wash other people's shit, sweep bars, screw
people up.... Yes, I even stole to survive another day. Being with
old women for money. Sleeping with them because they would dig
the Latin lover look, the *gaucho*[40] of the pampas,[41] the tango man.
So I wouldn't feel too bad and thinking that I could make a little

---

[38] TN: El Rastro is the most popular open-air flea market in Madrid (Spain). It is held every Sunday and public holiday during the year. A great variety of products (new and used) can be found at el Rastro.

[39] TN: Videla (Jorge Rafael Videla) (1925-2013) was a senior commander in the Argentine Army and dictator of Argentina from 1976 to 1981.

[40] TN: *Gaucho* is a Spanish term that commonly refers to a South American cowboy or resident of the South American pampas.

[41] TN: The pampas are extensive grass-covered plains of southern South America east of the Andes. The pampas are found principally in parts of Argentina, Uruguay, and southern Brazil.

fun of them, I sang them my signature number, *Anclao en París,*[42] in their ears while I mounted them. And that part was worth a few pesetas extra of tip that the old women felt obliged to pay.... After that I could never sing *Anclao en París* again. I couldn't even hear the whole thing. When it is played on the radio, I change it right away. I hear it and suddenly I see the painted faces, the wrinkles, the ridiculous poses, the heavy perfumes of those old women, the handful of wrinkled pesetas with which I could keep surviving .... And coming home at dawn, I would go from one pay phone to another to see if they were broken, or downright break them to get some coins out.... Yes, I did everything. I had to do everything. Except my thing... be myself.

DANIEL: But in the end you did well. You in your letters....

EDUARDO: Yes, in the end. After twenty... or a hundred countrymen–the comrades, who tell you that politics is the first thing, that you have to be a Politician with a capital letter, that you have to give a hand to the exiled militant–shut the doors in my face or sent me to see another one who they knew was not going to help me either, I finally found number one hundred and one, the first person who risked giving me a job without having the papers and lent me money to pay him back whenever I could; the one who at night, speaking softly, told me about *el paisito,*[43] about his family members who stayed behind in the Capurro neighborhood. We would drink *mate*, and his eyes would shine talking about the trees on 19 de Abril Street, the train tracks, the park where he sat down to look at the city .... Do you remember that the day after I arrived I went out alone? Well, I took bus #17 and went to look for Martín's place.... And there it was, just as he remembered it: the trees, the short stone wall.... And also, like him, I sat there and looked at my–"his"–Montevideo. And you know what? He was right. Looking from that short stone wall, Montevideo even looks pretty.... He was the first guy who helped me. Without asking me

---

[42]   TN: *Anclao en París* (literally: "Anchored in Paris") is a tango with lyrics by Enrique Cadícamo and music by Guillermo Barbieri. It was first recorded by the famous tango singer Carlos Gardel in Paris in 1931. In the song, the protagonist reminisces about the city of Buenos Aires (Capital of Argentina) from which he was been away for ten years.

[43]   TN: *El paisito* (literally: "small country") is the diminutive of *país*, which means country in Spanish. *El paisito* is an affectionate way used by Uruguayans to refer to their motherland Uruguay.

for anything in return. Then everything was easier. It was a matter of luck, of will, of not giving up, and thinking that if I failed I had the option to die.... Every time I saw the Manzanares[44] so dirty I said, "No, before throwing myself in there, I have to try again...." The Manzanares, you know, is a narrow river, in the middle of Madrid, full of foam and a sad brown color, polluted as you cannot even imagine.... To tell you that the Pantanoso[45] is cleaner and nicer....ANTONIO: Now you are already exaggerating....

EDUARDO: No, that's the way it is. I swear....

(The voices get softer, the light too; the only sounds that can be heard are the radio, the station changes, and someone speaking. Among others, the word "elections." Theatrical lights out. The light returns, accompanying only AMALIA, who enters with a lantern. EDUARDO, alone, sees her go by and applauds frantically.)

AMALIA: What's wrong with you? Is it Saint Vitus' dance?

EDUARDO: It's just incredible.

AMALIA: *(Looks everywhere.)* What is incredible?

EDUARDO: Even if it seems corny, I'll say it. It is wonderful.

AMALIA: But can you tell me what is incredible and wonderful?

EDUARDO: This, the blackout. I knew that my dear old UTE[46] could not fail me. It would not let me leave without giving me a real good blackout. *(DANIEL enters with a candle.)*

AMALIA: Leave it there.

EDUARDO: Lantern, candlelight. I cannot ask for more. Thank you, UTE, for letting me see the familiar and missed darkness.

---

44   TN: The Manzanares is a river that runs through the heart of Madrid. It flows south from the Sierra de Guadarrama before joining the westerly flowing Tagus River. After a 1,000-km journey, the water flows out into the Atlantic Ocean on the Portuguese coastline.

45   TN: The Pantanoso or Arroyo Pantanoso (literally "swampy creek") is a Uruguayan stream, crossing the Montevideo Department. It flows into the Bay of Montevideo and then into the Río de la Plata. It is one of the most contaminated water streams in the country.

46   TN: UTE is an acronym for *Administración Nacional de Usinas y Trasmisiones Eléctricas* (English: National Administration of Power Plants and Electrical Transmissions). UTE is Uruguay's government-owned power company which was established in 1912, following approval of a law establishing it as a monopoly.

AMALIA: Who knows how long the blackout will last and this one starts to celebrate like a little boy. Are you going to tell me that there are no blackouts over there?

EDUARDO: Yes, there are. But the ones here are unique. Just a little rain or a hole in the corner and that's it. Thank you, again, UTE, for this tribute. Now I can leave in peace.

AMALIA: Shut up. You're going to wake up your sister-in-law. Tomorrow she has to get up early.... You talk about leaving and it seems to make you happy....

EDUARDO: No. The blackout made me happy.

AMALIA: The fridge. I have to unplug it, otherwise....

DANIEL: I'll do it.

AMALIA: No, that's ok. I also have to find a rag. So it doesn't stain the floor. *(Exits.)*

EDUARDO: You don't have any idea how many times I talked about the blackouts. And about the names of the streets. They did not want to believe that there is no way to make Uruguayans use the new names. Street names change but people still cling to the old names. Who says "Lorenzo Latorre Street" rather than "Convención Street"? And José Batlle y Ordóñez? They all look at you weird as if you were flirting.... *(AMALIA enters.)*

AMALIA: Here, Daniel. Put those papers there too. *(He does.)* Are you going to stay or are you going to bed?

EDUARDO: I'll stay. Will you join me, Daniel?

AMALIA: *(To DANIEL.)* Look, then there is no way to wake you up in the morning, huh?

DANIEL: I'll stay for just a while.

EDUARDO: Oh, old woman. What do you call Sierra Street?

AMALIA: And what do you want me to call it? Sierra.

DANIEL: Fernández Crespo, mother. How many years ago!

AMALIA: Every time I go to the pension and retirement funds office, I tell the bus conductor to let me know on the corner of Sierra and Uruguay and he always lets me know. So, if he lets me know, it must be called Sierra. Or both ways…. What? Are you kidding me? Is it one of your jokes? *(The two, who were holding the laughter, now laugh out loud.)* Very funny. Before, when you lived here, you never laughed like this…. Well, the truth is that we did not see your face much. But when we saw you, you always looked serious.

EDUARDO: I changed, old woman, I changed.

AMALIA: I liked you better before.

EDUARDO: Serious, sad, bitter?

AMALIA: But you were here. Without those ideas of leaving all the time. *(To DANIEL.)* Do not stay long. See you tomorrow.

EDUARDO: You don't kiss me?

AMALIA: Since when?

EDUARDO: "Until tomorrow" is not enough for me today…. Are you embarrassed? Then, I will kiss you. *(He does.)* See you tomorrow, rest well. I love you. *(AMALIA pushes him away and exits. EDUARDO looks at her leaving.)* Why is it so hard for her?

DANIEL: She was brought up like that. Not showing what she feels. Keeping everything in. Keeping the good and the bad in and always keeping going forward.

EDUARDO: *(Staring at him.)* It's in the blood, right?

DANIEL: *(Not taking the hint.)* You had one thing left to name. *(EDUARDO looks at him without understanding.)* El Galpón Theater. Who calls it "Sala 18 de Mayo"?

EDUARDO: No one, right? One day I should write about how the memory of Uruguayans never fails. Neither with the passing of time, nor with dams, monuments, currency exchange tables, useless city mayors…. I should write about all that. *(Noise inside.)*

ANTONIO: *(Cursing can be heard from inside.)* … Holy shit. I ran into, I don't know what piece of furniture…. Because of this fucking blackout. And then the electricity bill ends up being the same or higher. *(Leaves a medicine bottle on the table.)*

EDUARDO: Do you take these?

ANTONIO: No, I took them from Marisa. I was going to throw them in the toilet, but with this blackout…. *(Goes to the garbage can.)* It's almost empty… she lives doped up with this. I hid it yesterday, but she must have more somewhere…. *(Throws it away.)* It's like sleeping with a dead woman. She even gets cold. And her breathing… the noises she makes. It seems as if she were going to choke at any moment.

EDUARDO: Does she always take these?

ANTONIO: Not that I know of. She's been like this for a few days.

EDUARDO: Do you know that they can cause addiction? Once, in Madrid, on a sunny day, I saw a demonstration of drug addicts. They celebrated Saint Canute day. It was incredible. Everyone cheerful with banners, carrying joints, syringes…. There were, I don't know, hundreds of people. They paraded and nobody said anything. What freedom, right?

ANTONIO: Debauchery.

EDUARDO: Stop. You speak like a hundred-year-old.

ANTONIO: What? Are you going to deny everything you told us? About drugs, porno shops, porn movies, Lola Flores's[47] boobs…?

EDUARDO: Lola Flores's boobs… which is like saying that Franco showed his tits. It was unbelievable. Because that is more or less the old woman's age, to say the least. But there she was, Lola of Spain with her two big tits, well-tanned in Marbella. It came out in all the

---

[47] TN: Lola Flores (1923-1995) was a well-known Spanish singer, dancer, and actress. She was an icon of traditional Andalusian folklore, recognized throughout Spain and internationally.

257

magazines and nobody was scandalized. There are many things like that… or worse. But it is logical within the context. Keep in mind that this is a Spain that came out of forty years of dictatorship, and suddenly was blown away and overwhelmed by democracy. It's a society that, when it finally could breathe, wanted to take all the air in at once.

ANTONIO: And is that why you are leaving?

EDUARDO: One thing doesn't have anything to do with the other one? I'm leaving because I have my things there. The businesses I left, the people who depend on me….

ANTONIO: Look at you. And you do not have anything here? No one who depends on you?

EDUARDO: Yes, of course, here I have all of you….

ANTONIO: Thank goodness. But, of course, you lean towards the stuff from there….

EDUARDO: I don't know where you want to go with all that….

ANTONIO: A beautiful question for you: where do you want to go?

EDUARDO: I cannot throw away what took me ten years to achieve. In fact, I should have already returned. Three weeks ago I should have been in Madrid….

ANTONIO: But how good you are! You break anyone's soul. You're giving us three extra weeks. Did you hear, Daniel? Your brother gave us the gift of three more weeks. What an honor! In Spain they must be crying. Eduardo, the man of the pampas, has not returned.

EDUARDO: But we have already spoken to the point of exhaustion, Antonio. My place is not here anymore.

ANTONIO: You get tired of talking about all this. So you have made up your mind. You are not going to stay, are you? It's a final decision.

EDUARDO: Nothing is final.

ANTONIO: Don't start with your made-up writer phrases. Your place is here. That is why you are the older brother. Here is where you have to be. With us. Helping us.

EDUARDO: You state it as an obligation. I helped all of you with….

ANTONIO: Yes, don't continue. You helped us by sending money. And is it there where your help ends? Do you think that's the end of your obligation? Mr. Eduardo sends us pesetas or dollars every so often and to him that seems to be enough… to send money…. And you think that money can repay the way all your shit fucked us up?

EDUARDO: Antonio….

ANTONIO: Antonio what? Yes, how you fucked us up. You fucked me up. You are the older brother. You should have been here, facing everything. You and not me. That was not my place, it was not my responsibility….

DANIEL: Calm down, Antonio. You don't know what you are saying….

ANTONIO: Stay out of this. I know what I'm saying. You both know what I'm saying. I'm not lying. You fucked up my life, Eduardo. You screwed me up real bad. I was here. And you were living the great life far away, very far away. Yes, yes, do not say anything, you had a horrible time, it was awful, you had to do all kinds of stuff. Your same old version. Poor Eduardo. But nobody said "poor Antonio." What was your situation compared to mine? You left, you disappeared, but I had to stay here. And I stayed paying instead of you, for your actions, your faults…. You don't know about my *Fe Democrática*,[48] do you?

EDUARDO: *(To Daniel.)* But what is he saying?

ANTONIO: Of course, no one wrote to tell you. Why make poor Eduardo feel even more worried, he has enough to deal with already? Yes, you did. Drugs, partying, Lola Flores's boobs…. And as for me, because

---

[48] TN: *Fe Democrática* (literary: "Democratic Faith" or "Democratic Commitment") was a document instituted in Uruguay by the military dictatorship to categorize people according to their ideology and alliance to the regime. There were three categories: A, B, C. People with category C were considered a danger to the regime and were not allowed to work in any government or public institution.

of you, they fired me from the job where I had been working like a dog for years without missing a single day…. Because the civil categories A, B and C came out…. You're not going to tell me that you did not know that. (*The other one tries to respond.*) Let me continue. Listen to me now. I've been listening to you for days. All the jobs began to ask for the *Fe Democrática*. It was a "dignified" way to fire people. And I, like everyone else, had to go to the police station to ask for it. And because of you, because of being your brother, because you had been in compromising situations, they fucked up my life forever. Forever, yes. I got tired of going from one place to another, of speaking. First demanding, then begging…. To everyone I said, "Look, it's not me, it's my brother's mess …." They showed me a thick folder like this, with your name in black letters. There were photos and data of the whole family, your signature and I don't know what papers… and me saying, begging, every time with less strength and more fear, "That's not me, those are about my brother. He is not here any longer, he is not going to return, consider that with this I will lose my job and I don't know how to do anything else, it's the only thing I learned to do in my life. Do you want me to sign something? That my brother is a delinquent, a rotten person? I will sign it, but do not make me lose my job…." And nothing. Nothing. You were the one who had done everything. They did not argue that. But, as your brother, I was also considered dangerous, and even more so. Because I was here, I had not left. The dangerous one, the delinquent one, was me, because you were in Barcelona or Marbella or fucking partying…. "And his wife had been with him gluing revolutionary posters and participating in all types of raids…." "My wife changed, she was so young at the time, and she did not know what she was doing…." And they told me that young people were the worst, and asked me if I knew that the majority of those who left were no older than twenty-five years old…. That my wife had been lucky… until that moment. I went to lawyers, to notaries, and they wrote a very nice letter for me in which I admitted that I had been wrong and in which I swore to God, and I swore on my mother's life, and on anything they wanted me to, that I had never thought that way, that my ideals were democratic, and asked them not to be mean and to please reconsider the *Fe Democrática* marked with a C and to let me work in peace.... I swear that when I signed it, I felt like throwing up. But I still took it to San José Street and Yí and in return they gave me a small card with my name and my file number. So, I also became a number and a file. They told me to come back the following week. And as soon as I stepped on the sidewalk, I knew I would not return. And it was not because of trampled pride, arrogance, or for any of all the worthy reasons that you would invent for some of your stories. I did not come back out of fear. As simple as that. I was scared to death. Scared shitless. So much that I never went by that street block again. And if I have to go that way, I take a detour. Do you know what it is to tremble when you see a soldier? Well, I would shake. Since that day I don't even go to the sidewalk without my identification card and if I am out and realize that I do not have it, I go back to look for it even if I'm already twenty blocks away.... Fear, tremors, documents, those seemingly small things are what my life has been about during these ten years. And you did not live through that.

EDUARDO: But you know well that I....

ANTONIO: What I know well is that I owe all this to you. And how can you erase fear, disgust for oneself? With the pesetas you sent us? With your letters, so beautiful, where you wrote that you missed us a lot.... while you were lying in the sun in Somosaguas?[49] No. I don't want to believe you. I don't want to, because it was not my duty to pay for your faults, for your false heroism. Who can give me back the Antonio that I once was? Can you make me go back to being who I was before?

EDUARDO: I suffered a lot too, Antonio. Even if you don't want to believe me. I also had fears. But you had our family and I was alone. You were able to see the old man die. I found out ten or twenty days later. You could close his eyes, throw a handful of dirt on his coffin. I had to admit to myself that he was not there anymore, when I had last seen him healthy, pruning grandpa's vines.... Who could I cry with?

---

[49]   TN: Somosaguas is an upscale residential area in northeast Madrid. It is considered the part of Madrid where Spanish royalty lives.

ANTONIO: How cute. And what did you do with all that pain? Write a story? A chapter of your great novel? No, you just sent more money. You increased the fee to better pay for your pain. It's true, you were not there and I was. I took care of him, washed him and smelled that sweet scent that was impregnating everything…. And the old man would hold my hand or try to caress me and would say, "Eduardo, my son Eduardo…." He did not see me, the one who looked after him day after day. Even that you stole away from me: the death of the old man…. And, now that you're leaving, you want to keep stealing from me, take more things. Do not move. I want to look at you. *(He grabs him.)* Tell me if it is not true.

EDUARDO: What do you want me to say?

ANTONIO: You know.

EDUARDO: No.

ANTONIO: Look at me straight. I don't have any shame left. I have no right to feel embarrassment. *(He shakes him and pulls EDUARDO towards him.)* Look at me, son of a bitch, I'm telling you. Like this.

EDUARDO: And… I'm looking at you.

DANIEL: Antonio, stop it.

ANTONIO: Stay out of it. This is not about you.

DANIEL: Don't keep doing this.

ANTONIO: Let go of me. You're always poking your nose everywhere.

DANIEL: Stop it, I tell you. You are going to make it worse for everyone….

ANTONIO: Now you are giving me advice? What do you know, you fucking asshole? Or you also want to tell me what to do? Since Antonio never says anything, never sees anything…. He endures everything. All of it. Even if they use his woman.

DANIEL: Shut up, Antonio….

ANTONIO: And why should I shut up? Am I offending anyone?

DANIEL: Knock it off. Say no more....

ANTONIO: Oh... because you knew it too. Everyone in this house knows it.... How hard you all must have laughed at me....

DANIEL: Nobody was laughing at you....

ANTONIO: But did you know about Marisa?

DANIEL: What difference does it make if I knew or not?

ANTONIO: A lot. You knew it and you stayed silent. You're just like this one. Of course, he is your admired brother, the one who tells you stories about greatness. Maybe he even paid you to cover for him....

EDUARDO: You like to drag everyone through the same mud, right?

ANTONIO: And who started it? You. You came back just for that, didn't you? To take her with you. It was not enough for you to sleep with her....

EDUARDO: No, it's not enough. Because a word of mine, a gesture of mine is worth to her more than the years that she spent with you. Do you want proof? *(Shouts.)* Marisa....

(DANIEL jumps and steps in between the two when ANTONIO attacks EDUARDO.)

DANIEL: But what do you want to do? Are you crazy?

EDUARDO: Stay out of this.... Let go.

DANIEL: No, not until you both stop it.

EDUARDO: Leave or I will make you leave....

DANIEL: Do it.

EDUARDO: You got an assistant.... But no one will silence me. Marisa....

DANIEL: But what did you come here to do? *(Hits him or tries to. EDUARDO, with one blow, pushes him forcefully.)*

EDUARDO: *(Challenging.)* Marisa.... Marisaaaaa.... *(ANTONIO pounces and both end up locked in a violent struggle. AMALIA enters.)*

263

AMALIA: What is all this shouting about? *(After a moment of stupor, tries to uselessly separate them.)* Stop, stop.... They're drunk.... They're crazy.... Help me. Do not just stand there.... *(Daniel walks towards them again.)* Stop, for God's sake. *(DANIEL manages to separate them, they are panting.)* What did you do to him, Antonio? Because it was you, right? I've seen you scowling at him for days. Why did you hit him? He is your brother....

ANTONIO: Yes, I hit him. I started it. Yes, comfort him, hold him. It was me, as always. Fix his clothes, wipe his face like when we were kids and he was always "right." Do it again, old woman.... *(Exits to the backyard.)*

AMALIA: Antonio.... *(EDUARDO starts to exit in the opposite direction.)* Where are you going? Eduardo?

EDUARDO: To my room....

AMALIA: Let me help you....

EDUARDO: No, I don't need anything .... *(Exits.)*

AMALIA: What happened to them, Daniel? What happened to my boys?

DANIEL: *(Strong, with repressed fury.)* They're not your boys anymore, Mom. They no longer are.

(Exits. AMALIA is left alone. She lets herself fall on a chair, defeated. Lights out. During lights out, the Los mareados *tango can be heard again. Lights come back when DANIEL opens the fridge to get some water. When he closes it, EDUARDO enters with a suitcase and a raincoat.)*

DANIEL: Are you ready?

EDUARDO: Yes.

DANIEL: But you still have like four hours.

EDUARDO: Yes, more or less.... But I'm leaving now.

DANIEL: And the others?

EDUARDO: I never liked goodbyes. If I leave now, it will be easier for everyone....

DANIEL: I'll go with you to the airport.

EDUARDO: No, you're staying here. You're not going to ruin the perfect plan, are you? Yesterday I arranged for a taxi to come pick me up. I'll take it and then I'll stay there these hours that I have left.

DANIEL: But so many hours....

EDUARDO: Not so many. It's going to be good for me. I want to be alone. Hey, give me a cigarette.

DANIEL: *(He gives it to him.)* But what about the old woman? She's going to be so upset....

EDUARDO: Daniel, since I marked the return ticket I'm not here anymore. Packing already makes you feel like you're not....

DANIEL: She is going to feel offended....

EDUARDO: She will get over it. Besides, I don't like to see her cry. Let me remember her grumbling, preparing food, going fast from one side of the house to the other.... Instead, I want to talk to you. As long as this last cigarette lasts.

DANIEL: Short conversation then.

EDUARDO: Enough. *(Pause. In an awkward gesture, he messes DANIEL's hair with his hand.)* Do not change, Daniel. Continue being the way you are. Do not think of us as examples. It's not helpful.

DANIEL: But how can you say such a thing....

EDUARDO: Let me talk. You just listen. There are things you can't doubt. You shouldn't doubt. You can't do like Antonio and I did, each one pulling in opposite directions, putting personal problems and frustrations ahead of everything. It doesn't work. You have to get those who are like you to unite. But real unity. The *paisito* is going to sprint ahead with everyone on board or it will not go anywhere at all. You can never forget, whatever they say, that a war happened

265

here. No war planes were flying over the city, no houses were destroyed, but there was a war. Do not fall back on the complicity of silence and fear that obliterated both your brother and I. You have to force yourself to argue, express your opinions every day–but opinions that are constructive–and then return to being like before. Or better than before. Are you going to heed this failure at all? Are you going to remember what I told you today, smoking my last Uruguayan cigarette? Look, I'll remind you when I come back in ten years…. Bertolt Brecht once wrote, "A people who needs heroes is not a fair people. A people needs men, people who live, not who die …." And you, Daniel, you have to live and fight. For you, for me, and for all those who are like me. You have to do what we, your brothers, could not do… what they didn't let us do…. *(Taxi horn.)* Bye kid…. See you ten years from now….

DANIEL: Bye, Eduardo…. See you in ten years…. *(They hug.)*

EDUARDO: You are not going to cry now, are you? You're not going to make a fool of yourself like the old lady, right? Here, give it to her. *(He gives him an envelope.)* It's money. If I gave it to her, she would not accept it and I know she needs it…. Oh, and in my room I left the other suitcase with clothes and other things. It's for all of you. There is the red sweatshirt that you liked so much…. *(Horn.)* The taxi…. *(Gets the suitcases and the raincoat. DANIEL tries to follow him to the taxi.)* No, no. Stay there…. Bye.

(Exits. Lights dim slowly. Lights out and the newscast on with information that says it's Election Day. Lights, the newscast continues, more noises in the street, chants, horns, etc. ANTONIO finishing his coffee. Fidgets with his voter ID card, he lights a cigarette, he gets up, he leaves the cup, he is going to leave towards the street, but he changes his mind and goes to the backyard.)

MARISA: Did you see Antonio?

DANIEL: No.

MARISA: He is going around in circles. He walks in and walks out.

DANIEL: He must have left already. They changed his voting location, right?

MARISA: Yes, he has to vote at the Malvín Experimental School. Completely different from the one he used to have. Your mother hasn't come back yet, right?

DANIEL: No. She left early. Even there, she has to be the first one in line....

MARISA: Is she always thinking about voting the same thing?

DANIEL: Always. Look, I talked to her over and over. But nothing. Even Eduardo, before leaving, tried to convince her. If he couldn't, he who has her wrapped around his finger....

MARISA: Who knows what he must be doing right now .... At what time will the results be known...?

DANIEL: Until the last moment, I thought that he was going to stay to vote....

MARISA: It must be nice to change countries like that, almost like one changes dresses. You sit eight hours on a plane, and when you get off you are somewhere else, in another time zone, with other people... and you mold yourself to those people, to those schedules, to that other place....

DANIEL: But you did not leave....

MARISA: I couldn't....

DANIEL: Or you did not want to?

MARISA: I couldn't. *(Changing the topic.)* If Eduardo had voted, we would have one more vote. Do you think we can win?

DANIEL: Of course. It can't be any other way.

MARISA: Now I am beginning to have doubts. I don't know.... There must be many people who think like your mother. And add those who change their minds at the last moment. Those who, whatever happens in the country, continue to vote the traditional parties by habit, fear, or whatever....

DANIEL: You're thinking about Antonio, aren't you?

MARISA: I see him disheartened, disinterested....

DANIEL: It must be because of everything that went on the last few days. But he isn't going to change his vote because of that.

MARISA: No, not change. But I don't know... I don't know what he's going to do. If he would just talk to me.

DANIEL: Should we go? I'm looking forward to voting. They stamp your voter ID, right?

MARISA: Yes.

DANIEL: First you accompany me and then I'll go with you.

MARISA: And then I'll invite you to have at least a coffee. We have to celebrate that we can vote again and your debut. Do you have the key?

DANIEL: Yes. They say that this is the best time to vote, that there are fewer people in line.... *(They start walking out.)*

MARISA: After coffee we can go around Montevideo and stop to talk to everyone, to follow the people....*(The voices get lost. ANTONIO enters. He takes off his coat, puts it on his chair, pulls out his voter ID, and turns it over. AMALIA enters.)*

ANTONIO: Finally, you are back. What happened?

AMALIA: Nothing....

ANTONIO: Did you go to Doña Angelina's?

AMALIA: No.... *(She sits, leaving her purse on the table.)*

ANTONIO: Are you going to tell me that you were at church this whole time?

AMALIA: *(Smiles sadly.)* It's the first thing they think about me.... You, your brothers, everyone. The old woman is not at home, the old woman is at church.... No, I did not go to church. I walked up to the door and could not go in.... I don't know.... I couldn't....

ANTONIO: Do you want me to make you some tea?

AMALIA: No. I just want you to stay where you are. I'm not sick, Antonio. I'm tired. I walked and walked.... I do not know where I walked. I could not stop thinking about everything, everyone... especially about you.

ANTONIO: Why about me?

AMALIA: Because of everything, you are the one who came to mind. Eduardo has his life made in Spain. He doesn't need us. Or he needs us in his own way. Daniel is young and has his whole life ahead of him. For him we are almost a drag. He has all the strength and hope of Francisco. You, on the other hand, you are like me. We put up with stuff, we endure, but there comes a time when it all turns out to be too much. We are not made to be alone. We need to have someone strong next to us. You have Marisa.... *(She anticipates his reply.)* Even if it's hard for me to admit it, she is a woman who can help you.... Just a while ago people in the street were turning around to look at me.... Even some kids were laughing, pointing at the old woman who was crying....

ANTONIO: You, crying in the street?

AMALIA: Yes, me. I cried for you, for me, for Francisco.... I failed Francisco.... All those ideas of his, those which drove me.... *(Soft smile.)* He used to tell everyone that I was ahead of my time.... Those ideas that I no longer have. They got worn out.... They are gone. They eroded them.... Everyone.... People. Those who I went to ask on behalf of your brother. The others who only promised me help if they could get in return a piece of the pie, money, a statement, or to betray some poor guy.... They were all thinking about getting something out of it for them. Everybody. Lawyers, politicians, policemen, people in the neighborhood.... I'm... I don't know... tired, disheartened... without faith. *(Looks in her purse. Gets her voter ID.)* Look. I voted. Look at the stamp. Take a good look. You know what? That's it. I did not vote for change, as you all wanted me to, nor did I vote to continue this way.... No, I voted for nothing else but to get the stamp, thinking that if I did not vote, I would not be able to collect your father's pension payment.... So, you see. In that I failed Francisco. By submitting the empty envelope just to be able to get the money, I know I failed him.... And I left the voting booth with all that inside of me. I started walking without even thinking. I wanted to get somewhere, somewhere.... *(ANTONIO caresses her.)* But now I'm okay. Don't worry. *(Stands up with difficulty.)* And you? Did you already vote?

ANTONIO: No. I was going to go when you came....

AMALIA: But there is not too much time left. It is until....

ANTONIO: I'm going now. I will get there in time. You should rest for a while.

AMALIA: Yes....

ANTONIO: Go relax.

(She leaves very slowly. He watches her go, he lights a cigarette, he is going to put the lighter away, and then stops. Los mareados can be heard in the background. He fidgets with his voter ID in his hands. Looks around. He starts to burn the voter ID. At the same time, the newscast is giving the results of the elections, the light dims and the tango gets louder. In the end, the light is only focused on the voter ID which is burning. The election results and the music blaring.)

THE END

Just Yesterday:
Life Histories Impacted by Dictatorship and Exile

Lourdes Martínez Puig

Just Yesterday–initially entitled "Penas de apenas ayer"[1]–received mention in a contest organized by the publishing house Monte Sexto and the café Sorocabana.[2] For this play, Dino Armas was selected Best Author of the Year by the theater section of the Montevideo newspaper *El País* in 1995 and was furthermore named Best Author of the '95 Season by *Sábado Show* magazine. The play premiered in 1995 in Montevideo at El Tinglado Theater, under the direction of Claudia Pérez.

We believe that in *Just Yesterday* the issues of dictatorship and exile intertwine in a basic way with the breaking down of a family that suffers the pain, the loneliness, and the resentments brought about during the interruption of the democratic order in the country. In this sense, we agree with Myriam Caprile's statement: "The axle around which revolves this family, composed of a mother, three sons, and a daughter-in-law is the difference in ideologies, ten years lived in Uruguay and ten lived abroad by one of its members. Two worlds that get juxtaposed and merged in a strange crucible of unconfessed feelings (love and hate)."

With this play, Dino Armas makes us reflect on the consequences of the dictatorship, the exile, and the disintegration of a family that suffers heartbreak and powerlessness in the face of the separation caused by ideological persecution and marginalization.

The dramatic characters in the play–Eduardo, Marisa, Antonio, Amalia, and Daniel–present their life stories impacted by dictatorship and exile. The play emphasizes the human dimension of these characters. This emphasis allows the reader and the spectator to understand the emotions and life experiences of those who sought refuge abroad and also of those who stayed in the country.

It is important to point out that when we refer to dramatic characters, we are following José Luis Barrientos's use, which distinguishes between the stage

---

[1] Translator's Note: "Sorrows from Just Yesterday."
[2] Note from the original Spanish editors: In 1987.

person (the actual actor), the fictitious character (the role), and the dramatic character. He defines the latter as "the embodiment of the fictitious character in the stage person or an actor performing a role" (154-155).

Each one of the characters made different decisions, both during the dictatorial period and in the face of the call to democratic elections in Uruguay (after ten long years). Their life histories reveal the deep wounds–which still remain open–and the silenced resentments left behind by their experience of the dictatorship. In this regard, Jorge Arias, referring to the staging of the play, said, "Over the course of *Just Yesterday*, almost the entire military dictatorship has passed: the audience claps strongly [at the end]. Perhaps because everything that is barely touched by the story is still sensitive and bleeds; perhaps we have so little that a mere allusion is enough to satisfy us" (n.p.).

The play constitutes a picture of Uruguayan society in the years between 1973 and 1984, the year of the call to elections that marks the return to democracy in Uruguay. The playwright presents, without judgment, a multiplicity of points of view and decisions embodied in the characters, maybe because each one of them represents a different sector of Uruguayan society, illustrating how each social group faced the dictatorship and how they reacted to the return to democracy. This is what the play is about: life histories that could have been the histories of any of the readers and spectators who endured the Uruguayan dictatorship.

Taking this into account, Dino Armas presents different visions of the same historical event; in this essay, we focus on the perspectives of those who remained in the country and those who went into exile.

Eduardo's character embodies the point of view of those Uruguayans who, because of persecution due to their political ideas, had to go into exile and seek refuge abroad in order to survive. On the other hand, the characters of Antonio, Marisa, Amalia, and Daniel stayed in Uruguay and suffered the consequences of doing so, including the rejection and social marginalization endured by the relatives of those persecuted for thinking differently.

These two different point of views are complementary, because together they allow us to better understand a historical event of the magnitude of a military dictatorship, which, among other consequences, provoked the family and social upheaval caused by the forced migration of many Uruguayans who had to choose exile in order to survive.

Eduardo's letter, which the playwright presents at the beginning of the play, has a temporal and spatial frame that turns out to be very significant: "Madrid. December 31, 1973. January 1, 1974" (201). Thus, the writer introduces the issue of migration as a consequence of the dictatorship. From afar, Eduardo describes the place and circumstances in which he finds himself: in the middle of the racket made by people–because in Madrid they are seeing the New Year in, with twelve grapes cramping his hand, pushed by people, dodging the cider bottles being thrown off the balconies. In the middle of that hubbub, the character feels the need to express the great loneliness he feels due to being far away from his family. In this view from exile, Eduardo's situation contrasts with the rejoicing around him.

The distress, the cold, and the loneliness that overwhelm him lead him to reminisce and yearn for his family, his house, and the familiar smells. His memories of his relatives and their usual actions reflect the homesickness that envelops him. A second contrast is marked thus between the family gathered in Uruguay and Eduardo's loneliness in Madrid, wishing that his only desire–returning–would come true, even though this is impossible for a political exile in 1973-1974.

This very heartfelt letter moves the reader and spectator. It communicates the loneliness of someone forced to remain far from his country and his family only because he thinks differently from a political point of view and because this different way of thinking is not accepted by a dictatorial government.

Eduardo's letter is the starting point which allows the playwright to chronologically situate the reader and spectator before presenting the life histories of Eduardo, Antonio, Amalia, Marisa, and Daniel, impacted by dictatorship and migration in their different temporal stages:

a) The past lived by the characters, the wounds left by the dictatorship, and the consequences of exile.

b) The present, Eduardo's return, the reunion with the family; the outburst of reproach, love, and hate repressed during the many years of absence; the jealousy of two men who outline a love triangle with Marisa.

c) An uncertain future and a glimpse of hope in the return to democracy after the call to elections that ends the dictatorship.

273

The passing of time in the play is strategically indicated by the playwright through the dates of the letters: Eduardo's, written on December 31, 1973, and Antonio's, written on January 15, 1980. In addition, the radio program broadcasting news of the period also constitutes a guiding thread and a dramatic resource that allows the positioning of the characters' life histories in time: the beginning of the Uruguayan military dictatorship, the year 1980, and finally the call to elections that foretells a new democratic government in Uruguay.

It was previously pointed out that the dictatorship had significant consequences, some of which are presented by the author throughout the play. On one hand, we see the breakdown of the family bonds, the rupture of affective relationships, and the disintegration of the families that had to accept and suffer the exile of one of their members. This dismembering of families was caused because exile was the only possible alternative to save the lives of those persecuted for their political ideas.

Another consequence of dictatorship is expressed by Amalia when she recalls the past upon the return of her son Eduardo, who the family had not seen in years. In the dialogue with her son Daniel, Amalia explicitly mentions the social rejection and marginalization suffered by the family due to Eduardo's political ideas and exile. Feeling devastated and with the pressing need to talk, Amalia refers to the ideological persecution, the lack of freedom of expression, and the absence of tolerance suffered during the dictatorship. She also mentions the influence and power of the media, manipulated by the de facto government, and the rejection suffered by the entire family even from their own friends.

Amalia needs to remember and express what she felt and lived through when her son was persecuted in the times of the dictatorship; she says, "It was as if everyone in this house were a leper, when all your brother had done was think differently..." (223). The image used by Amalia clearly suggests the rejection, the discrimination, and the contempt suffered.

Dino Armas reaches a balance between the relaxed moments and those with greater dramatic tension. Two examples of relatively relaxed moments are when Antonio and Eduardo walk with their arms around each other towards the table after the older brother has sung the tango *Los mareados*, imitating Julio Sosa,[3] and when Antonio remembers with nostalgia a story their father used to tell them.

---

[3]   TN: Julio Sosa (1926-1964) was a Uruguayan tango singer, nicknamed "El Varón del Tango" ("The Man of Tango").

The atmosphere is relaxed because the brothers are celebrating being together one more day. The playwright thus succeeds in creating an atmosphere in which the characters are able to reveal what they feel and what they have missed during the many years of separation.

Eduardo's speech following the anecdote remembered by Antonio represents the point of view of those who left the country, that is, the view from exile. Eduardo complains about the loss of his identity and the changes suffered by having to live abroad. He feels he lost the opportunity of becoming a great writer and writing a great novel. He feels the dictatorship took away all the opportunities of achieving the goals he had set for himself on a personal, family, and professional level. These reproaches—addressed perhaps to life or dictatorship—have been kept locked away for a long time, hence the character's need to vent within a family setting.

Eduardo declares, "It was a very high price that I had to pay. I lost my identity. […] I am a foreigner here and I am a foreigner there. I have lost my history" (251). Eduardo's words show he does not feel at ease anywhere. The loss of his identity—from having been forced to go into exile—is what makes him feel a foreigner in his own country and also in Spain. Eduardo feels he has no roots and feels the pain of the uprooting. He perceives that—even though he returned and is with his family—he cannot be the same person since he has changed. The changes produced in him as a consequence of living in exile for ten years lead him to become aware that in the present he is "an old guy, too old already, who does not know where he's going or who he is" (252). This last phrase synthesizes his loss of identity; the character becomes aware of the life stage in which he now exists. The feeling of rootlessness that Eduardo experiences is, perhaps, what allows us to understand the character's decision to go back of his own accord to Madrid.

Eduardo also mentions his life experiences in Spain during the exile. He remembers the cold, the hunger, the loneliness he felt. He describes the survival strategies he had to put into play in order to be able to eat, and he is aware there were things he would never have done in Uruguay, but the situation of poverty and squalor he experienced as an exile forced him to carry them out. In short, Eduardo expresses what exile meant to him and his need to live in another country and abandon his family for political reasons.

There is a fundamental moment in *Just Yesterday*, which constitutes the axle around which the entire play revolves, because it allows us to fully comprehend the life histories embodied by the characters: the fight between the three brothers and, especially, the confrontation between the two older brothers, Antonio and Eduardo. Through this, the playwright lays out a contrast between two different perspectives of the Uruguayan dictatorship. The two points of view are distinct but complementary, allowing the reader or spectator to understand how the consequences of the dictatorship were experienced.

How does the playwright succeed in creating the moment of higher dramatic tension in the play? In the confrontation between the older brothers, Antonio's reproach, anxiety, fear, and rancor emerges. Now it is he who needs to vent, but in so doing, he lays bare the deep and still-open wounds that dictatorship and migration have left in the souls of the members of this family.

The trigger of the confrontation between the older brothers is Eduardo's decision to return to Spain in spite of the upcoming elections in Uruguay, which mean he no longer needs to live in exile. Nevertheless, Eduardo is determined to leave his family and his country once more, and he explains his reasons for going back. His decision and the arguments he puts forward provoke an angry reaction from Antonio, who finally decides to express everything he has kept inside for so many years. Thus the verbal confrontation between the brothers.

Through Antonio's speech, the playwright presents the point of view of those who remained in the country–of those who experienced the dictatorship firsthand. Antonio's perspective reflects the suffering that the members of this family had to endure because of their kinship with a political exile, especially due to discrimination on social and occupational levels.

Antonio's reproaches increase gradually. He starts from a vague recrimination, but then he moves to a more personal, more intimate reproach: "You fucked up my life, Eduardo. […] I had to stay here. And I stayed paying instead of you, for your actions, your faults.... You don't know about my *Fe Democrática*,[4] do you?" (259). Antonio's recriminations towards his brother are due to his belief that the situation lived by Eduardo in exile cannot be compared to what he had to live through during the dictatorship in Uruguay. At the beginning, Antonio generalizes his suffering, but then he pauses to explain a particular event–the loss of his job, which is directly related to his family ties with Eduardo. Antonio explains that during the dictatorship every worker was forced to request a *Fe Democrática* at the police station and they were put into lists with the categories

---

4   *Fe Democrática* (literary: "Democratic Faith or "Democratic Commitment") was a document instituted in Uruguay by the military dictatorship to categorize people according to their ideology and alliance to the regime.

A, B, and C. The loss of his job was linked to his placement as a worker in the list with category C because of his brother's and Marisa's activities. As Antonio expresses it, "But, as your brother, I was also considered dangerous" (260). The playwright succeeds in communicating Antonio's deep pain, anguish, and fear because of something related to his kinship with Eduardo.

His state of distress becomes even more pronounced when Antonio acknowledges that this job was the only thing he had learned to do in life. He suffers and feels powerless, because he had not done anything to justify the rejection of his Democratic Commitment, yet he was fired. His only "crime" was to be the brother of Eduardo, who had fled to Spain in order to survive. Nevertheless, Antonio was considered the "dangerous one, the delinquent one" (260).

The atmosphere intensifies. Antonio reproaches his brother for avoiding the situation over these ten years, while the rest of his family had to live in the country and bear the dictatorship's abuses. Because of it, Antonio has changed, as indicated by his rhetorical questions: "Who can give me back the Antonio that I once was? Can you make me go back to being who I was before?" (261). These questions do not call for an answer because deep down Antonio knows that there is no way to erase everything they endured. Still, he needs to make his brother understand that, even if the latter suffered in exile, they also suffered staying in the country.

Eduardo defends himself and replies to his brother's reproaches. He reasserts that he has suffered much and explains the loneliness he experienced. The military dictatorship also left deep wounds in him due to the impossibility of returning to the country. For example, he could neither spend time with his father during his last years nor be present at his deathbed. The intensity of Eduardo's pain can be understood since it is a pain experienced alone, at a distance, and an anguish that could not be shared with loved ones, who were perhaps able to find solace in the company of each other. Exile is difficult to comprehend for Antonio, who seems shut in his own pain, simply because he has not experienced it. How is it possible to understand the loneliness, the suffering, the nostalgia for shared places and moments, the intensity of these memories, and the fear of losing loved ones, if one has not lived through the experience of emigration?

In this dialogue between Antonio and Eduardo, each character attempts to explain to the other what he has lived and suffered in all those years they have been apart. In spite of Eduardo's explanations, the issue of their father's death unleashes a new reproach, since Antonio's permanent care of his father was not recognized by the latter. These wounds remain open within the family. Jealousy is added to the reproach between brothers and between men, as it is hinted that Marisa, Antonio's wife and Eduardo's former girlfriend, is cheating on Antonio.

The stage directions indicate that the tension has reached its limit: the reproach, the jealousy, and the distress, repressed for so many years, lead to a verbal confrontation that inexorably results in a physical confrontation. In that regard, Armas expressed in the interview "On *Just Yesterday*":

> [...] the fight between the three brothers and the reproaches repressed for years, the jealousies, the hates, the fears, the differences [that] blow up and managed to move me when I was reading it, as much as the actors were moved when they were performing it. I have patently clear in my memory that scene in the theater and the unconcealed crying of the two older brothers, an emotion that would reach the audience and pierce the representation barrier and settle in the auditorium as truth. (285)

In sum, a contrast is observed between the life histories of Eduardo and Antonio, traversed by the Uruguayan dictatorship. Eduardo's and Antonio's points of view, however, are two complementary perspectives of the same historical event: by those who endured the dictatorship, stayed in the country, and faced the consequences (Antonio, among others), and by the ones who decided to go into exile as a way to save their own lives (Eduardo).

Concerning the female characters, the conflictive relationship between Amalia and Marisa stands out, characterized—as far as it is reflected in the play—by lack of communication.

The image that Marisa presents of Eduardo, one that his own mother does not want to concede in her eagerness to make others responsible for her son's exile, turns out to be quite interesting. Marisa lists the actions that Eduardo—as well as other militants—carried out in the past so as to fight against repression. Her description of Eduardo—who, from her point of view, was neither a criminal nor a hero—allows her to reflect upon the events during the dictatorship and enumerate its consequences: deaths, torture, and years of imprisonment for those people who thought differently and fought against the dictatorship.

There is also a confrontation between Marisa and Amalia, which is anticipated by the stage direction: "*Lightning and thunder*" (236). The storm that breaks in the exterior world reflects the storm in the interior world of the characters, who succeed in overcoming their lack of communication for a moment and dare to express the "truths" and criticism that have been repressed for so long. The confrontations between Antonio and Eduardo on one hand, and Amalia and Marisa on the other, are testimony to the deep wounds, the latent rancor, and the disintegration of a family embroiled in conflicts caused in good part by dictatorship and exile.

Finally, it is indispensable to highlight Eduardo's words to his brother Daniel at their farewell, since they allow us to fully comprehend the true meaning of the dictatorship:

> You can never forget, whatever they say, that a war happened here. No war planes were flying over the city, no houses were destroyed, but there was a war. Do not fall back on the complicity of silence and fear that obliterated both your brother and I. You have to force yourself to argue, express your opinions every day–but opinions that are constructive– and then return to being like before. Or better than before. (265-266)

Significantly, in the play's dénouement the playwright presents the different decisions made by each of the characters in the face of the call to elections for the reinstatement of democracy in the country, decisions which reflect different ways of thinking.

In conclusion, it is possible to say that Dino Armas presents an unbiased picture of the society of the period. He observes and shows diverse points of view so the reader and the spectator achieve a global outlook that incorporates a simultaneity of standpoints regarding dictatorship, exile, and the emotions that the reinstatement of democracy arouses in different social sectors.[5]

---

[5] Essay translated by Álex Omar Bratkievich.

Works Consulted

Arias, Jorge. "'Apenas ayer", de Armas en El Tinglado." *La República* [Montevideo] April 2, 1995, Crítica y Teatro.

Caprile, Myriam. "'Apenas ayer' de Dino Armas en El Tinglado. Excelente texto y buenos actores en una obra realista y uruguaya." *La Mañana* [Montevideo] March 31, 1995, Cultura.

García Barrientos, José Luis. *Cómo se comenta una obra de teatro. Ensayo de método.* Madrid: Editorial Síntesis, 2003.

Martínez Puig, Lourdes and Dino Armas. "On *Just Yesterday*". *On the Scene with Migration and Dictatorship: An Interdisciplinary Approach to the Work of Uruguayan Playwright Dino Armas.* Dir. Gabriela Christie Toletti. Norfolk: New Dominion Press, 2018. 281-288

On *Just Yesterday*

*Interview with Dino Armas conducted
on March 03, 2014 through a questionnaire
previously prepared by Lourdes Martínez Puig*

LMP: Lourdes Martínez Puig

DA: Dino Armas

LMP: **How did the play *Just Yesterday come about*? Why did you write it?**

DA: The play arose from a contest call from Editorial Monte Sexto and the iconic Café Sorocabana. The call was attractive, since it was the first in democratic times, it promised the publication of the first prize, and there was a good panel of judges.

The play obtained a mention. I remember presenting it with the title "Penas de apenas ayer,"[1] which came [to me] walking on the beach in Atlántida. I had the play all finished and I was considering another title, taken from a poem by Neruda, "We, of that time"[2] (the poem goes on, "are no longer the same").[3] But I read that an Argentinian play had that title and, stepping barefoot on the sand, a thought came, "Sorrows from Just Yesterday," which the director of the play very sensibly cut to *Just Yesterday* at the time of the premiere for marketing reasons: removing the word "sorrows," which might put off a sector of the audience, and shortening the title so as to make it easy to remember. And, for me, it was better; that simple *Just Yesterday* better captures the entire play and talks about a recent past.

I also remember that I used "Gaudí" as my pseudonym.

LMP: **What life experiences during the dictatorship in our country left a mark on you? To what extent did those experiences influence the writing of this play?**

---

[1]   Translator's Note: "Sorrows from Just Yesterday."
[2]   TN: In Spanish, "Nosotros los de entonces."
[3]   TN: In Spanish, "no somos los mismos."

DA: Reading the play now in order to answer your questions and without having reread it until now, nineteen years after [the premiere], I was surprised by the strong criticism and pain in the play, of which I might not have been so aware at the time. There's a heavy burden from a moment of fear, tension, reproach, and division, both within society and within this family. All those emotions were felt by the Dino of that time and his partners, friends, and relatives. The image of my mother, her church-going and her promises can be found in the play–also my father with his socialist ideas and his atheism and idealism (which he passed on to me and my sister). There's the neighborhood–my neighborhood, el Cerro– with its militancy, its workers from the meat plants, its immigrants; a combative neighborhood, with its own ideas, separated just by a bridge (over the Pantanoso) that could be opened or closed when there were strikes. There's the Dino that was denied the Democratic Commitment and stigmatized with the letter C[4] (they caused that boy, who didn't know anything else besides being a teacher, to live in fear). Everything that Antonio narrates and his vicissitudes going to San José and Yí[5] (the file and pictures he's shown, the issue of the green-colored card with a file number) is what this author lived through... this author, who year after year would review the lists of primary school employees who were not allowed to work in public schools and who had to work in private schools with double shifts and, even sometimes, had to teach private lessons in order to survive. And the fear... that fear that gets in your bones and made me return home if I didn't have the ID card on me. The fear of talking to people, the fear of raids and of simply going by a police station.

My crime was to participate as actor in events in front of the newspaper *El Popular*, on the street, with Grupo 68, a theater group that didn't have a theater but was very active politically. Those performances were kept on record in photographs, as was the photo of the young Dino, in a white raincoat, next to Líber Arce's[6] coffin, on the front page of *La Mañana*. The performance of the group at Centro Cultural Uruguay-China[7] doing Bertolt Brecht's *Die Gewehre der Frau Carrar*[8] also had an effect, as well as being informed on by some theater "mate."

---

4   TN: Cfr. Chapter Six, "*Just Yesterday*: Life Histories Impacted by Dictatorship and Exile," 277.
5   TN: The Police Headquarters in Montevideo.
6   TN: Líber Arce (1940-1968) was the first student killed in a confrontation with the Uruguayan police forces (two more would die the following month). He became an emblem of the opposition against the government's repression.
7   TN: "Cultural Center Uruguay-China."
8   TN: Known in English as "Señora Carrar's Rifles."

How much is biographical in *Just Yesterday*? Almost everything, if not everything. From the narrated militancy and its consequences to minor data. I'll point out some:

- The letter with which the play opens. It's dated in 1973, but it's an experience I had in '82: our first trip to Europe with Hugo,[9] a 45-day tour—there aren't tours like that anymore; on that tour we met Graciela Balletti.[10] Everything told in the letter is the experience we had that New Year's Eve in Madrid.

- And, next to that memory, the other one, the backyard at my house with its vine arbor.

- Except for the piece about the father preparing the salad, everything else is true and just like that. The tablecloth and glasses that were used only at that time and then put away until the next year, what was eaten…. (Reading it, a wave of tenderness came over me.)

- The scene described at the mental hospital, retaken later in [the play] *Pagar el pato*,[11] but here it's told more truthfully: there's the grandmother, the mother, and the child.

- The references to the rural schools made by Amalia.

- The Kendall cigarettes (they don't exist anymore), which were what I used to smoke.

- The photos of the picnics and the grandparents stored in a box (later retaken in [the play] *Rifar el corazón*).[12]

- The meal ritual with its gnocchi ([also] see *Rifar el corazón*).

[Other references in Just Yesterday]:

- Gavioli's[13] face illuminated by the colored lanterns, lifted from the movie *Picnic*. Do you remember Novak (I saw her yesterday at the

---

[9] TN: Orlando Hugo Ponce, history teacher, friend of Dino Armas.

[10] TN: Argentinian actress and theater director who has staged and starred in several of Armas' plays.

[11] TN: *Pagar el pato* is a Spanish idiom used when someone suffers the consequences of another person's actions, close in meaning to "taking the rap."

[12] TN: "Raffling the Heart."

[13] TN: Romeo Gavioli (1913-1957) was a musician, conductor, and singer of tangos and candombes.

Oscars and they used *Vertigo*'s music for her entrance) and Holden's dance and their faces illuminated by the garlands of colored lights? And there's also the thing about the two faces [which also appears in] *Pagar el pato*[14] and *Lucas*.[15]

• The game of the three bears (like Hansel and Gretel in *Ave Mater*). Here it's great (the author is so humble!) how they go from a game and laughter to the veiled threat of "Who slept in my bed?" (250)

• Doesn't Eduardo resemble Silvana[16] in his story? He says of himself, "an old guy, too old already, who does not know where he's going or who he is." (252)

LMP: The structure of *Just Yesterday* doesn't seem as clear as the one laid out in other plays. If we use as a guide the stage directions in which the word "blackout" explicitly appears, it would seem the play is divided in six or seven scenes. What is your opinion regarding its structure?

DA: I wrote *Just Yesterday* without making previous outlines like I do now. It's a play that grows out of impulses (it gushes out, I'd say). The characters, with their stories, carry it forward and the author, next to them, is telling his own story. I vaguely remember that there were no corrections nor many rewritings. I must've written like this and that's how it ended up.

Reviewing it now at a distance, many things about the structure surprised me, [such as] the insertion of those news bulletins to locate the spectator. The dialogues between the characters—despite the political subject—are not propagandist (very easy mistake to make when one deals with a subject like this). There's politics and being political, but the human prevails: the passions, weaknesses, and nobilities of these characters who live the ups and downs of the times and of their lives. They're not spectators of the moment: they live the moment. They can't distance themselves because they are living it now. I was surprised by Eduardo's occupation: short-story writer, among other things. I used to boast of never having a writer

---

[14] Note by LMP: In *Pagar el pato*, Roma—the main female role—has one perfect side on her face, whereas the other is traversed by a great scar that deforms it. That is the reason for Omar—leader of a commercial network of beggars—choosing her, because she is an unusual person who will awaken compassion in the people who travel on Montevideo's buses. Thus she will be able to go begging and obtain the money which will undoubtedly enrich Omar.

[15] Note by LMP: In *Lucas o El contrato* [TN: "Lucas, or the Contract"], Lucas is also an unusual person, since he is sick; one side of his face is perfect and the other is deformed. Lucas is a 23-year-old man who remains hidden in the upstairs room. The audience never sees him.

[16] Character from *Rifar el corazón*.

as a character in one of my plays and there I had this short-story writer who wanted to be another Benedetti[17] or another Galeano.[18] Luckily, I didn't put him as a playwright. It annoys me enormously when playwrights place an author at the navel of the world. I'll give you a very clear example: I really hate Arthur Miller's *After the Fall*, where he tells his story with Monroe. But… you saw how, next to wanting to be a short-story writer, I include that he likes to be a tango singer, another Julio Sosa.[19] That makes the character more human and brings him closer to my gallery and doesn't place him on the Olympus.

Of the structure, I can tell you that I liked the alternation between quotidian situations and tense moments. There are three, at least, that were very well resolved by that author from [1987].

[One is] the scene of Marisa and Amalia preparing gnocchi, with a storm outside and inside of them. The formal treatment ("usted"), Amalia's criticism regarding a woman having to be younger than her husband…. The scene grows slowly and mutedly until almost getting physical.

Another scene that I liked is the one between Eduardo and Marisa, which ends when she answers his whistling but first hesitates and looks at Daniel. The prior dialogue between Marisa and Eduardo plus that scene ending in silence surprised me. And it still surprised me even more that the adultery was carried out. It was and is daring.

Finally, the fight among the three brothers and the reproaches repressed for years, the jealousies, the hates, the fears, the differences [that] blow up and managed to move me when I was reading it, as much as the actors were moved when they were performing it. I have patently clear in my memory that scene in the theater and the unconcealed crying of the two older brothers, an emotion that would reach the audience and pierce the representation barrier and settle in the auditorium as truth.

After reading it, I believe it's the more Sánchez-like[20] of my plays, maybe along with *Día libre*.[21] That realistic theater, with that family (maybe another

---

[17]   TN: Mario Benedetti (1920-2009) was a Uruguayan journalist, novelist, and poet.
[18]   TN: Eduardo Galeano (1940-2015) was a Uruguayan journalist and writer.
[19]   TN: Julio Sosa (1926-1964) was a Uruguayan tango singer, whose nickname was "El Varón del Tango" ("The Man of Tango").
[20]   TN: Florencio Sánchez (1875-1910) was a Uruguayan playwright.
[21]   TN: "Day Off."

En familia?),[22] which deals with the quotidian, the present, the evoked and lost past, and a future with more questions than certainties. And a similar ending, maybe in another key, but with an Antonio that could be another Quixote, as was Damián (*En familia*).

LMP: Do you think this play can be understood beyond the Uruguayan borders? And if so, why?

DA: I think that the play has a historical frame that must be respected each time it's performed in Uruguay, because the events happened at that time and like that. *Just Yesterday* is like a photograph of that moment. It is where theater and sociology combine. If a student from today or an ordinary person would read or watch *Just Yesterday*, s/he would know what society was like at that moment; s/he would know that there was a chain of grocery stores called Manzanares; s/he would find out about the tangos that were heard at that time and that there were people who dreamed of singing like Julio Sosa or writing like Benedetti or Galeano, that there was—there is—a place in Capurro from which Montevideo looks nicer, that there were blackouts and street markets, etc.

But it can also be performed in other countries. There have been dictatorships everywhere and in every place there were Eduardos, Antonios, Marisas, Daniels, and Amalias. The dictatorship is the historical frame, the fresco, the background picture where these five characters tell their sorrows and joys, their successes and their failures, their pettiness and greatness, their loves and dislikes. The life throbbing within them is what matters and what allows [the play] to be understood and felt by any spectator anywhere in the world.

LMP: This play was staged only once in Uruguay, in 1995, after democracy had been restored.[23] Do you have any memories regarding that staging (audience reactions, moments that were best liked, etc.)? How did you feel watching that performance?

DA: I remember the realistic mise-en-scène, where even the humidity on the walls of the house could be seen, and the performance by the quintet of actors, in which a great veteran actress called Marisa Paz would shine and give an acting master class performing the role of Amalia. I remember the scene of the fight between the three brothers, in which their contained emotion and anger would

---

22   TN: "With Family." One of Florencio Sánchez's plays, which had its premiere in 1906.
23   Note from the original Spanish editors: Uruguay's democracy was restored in 1985. The play was written and submitted to competition in 1987. The premiere took place in 1995.

be transmitted to the spectator and it would make me tear up, accompanying the crying of those men on the stage. I remember the good direction by Claudia Pérez (professor of literature and a graduate from the School of Humanities). I remember the change she made to the ending, which the author accepted (because the author believes and supports all the directors of his plays). The ending with Antonio burning the voter ID card was left out. Antonio exits and stays at home without voting, and Amalia, on stage, under a lamp, sitting on a sofa–I think brown–would cry, and the theme sung by Gavioli, *María del Carmen*, would play, and, little by little, Candeau's speech at the Obelisco[24] would be heard louder and louder.

Now that I wrote "Gavioli"… to those picnics at La Dominga (which were the picnics where the parents of the child Dino would go during his childhood, where his father would dance pasodoble with great elegance–as Amalia's Francisco would do, and [for which] Dino's mother would have–as Amalia–a *croquignole* done) Gavioli never went, but all that is said about him was like that, and the child Dino remembers reading the news on *El Diario*. But my point is this: perhaps, unconsciously, the playwright puts Gavioli there because he was famous for his strong communist militancy, which he would not hide; in fact, he would make it visible by going to Bella Unión to sing and support the sugar workers.

LMP: **I believe we can observe a change in the characters of Amalia, Antonio, and Marisa if we compare their past attitudes (the certainty in fighting for their ideas, their energy) with their resignation and disbelief, their disillusionment at the life stage in which the play presents them. How would you explain that change? For example, why did Amalia cast a blank vote and why did Antonio choose not to vote and to burn his voter ID card, especially at the historical moment of reinstating the democracy? What influenced you as a playwright to resolve it in that way?**

DA: The playwright, by narrating how each character behaved that day (the first under democracy), sought to represent each segment of society and their behavior. Let's see if I explain myself: there's the person who is abroad and can't vote because there is no consular vote (Eduardo); there's the one who keeps voting for the

---

[24]   TN: Alberto Candeau (1910-1990) was a Uruguayan actor, theater director, and writer. He was the only speaker at the event known as "Acto del Obelisco," celebrated on November 27, 1983, which was the last Sunday of November (the day when elections have been traditionally held in Uruguay) of 1983, in front of the Obelisk of Montevideo (which had been dedicated in 1930 to honor the signers of the first Uruguayan Constitution of 1830). Candeau read a proclamation calling for elections on the last Sunday of November 1984.

ideals she had and still has and are faithful to her doctrine (Marisa... precisely the "bourgeois" [230], [as] Eduardo says); there's the one who goes to exercise the [right to] vote for the first time in all its novelty (Daniel); there's the one who betrays her ideals and votes to get the little stamp, for fear of the dictatorship recurring, the one who votes for the safety of others (Amalia). Regarding that vote, it reminds me of the plebiscite for the [green vote] and the [yellow vote], where the majority voted for the [yellow vote], even in a democracy, due to the fear still hovering over the society.[25]

Lastly, [there's] Antonio's position, who chooses not to vote and makes of this an explicit act by burning his voter ID card (due to resignation, disbelief, disillusionment, precisely the same that is felt or perceived in these moments–2014–among certain militants in the left).

Perhaps we authors, on some occasions, because of some kind of sensitivity, perceive facts or emotions, which appear in [the] plays and later manifest themselves in reality. It's like a magical thinking that accompanies me. I have always used, for example, names of cities and/or countries that I did not know and then fate takes me to them and they're just like I described them, even without having been there. It happened quite clearly in the only film script I wrote: there the action was set in Montevideo–my city, aside from Chicago and Havana, cities that I got to know afterwards.

Let me add something important: since each one of the five characters takes a different stance at the moment of voting, the playwright balances the scales. He shows all the ideological positions, but doesn't lean towards any. He shows them, he doesn't judge them. Had he supported one or the other, the play would have become a pamphlet, a script. And that's not what was sought.

LMP: **Thank you very much.**[26]

---

[25] TN: In 1986 the Uruguayan Parliament passed a law (Ley de Caducidad de la Pretensión Punitiva del Estado, "Law on the Expiration of the Punitive Claims of the State") granting amnesty for the crimes committed during the dictatorship. In 1989, Uruguayans voted in a referendum as to whether they wanted to keep or repeal the law. The vote for keeping the law was printed on yellow paper (hence its popular name, *el voto amarillo* ["the yellow vote"]. The vote for repealing the law was printed on green paper (*el voto verde* ["the green vote"]). The "yellow vote" won by a margin of 57% to 43%.

[26] Interview translated by Álex Omar Bratkievich.

A High Price to Pay

Marcelo de León Montañés

I have lost my history. They stole it from me, they erased it ...
(Eduardo, Just Yesterday.[251])

Just Yesterday deals with the dislocation of a family as a result of the tremendous social dislocation of 1973. Exile, uprooting, breakups, nostalgia, reencounters with a past that is close and distant at the same time are observed and felt in a fascinating storyline of personal histories entangled with the nation's. The exile of the oldest son, Eduardo, is an individual and family drama, in a culture where family and homeland occupy priority places at the time of weighing decisions.

Just Yesterday presents both faces of exile: from the people who left and from those left behind. Uruguay had not experienced a mass emigration since the Redota[1] and, therefore, even though Uruguayans knew about the immigrants' mourning, they were unaware of the mourning of their emigrated compatriots, uprooted, alone, and facing an unfamiliar reality.

In every story there is more than one version. Here the characters have created two versions of themselves, an epistolary one and a hidden or half told one. The reconnection in person will decide which the true one, if any is, or whether both will join so as to achieve a real picture. On the other hand, how much is left of what they were before the tumultuous alteration of courses? As reflection of the vicissitudes in life itself, there arise central themes and rich lateral secondary themes. Dino Armas admirably penetrates the complexity existing behind even the apparently simple, routine, common, be it the street market, gnocchi, the *mate* in the kitchen, or expecting Mom to wash the jeans.

---

[1] Translator's Note: Popular name given to the 1811 mass migration of 16,000 Eastern Strip inhabitants during the Independence Wars. After an armistice between the Spanish authorities and the Revolutionary Government of Buenos Aires, mainly for fear of retaliation, they followed General José Gervasio Artigas, who had been assigned to a Northern post, expecting his protection. The name is a local slang variation of *derrota* ("defeat").

289

The following paragraphs explore some of these items within the depth of this memorable story molded in Uruguayan culture and history, reverse migration, and the sociopsychological dynamics of the heart-shaped country.

Just Ten

Ten years passed between Uruguay's return to democracy and the premiere of this play in 1995. Ten also separated Eduardo in political exile from his family. If twenty years are nothing, what about the ten of exile? Ten more years are foretold, as if a cycle had been established after finding out that one decade, or *that* decade, was neither just nor yesterday. It hardly could have been, given the colossal facts that marked it. "Who is going to give us these ten years back?" asks Eduardo (250).

The fall of the constitutional government in 1973 could not but provoke a domino effect in the smaller social components, that is, the family and the individual. A predictable life schema of little change ended. Uruguay changed from a stable to an unstable democracy and ended up under a tyrannical government. The country of advanced social legislation was now violating personal rights; the receiver of immigrants was expelling its citizens. The familiar traditions of cohesion, belonging, duty, as well as the profound attachment to the homeland (two of the emigrants in the story are political exiles) and to living close to one's own ("I wanted [...] [t]o have us, all of us, here, together, or near..." [218]) received an enormous blow. It left empty spaces. Many suffered the worst fate; others, like Eduardo, managed to flee and face an infinitely more benign course, although at a high emotional price (mainly but not uniquely).

The "Who is going to give us [...]?" employs a plural pronoun ("us") since the loss is collective. Can it be overcome? That past, is it *just yesterday*? Questions surface about the exile and the return. Even though there is a *Return*,[2] it is not the "humble hope" of that tango that is heard but the "wounded" lyrics of *Los mareados*.[3] It is as if Armas were saying, "The reader is warned."

The plot alludes to the evolution in national politics in those years but does not explore it in detail. This evolution affects the protagonists, triggers traumatic events (rushed separation, breakup, engagement with bad auspices,

---

[2]   TN: *Volver* ("To Return") is an iconic tango composed in 1934 by Carlos Gardel (music) and Alfredo Le Pera (lyrics).
[3]   TN: "The Tipsy Ones."

unemployment), and reveals personalities (patriotic illusion, lost or found ideals), but in *Just Yesterday* the private tragedy, behind closed doors, is more important; the macrosocial one already has abundant academic material.

To Be and Not to Be, and to Be without a Certain Course

The brothers Eduardo, Antonio, and Daniel, their mother Amalia, and the daughter-in-law Marisa constitute a family in Uruguay, which by the '70s and '80s had melted the multicultural yesteryear into a common identity. Armas makes the latter surface in knowing winks to Montevidean or national folklore ("from Manzanares, because they have them at a better price and they are on sale" [202]; "Thank you, UTE,[4] for letting me see the familiar and missed darkness" [254]); expressions that, if not unique, at least have become ingrained ("estamos como estamos" [Armas 202]; "Dale Juana con los canastos" [Armas 202]);[5] references that can only be understood in Uruguay ("She brought it from Chuy")[6]; the use of "gringo" (Armas 205, 200)[7] as synonym for *foreigner* and not *person from the U.S.*; the weakened religiosity; the longing for some past which must have been better ("We had such good times!" [224]); the complaint next to the strength that maintains social cohesion even under the worst circumstances; and so many more details (the street market, "y chau" [Armas 201],[8] Gardel, pasta, etc.).

If before it was possible to discover our own characteristics through the perception of the foreigner in Uruguayan land, with reverse migration it is the Uruguayan (Eduardo) in foreign land who contributes brushstrokes to the portrait of his own country and people: "They did not want to believe that there is no way to make Uruguayans use the new names [of streets]" (255). The regional aspects are also found in the language, the dialect, the "codes, [the] subtexts, [the] implicit references" (251).

Eduardo loses part of his identity in those ten years being apart, enough time to blur the culture of origin and to add new elements from the adopted one ("I stand in front of a window display and think 'escaparate' rather than 'vidriera';

---

4   TN: Administración Nacional de Usinas y Transmisiones Eléctricas (National Administration of Power Plants and Electrical Transmissions, UTE for its acronym in Spanish) is Uruguay's state-owned power company.

5   TN: In *Just Yesterday*, the English translations are "we are in the situation we are" (216) and "you can't let it go" (216).

6   TN: Chuy is a border town where people can buy goods at cheaper prices (duty free).

7   TN: In *Just Yesterday*, the English translation is "Italian" (213).

8   TN: The English translation is "and that's it" (215).

and my suitcases are 'maletas,' not 'valijas'; and you laugh because I say 'vale'" [251]),[9] but insufficient for him to identify with his new land. Worse still, he uncovers a myth of his Uruguayan identity: a person from Uruguay, which looks towards Europe and turns its back on Latin America, learns that Europe does not consider him European and he ends "[d]ressed up as a Latin American" (252) in order to make a place for himself in the old continent at the expense of lying.

With Family

Identity is also personality. Armas recreates phrases, attitudes, gestures that are an expression of very Uruguayan personalities. It is difficult to perceive what is typical in our own culture without an external contrast, but an effort to think abstractly or interaction with immigrants in the modern country helps in detecting what is characteristic in the national culture.

Just Yesterday shows a very tight-knit family in which offspring take shelter at their parents' home, children take care of their elders until their death (Antonio and his father), and several generations live under the same roof. The blood code prevails, the one which puts the clan ahead of the tribe: "Why did you hit him? He is your brother," says Amalia scolding Antonio (264).

Solidarity and affection are positive bonds, but there are also negative ones: the bonds of need ("He doesn't need us" [269]) and guilt ("since your mother asks something that is for the good of all of us, no, Mr. Daniel feels annoyed" [222]), the passive-aggressive behavior that masks anger and perhaps comes from frequent interaction within a reduced physical and human space ("you are not one of those who gets nervous about a summer storm" [237]; "What could happen here without you knowing?" [237]).

Exile altered the internal equilibrium. Eduardo is shown signs of affection upon his return but seems to confuse affection with freedom to act without restraints. In turn, the family interprets Eduardo's affection to mean he will assume responsibilities that were interrupted by exile. Both sides will discover how much bonds can be altered by ten years and an ocean in between. Whoever dreams of returning to a past model will find that profound changes affect the most legitimate of expectations and foundations as solid as a family's.

---

9   TN: "Escaparate," "maletas," and "vale" are lexical items characteristic of the Spanish dialects spoken in Spain; "vidriera" and "valijas" are characteristic of the Spanish dialects spoken in Uruguay.

A member leaving a small community upsets the group. Marisa, Eduardo's girlfriend in 1973, is about to enter the in-law family when her boyfriend's exile begins. Antonio attracts her into the circle again and seals her entry through marriage. Did he expect to repair the sentimental void left by Eduardo in the same way he had fulfilled Eduardo's filial void: taking charge of the unfulfilled responsibilities?

Family conceptualized as a whole can attract a kind of modern collective biblical guilt ("the way all your shit fucked us up"), by coincidence or because of the Judeo-Christian roots of Uruguayan society. Antonio complains about the collective ("how you fucked us up") and individual ("You fucked me up") punishments due to someone else's actions. It is clear that there were not just one but several prices he paid because of his kinship, such as losing his job ("because of being your brother, because you had been in compromising situations" [259-260]) and depending entirely on his wife's income.

We Are All Different Now

Eduardo assumes that certain spaces from his previous life remain intact; however, he acknowledges he has changed. Marisa, whom he expects to remain unchanged, notices his change. Daniel, too young to remember his brother from before, is still of the opinion that he is the same. Eduardo replies with a heavy truth: "You say it like everyone else, almost like an obligation or because it sounds good" (250). If a repeated lie turns into a reality, reaffirming that there was no change establishes the illusion that that decade is just a day ago and avoids the painful (uncomfortable, at any rate) certainty that much has definitely become part of the past.

Nevertheless, there is an unquestionable change indeed, the one caused by the very presence of Eduardo. "Antonio is another person since his brother is here" (222), thinks Amalia. Her comment points to the happiness of reunion, but the remark will later slip through the twists and turns of the story, in which people's moods change for reasons other than the happiness of a delayed embrace. By the end of the play, Daniel's enigmatic reply to Amalia's comment, "We are all different now," acquires its full meaning.

Men and Women

A patriarchal society draws clear lines between genders. Men and women are shaped within molds that specify their gestures, attitudes, habits, language, and thought. At the same time, men and women, even within their roles, act in distinct ways, in this case–clearly–in the form of facing the breakage caused by emigration.

The men in *Just Yesterday* received their model of manhood and manliness from their father, Francisco, to whom they turn in their memories over and over (also to the grandfather, but his evocation only adds another masculine referent). This absent/present paternal image coincides with a paternal figure from another time, absent/present even in life, a domestic hero who reigns (although does not always rule), noble or ennobled in the family altar of his wife's devotion and his children's admiration. This exaltation forges Eduardo's goal, before the exile, of "fulfill[ing] the old man's dream" (239-240).

Eduardo embodies the man who looks at the most obvious images of the culture to carve his own masculinity: his father, tango, the "Man" of tango (Julio Sosa[10]). Since Francisco's death took away the main masculine figure from the family, it is not preposterous to think that part of the joy at Eduardo's return could be the expectation of his replacing the missing masculine cornerstone.

The paternal mold, filled by Antonio, has lost its verve, not in masculinity but in personality (Antonio is basically submissive and does not rebel), and has faded in Daniel, who perpetuates the division of labor ("Mom, wash my jeans. I left them on the bed" [219]) without fitting entirely into the mold of men from another time. Maybe Daniel heralds a new country and a new definition of man.

Eduardo's exile interrupted the natural evolution of intergenerational relationships. Among other things, it caused him the sorrow of not sharing the last moments of the father he wanted to make proud. As for Daniel, although he lived with Francisco for some time that did not go beyond his teenage years, he still seems to have grasped his father's brand of idealism. Daniel was also deprived of the model of his energetic brother, so there was little he could receive directly from him; therefore, the emotion in the final embrace with Eduardo could be due not only to the obvious reasons given the departure of a close relative,

---

[10] TN: Julio Sosa (1926-1964) was a Uruguayan tango singer, nicknamed "El Varón del Tango" ("The Man of Tango").

but also to the parting of a masculine referent created–and perhaps idealized–through letters and family stories, briefly embodied in his return, and lost with a new farewell. After all, Eduardo could very well accompany Francisco on the family altar, not for his behavior (which differs ethically from his father's) but for Amalia's extolling treatment of him.

Finally, Antonio's example to Daniel differs from Francisco's and Eduardo's: an enduring, resilient man ends up fearful and unhappy. On the other hand, Daniel the man will carry the traces of growing up under a dictatorship. The young man watches everything, participates little, protests some because of domestic issues yet parts discreetly with the past when he understands it vanished (such as tearing a photo) and harbors hopes of a better future, always within a prudent emotional reservation. He is the young man of a country traumatized by recent violence.

For the three men, the distribution of roles–supported by the women of the house–is so natural that not even being exposed to other cultures or relying upon themselves for everything, as in Eduardo's case, has altered it (emigration does not necessarily alter the essence of who we are, which remains or becomes clear if it was not visible). Amalia's memories of the picnics of her youth could be transferred to the present of the reunion without anachronism: "Women would put the food we had brought on a large table, and while men played soccer or cards, we would cut everything" (224).

Of women, there are two psychologies. One is Amalia's, typical mother from our culture (and Hispanic, Italian, Greek, Jewish, Mediterranean in general), devoted to her children, generous, meticulous, and also overprotective ("Reassure Mom because I think I'm hearing her wonder if I'm wearing warm clothes," writes Eduardo from Spain [202]), who would like to think of herself as omniscient ("In the end, everyone knew more about Eduardo and about our life than me, his mother..." [223]). She allows herself to break her strict codes of composure (taking off her shoes was "her only concession to the summer" [202]) when overwhelmed by grief ("You, crying in the street?" asks Antonio surprised [269]). Weak when she can be, she is strong when she must and "endured [a raid] on her feet" (218). Wonderfully portrayed, Amalia is a Uruguayan woman who knew how to combine the roles of partner, wife, and mother. Grumpy, affectionate, righteous, devout, wise, intransigent, flexible, a multifaceted embodiment of the matriarchy hidden behind a patriarchal façade ("if she is not the first one to arrive [at the street market], she thinks it will be suspended" [210]), she proves the weaker sex is not such.

As a mother, she develops a tighter mother-child connection than other cultures'. Her children, whom she does not always recognize as adults (she scolds Antonio for hitting his brother), are an extension of herself, flesh of her flesh, ethics of her ethics. Their mistakes, therefore, do not exist, are justifiable, or can be mitigated. She does not conceive of blaming Eduardo for the activities that pushed him into exile. Curiously, she does not exculpate him by blaming the official authoritarianism but people close to him: the bad influence of his friend or girlfriend. The drama, again, occurs behind closed doors.

Amalia evolves, which adds allure to her character. She does not stagnate in one way of thinking; she transforms ("I was all of those and none of those I am now" [218]) according to the lessons given by life. She got her wisdom and strength (which she does not perceive since she believes she "need[s] to have someone strong next to [her]" [269]) from the world, not from her insufficient formal education. There is a young Amalia, another who withstood raids, another with an exile offspring, and one with an emigrant son…. The entire family carries joys and sorrows, but if the others live and think from within their places according to how another impinges (positively or negatively) on their space, Amalia is able to take distance, observe, and summarize the character and role of each one without necessarily starting from their interrelationship with her. It could be said that in insight and understanding she perhaps surpasses everyone, from Francisco to Marisa.

Marisa is more of a contemporary woman. She shares with her mother-in-law the determination and an apparently greater maturity than the men of the house. She is, furthermore, provider of her home. She was politically active and participated in "gluing revolutionary posters and participating in all types of raids" (260), and even though she refers to conviction in the cause ("We thought we would change the world…" [231]), her genuine motivation was love ("[…] everything I did, I did with you. Only for you…" [231]). Even so and despite such dedication, she knew how to balance the emotional and the rational. She is an emotional woman with a practical logic. As does Amalia, she conveys fortitude. There is embitterment but not a bitter character. There is reproach but it is not gratuitous. She has weaknesses yet she sacrifices herself so as not to hurt.

If we compare the two femininities with the three masculinities, a noticeable difference can be observed in their skill to deal with the challenges of life and to rise after a fall.

Ulysses's Weeping

Until the '50s (technically until the '60s), Uruguay was a recipient of immigrants. What had been left behind? What stories did the people who returned tell? The reversal in the unidirectional migration would answer many questions. The first important flow of emigrants occurred because of the democratic deterioration towards the end of the '60s and the dictatorship that ensued. In Eduardo, Armas collects ahead of its time various aspects of what is today called *Ulysses Syndrome*, whose characteristics are stress and multiple bereavements, caused by–among other factors–the violation of the attachment instinct due to the separation from beloved people and places ("Alone […]. Who must have invented such a short word for something as big and tremendous […]?" [202]; "his eyes would shine talking about the trees on 19 de Abril Street" [253]), the despair ("[they] shut the doors in my face" [253]), the fight for survival ("Hunger, cold" [252]), and the end put to projects and dreams ("The desire to be another Galeano, another Benedetti, maybe an Onetti, it remained that, a wish" [251]).

Heartfelt and eloquent is this less familiar story of emigration, whose intensity is still very vivid for Eduardo because it happened *just yesterday*. Regrettably, there is no receptive audience. Some belittle the bereavements of emigrants because of the false idea that they must have had a great time if they moved to a more developed country ("And you were living the great life far away," retorts Antonio [259]) and that they distanced themselves from the problems of their own people ("very far away" [259]); others dismiss the trials on the way if material success is achieved. Faced with Eduardo's moving account of squalor and decadence, Daniel adds, "But in the end you did well." His "in the end" means that the result is what matters, not the preceding journey. Eduardo replies with identical words but inverts their interpretation to highlight, precisely, that what detracts from the result is that it happened only "in the end" (253).

Antonio counterposes his own Via Dolorosa, caused by Eduardo: "You fucked up my life, Eduardo. You screwed me up real bad" (259). Pain and the misperception that everything shines for the emigrant destroy any possible empathy towards his brother, for whom he shows a brutal disdain: "Yes, yes, do not say anything, you had a horrible time, it was awful, you had to do all kinds of stuff. Your same old version" (259).

A shared world is lost. The hardships experienced by those who left are ignored (the emigrant at least partially knows the reality of those who stay since it was his own), but the sharing of the positive or neutral is also missing. In ten years, the emotional gap is enormous: "[…] you did not smell the scents of El Rastro in the summer, nor did you see the Guernica painting; you did not see how choked up I was…. I cannot be the same person for you, because you don't know everything I did, everything I went through…" (252). In Spain, in December of 1973, Eduardo writes, "Even the cold separates me from you" (202). He was already experiencing the bereavement and the "even" indicates that he was reviewing a solid list of separating items. The paths bifurcated. Can they reunite? The question is implicitly asked: "For us you will always be the same"… (252).

Both Eduardo, who left, and Antonio, who stayed, consider those years lost. Eduardo adds one or two positive or anecdotal comments to his statements; the rest of his memories in exile are negative. He does not consider the positive balances since they do not compensate for the losses and only came with time. Antonio's presentation of facts is gloomier, exclusively negative (unemployment, permanent fear, sentimental unhappiness). The joy because of Eduardo's return is his illusion of balancing the scales.

Person-Country

In the masculine characters there are glimpses of Uruguayans from partially overlapping historical periods who endure differently the collective trauma of a dreadful time. Francisco was the peaceful idealist ("He never got to…" [240]), a socialist from an agonizing Switzerland of the Americas; he died during the dictatorship, in a definitive burial of the country of his youth. Eduardo fits into the Uruguay of increasing conflicts, violence on the rise, and worsening economic, social, and political crisis…. It is the second half of the '60s and beginning of the '70s; afterwards, it is the Uruguay of a diaspora.

Dictatorship, persecution, disappearances created Antonio's Uruguay. Frightened, he endures without protesting or because he does not protest ("you're never going to rebel, are you?" [209]); sometimes he lies ("when I signed it, I felt like throwing up" [261]) or betrays, not out of complicity but survival ("Do you want me to sign anything? That my brother is a delinquent, a rotten person? I will sign it, but do not make me lose my job…" [260]). He is or has become incredulous; instead of living in the past out of longing or in the future out of illusion, he lives in the present because it is real or out of inertia. The origin of the terrified Uruguay/Antonio (his words: "fear," "scared to death," "[s]cared shitless," "to tremble when you see a soldier," "tremors" [261]) was maybe born out of an adapted, conformed (conformist?) Uruguay/Antonio, follower of a cause "by habit, fear, or whatever" (267). He is not cowardly but docile: he "never says anything, never sees anything" (262), and needs "someone strong next to [him]" (269). Opposed to Eduardo (as in their positions at the beginning: with their backs towards each other), neither of them is Francisco.

Daniel belongs to the generation raised under a dictatorship, a product of the change in the country and the formative influence of a totalitarian regime. Cheerful until '73 ("You were not like that as a boy. What I remember most about you was your laughter..." [244]), he is now a reserved, "awkward" young man, who is "always shutting himself up, hiding" (244). This fictional character could well be one of the real university students whom a professor asked, amazed, when he found out they tolerated without opposition unfair treatment from another professor, "Boys, what happened to you?" Dictatorship happened to them: perceiving the fear in their elders, learning to keep quiet and not argue against the system. Daniel must have experienced his own and others' fear during the raid on his home or Eduardo's hasty departure; without a doubt he sensed it in Antonio, with the aggregated value of being a close masculine image. Nevertheless, he is the only son with a real interest in the return to democracy: "I'm looking forward to voting" (268). Does he represent a revived hope and will he be the one who–in Eduardo's words–will be able to "do what we [...] could not do... what they didn't let us do..." (266)?

Eduardo throws up his hands, turns his back on the country of his broken dreams ("If [he] had voted, we would have one more vote" [267]), and faces his failures. Antonio turns his back on a democratic promise undermined by the terror created during the regime, and, in the first act of rebellion, showing his disgust over his own broken dreams, burns his voter identification card. Fortunately, there still remain Daniel and others like him. An old Uruguay regains life: "He has all the strength and hope of Francisco" (269).

Amalia compares herself to Antonio and feels similar to him. While this is true in endurance, they radically differ in other aspects. If the males were static depictions of Uruguayan sectors, the women would be dynamic portraits, with elements of the former plus some of their own. Amalia is strong even if she thinks she needs someone strong next to her; she has had driving ideals–although she is now disenchanted–and not even in their transformation into pragmatism ("I voted for nothing else but to get the stamp" [269]) is there inertia or apathy. She navigated through a dark period staying on her feet, but she does not overcome the disillusionment about her fellow "[l]awyers, politicians, policemen, people in the neighborhood" (269), selfish and opportunistic at a critical moment.

Marisa is a somewhat contrary dynamic portrait: she comes from disenchantment and heads towards hope. Of course, like Amalia, she remains beside her husband (even though the love that united her parents-in-law is missing). Two women that barely tolerate each other but know how to live together anyway, they traverse a similar journey in opposite directions and illustrate how some people handled their conflicts at the time. Marisa is not maturing into weariness or hopelessness. The young woman who followed her boyfriend at clandestinely putting up posters threw away the romantic games of Eduardo's Asiram to become Antonio's Marisa. A very confident woman, she lives the present, celebrates the future, and shuts down the past: "Before…. Who remembers before?" (230).

Symbology

Tango (habitual companion of Armas' work) and its often heartbreaking emotional charge has linked generations and served as a connection with the legacy of immigrants since it takes up their melancholy, nostalgia, and frustration. In *Just Yesterday* the sentimental power of tango is tapped through Eduardo, who, by repeatedly singing it in Spain, must have experienced again the immigrants' tears underlying the lyrics. The musical genre fulfills a double function for the exiled Eduardo: on one hand, it is the funny anecdote he tells during the honeymoon of the reunion (which lasts until happiness diminishes and less pleasant emotions appear) and thus he remembers himself singing tangos to the "Spaniards" (251); on the other hand, he reveals the hurtful side of the same anecdote, the story of the emigrant who sang "to eat" from the charity of the passers-by (252).

Daniel keeps himself outside of the tango references and does not even participate in the round of drinks with his brothers at the bar, one more traditional exhibition of masculinity to which Daniel remains unconnected. Daniel grew up when tango, like the world of his elders (from Francisco to Eduardo), was losing currency. The common cultural road between generations was narrowing and Daniel's generation was diverging towards a different path that would eventually make tango and former values, as well as the spirit of Francisco's generation, reemerge.

One might think that the story of a Rioplatense return should be accompanied by *Volver*, a tango which is mentioned only once, in passing, and next to *El día que me quieras*.[11] Given that *Volver* is sung from the perspective of a person alone with his thoughts, in a discourse with hopes of a happy ending for the returning traveler, the unfolding of *Just Yesterday* immediately reveals its inadequacy for the story. In its place, Armas chose *Los mareados*, whose lyrics abound in elements suitable to the intimate tragedy of practically every character: misfortune, laughing in order not to cry, not seeing each other, diverging paths, love, regret, and the remains of something that disintegrated. Lyrics oriented towards romantic love extend to other affections and sorrows. Its first word, "strange," warns the spectator about the nature of the encounters to be witnessed; the last phrase, "look at what remained," summarizes the spectator's reflection.

Much more can be discovered....

The contrast in masculinities is already foreseen in the opening, with two standing men, in opposite positions, prelude of the struggle that will develop between the brothers.

Antonio mentions his grandmother's madness. Mental disturbances appear in other plays of Dino Armas since the playwright gathers human fortunes and misfortunes or the terror of suffering the latter. The ghost of dementia is born out of or increases the fears suffered by Antonio. When it is mentioned, it incidentally allows the spectator to start taking pity on Amalia, who, before losing a loved one because of political exile, had already lost another because of the exile of reason.

Eduardo reminds us of the prodigal son from Luke's Gospel, whose return causes the rejoicing that the other son, obedient and reliable, does not get. In the end, resentment is inevitable ("comfort him, hold him" [264]). One might ask whether the different positions correspond to those of Uruguayan society towards its repatriates.

---

[11] TN: "The Day that You Love Me."

301

For Me, For You All...

A part of the drama of exile is what is lived there and not lived here, and vice versa. Part is that an idyllic phase might sometimes be an ephemeral illusion followed by pending accounts and sad anecdotes. A part resides in the incomprehension of one side regarding what happened to the other during the time apart.

Another part, the most devastating, is the dissolution of identity, which provides the secure feeling of knowing who we are and, paraphrasing Rubén Darío, where we go and where we come from. The known world collapsed for Eduardo: "I am a foreigner here and I am a foreigner there. I have lost my history. They stole it from me, they erased it ten years ago [...] That's what I am now, what they made me become: an old guy, too old already, who does not know where he's going or who he is..." (251-252). This major loss is exacerbated when the empathy of others fails, as happens to Eduardo. His story depicts the exile who is safe from physical victimization but affected by severe emotional grief.

Thus a fifth part of the drama of exile is better understood: the attempt to resume a former life as if time had not passed. Eduardo's advances towards his sister-in-law is perceived under a different light if it is considered a desperate–however selfish–attempt to recuperate the gone past.

Eduardo's final decision delivers the final blow to the collective fantasies built over the correspondence and the half-truths ("You only know what I put down in the letters" [252]) that have been dying since his return. In almost every character, a "soul clinging to a sweet memory" (*Volver*) opens its eyes to say, "Three things bear my wounded soul: love... regret... pain..." (*Los mareados*). Eduardo, Antonio, Marisa, Amalia, and–to some degree–Daniel could make the lyrics of this tango their own.

The question that remains open is: who will make their own, "Today you will become part of my past, the past of my life"?[12]

---

[12]   Essay translated by Álex Omar Bratkievich.

Works Consulted

Armas, Dino. "Apenas ayer". *Migración y dictadura en escena: Un análisis interdisciplinario de la obra del dramaturgo uruguayo Dino Armas*. Dir. Gabriela Christie Toletti. Norfolk: New Dominion Press, 2017. 189-250.

APPENDIX
Conversation on Life and Theater

Interview with Dino Armas carried out on June 17, 2014
By Gabriela Christie Toletti

Gabriela Christie Toletti talking with Dino Armas
(June 17, 2014)

GCT: Gabriela Christie Toletti

DA: Dino Armas

GCT: **Good afternoon. We are at the home of the great playwright and my dear friend Dino Armas, in Montevideo, Uruguay. Dino, what a great pleasure to be here with you! Thank you for receiving us.**

DA: My pleasure.

GCT: **Thank you very much. I'll ask you some questions about your childhood and your family life. Which people from your family life, from your childhood, left a mark on you as a person and as a playwright? How are your childhood and your story reflected in your playwright career? I'd like to know a little of you as a child.**

DA: I was born in Villa Cosmópolis,[1] in "el Cerro de Montevideo."[2] I was a child overprotected by his mother, and I was an asthmatic child. That affected me, especially because I couldn't play with the other children. I would spend a lot of time in bed with medications and the only thing I had was reading.

GCT: **So that's when your interest in reading was born.**

DA: Yes, that was essential, I believe. Besides, several peculiarities of my childhood influenced my life and later my dramaturgy. For example, there was my healer grandmother.

GCT: **As in *Doña Mercedes*. That work is autobiographical, isn't it?**

DA: It's completely autobiographical. I say that my grandmother saved me twice: once when she cured me from my childhood asthma (she healed me exactly as is told in *Doña Mercedes*) and another time when I was a months-old baby and had these convulsions—so I was told—and she healed me with hot bricks.

GCT: **How interesting!**

DA: Yes. That's why I say that my grandmother saved me twice. Then I was an atypical child in a neighborhood where people used to play ball games, all those

---

[1] Translator's Note: "Cosmopolis Village."
[2] TN: *El Cerro de Montevideo* (literally: "Montevideo's Hill") is a hill adjacent to the Bay of Montevideo. One of the neighborhoods located on it is called *Villa del Cerro* (literally: "the Hill's Village") or, simply, *el Cerro* ("the Hill").

boyhood games in which I couldn't participate because the asthma was always there on my back. It was also detrimental for my schooling since, in addition, I had to repeat a grade. But that was useful in a different way, because becoming interested in reading was positive.

GCT: **Reading, which leads you to introversion, introspection, and observation....**

DA: Exactly, introversion and observation, which led me to observe all the surroundings that are later reflected in my works. What's more, there were my parents: my father, who was socialist and atheist, and my mother, who was a believer. My parents were children of Spanish immigrants. All that hodgepodge I had, in a very peculiar neighborhood, a working-class neighborhood of people who worked at the meat plants but with a lot of culture, with libraries, with a lot to offer theater-wise....

GCT: **A very special and fantastic neighborhood, with all that mixture of immigrant cultures and with characters as original as Doña Mercedes.... *Doña Mercedes* is a short story: have you also dabbled in the short story genre or is this your only short story?**

DA: Well, I have another. But they're only two short stories because I always tended towards the theater.

GCT: **How did the idea of writing *Doña Mercedes* come up, then?**

DA: Because I was asked by a newspaper from El Cerro to write something about a character or about my life and I wrote *Doña Mercedes*, which was later staged as a play. But the experience I have of my childhood is just like it's explained in the short story. And it has magical realism: there's the thing about the belief that salivating into a live fish could get rid of my asthma.

GCT: **And it did, right? You don't have asthma anymore!**

DA: It got rid of it completely. I never had asthma again. There's faith, isn't there? What one wants to believe and doesn't want to believe; that's the positive part. And my grandmother, I remember, was such a character, just like it's told there. What is not told in the short story is that she made a lot of money as a healer. She had a two-story house in El Cerro, which at that time was something only rich people had.

GCT: [**It was**] **uncommon.**

DA: Yes, and she also had a house in a resort town. Later she bought other houses in El Cerro itself. She was very efficient in her work.

GCT: **It's so interesting that you wrote this autobiographical short story about your grandmother…. There are many autobiographical elements not only in this but also in many of your plays, right?**

DA: Yes, yes, without doubt. In all my plays there is something autobiographical. For example, in *Feliz día, papá,*[3] which is set at a health clinic and [in which] the three sick people in the clinic die on the day a soccer game is played between Uruguay and Chile, my father was also admitted to a hospital; there's a lot of me in that play.

GCT: **Since there are many autobiographical elements in your plays, do you think there is something cathartic and therapeutic about them? Do you think that the act of writing is cathartic and, up to a certain point, therapeutic, not only as a way to process personal conflicts, but also as a way to process social situations in which you find yourself involved?**

DA: It seems as if we have always talked about these subjects, doesn't it? [They laugh.] Because I say that theater saved me from madness and is therapeutic. In my family there were actual crazy people.

GCT: **Then, theater [was a] way of channeling that madness.**

DA: Yes, of getting all that out. When one writes a play, one gets exorcised and expresses not only one's feelings but also everything that surrounds us. For me, it's therapeutic. It's healing.

GCT: **And it continues to be healing, right?**

DA: Yes, yes, it continues to be healing. And, besides, now that my plays are being analyzed as a group (for example, for this book), it's being understood that it's always the same world in my plays, Dino's world.

GCT: **Dino's interior world.**

DA: Yes, and that's why writing is healing and therapeutic and I advise it as

---

[3] TN: "Happy Day, Dad!"

something cathartic. [He laughs.] People can write what they feel, not necessarily only in the form of a play.

GCT: **It can be a diary, a short story, isolated thoughts, etc.**

DA: Yes, yes, all that is useful as something cathartic. But–moreover–I am a shy person in real life. I don't talk as much as in the interviews. I talk less. Therefore, the way I have to express myself is writing.

GCT: **Your way of communicating with the world is through writing.**

DA: Yes, it's the way of expressing what I feel inside.

GCT: **Otherwise, all those feelings remain there.**

DA: Yes, otherwise all of that remains there and sometimes it's unhealthy. It's good, therefore, to get it all out.

GCT: **It's a way to exorcise and free yourself from all those emotions. Since you are, as you say you are, a little shy, how was it that you got interested in teaching, where you have to be in front of a class? I have also thought about how teaching could have influenced your writing career and vice versa. What relationship is there between the two?**

DA: Well, let's go by stages. I was a teacher but not by vocation.

GCT: **At the beginning or throughout your teaching career?**

DA: It was at the beginning but it wasn't noticeable. Maybe also because, not having a vocation, I tried to do my job in the most professional way possible.

GCT: **Why, then, did you work as a teacher?**

DA: Well, we have to go further back. I was a teenager who knew how to draw very well. I am from the times when parents imposed careers on you. Given that I drew well, my father said, "He's going to be an architect"; so they signed me up at the School of Architecture. There I passed Drawing, I passed Art History, I passed Literature, but I couldn't pass Math. Then came a certain age when I was already grown-up and had to work somehow. I looked for the shortest possible path to a job and that career was teaching. Later, I came to like the career. And I ended up, when I worked in El Cerro Norte, in some deprived neighborhoods, feeling that my job as a teacher was really worthwhile.

GCT: **You felt that you were making a difference with your work.**

DA: Yes, that it was important social work. Besides, I always had good relationships with the children and excellent evaluations as a teacher. But, like I said, at the beginning I started without a vocation.

GCT: **Do you think there's a connection between teaching and the theater?**

DA: Yes, without a doubt; teaching is acting.

GCT: **It is like that for me, too. I am an actress every day I teach.** [They laugh.]

DA: That's why. And one has to be there every day; even if something's happening or that day one doesn't feel well or one feels sick, one needs to be in good spirits. You have to work, the students have to see you well and one needs to pass on the knowledge. And, to transmit the knowledge, you have to hook the students somehow. Besides, when one works with children, there's the affection from the children. I have former pupils, now adults that remember me and come to visit me (for example, a student that now lives in Barcelona tracked me down on Facebook and came especially to my house to visit me), so the memories the students have of me are good.

GCT: **I vouch for the good memories of your pupils. In fact, I talked with one of your former students from Queen's School who remembers you affectionately as the teacher who always had all the children under his wing.**

DA: Yes, those were my times at Queen's School. And I have to greatly thank Queen's School. It was during the dictatorship years…. I was a category C citizen, which meant I couldn't work for the State in any public position, at any public school. Queen's School would open its doors to everyone who had political problems. It was a very good school. I always remember the principal, Patricia Hormaeche. One has to be thankful for those things, those opportunities…. But you were asking whether teaching influenced my plays.

GCT: **Yes, and I'll add something else: as a writer and with your teacher training, do you feel that there is a didactic duty in your plays? Do you feel the educational duty of communicating a message, of teaching? I also wondered whether teaching is actually teaching to think.**

DA: [He nods smiling.] Yes, it's exactly that. You put it perfectly! For example, my plays are very photographic; they show moments, like *Just Yesterday*. So showing a proposal or a problem that exists in the country and making people reflect is teaching, teaching how to think and not taking sides (because otherwise the play turns into a pamphlet), showing what it is and, afterwards, letting the people think.

GCT: **It's a didactic task in the sense of teaching a type of mental operation. Writing is teaching and teaching is acting.**

DA: [He nods and laughs.] It's like that. Writing is teaching and teaching is acting. By the way, speaking of didactic, the characters of teachers appeared in my plays after I retired, not during my teaching career. When I was able to distance myself from that world, when I stopped belonging to the education world, I was able to write about teachers. Before, teachers had never appeared in my plays.

GCT: **Were you inspired by teachers you knew throughout your career to create characters such as the teacher in *Present, Señorita*?**

DA: Yes. *Present, Señorita* is a summary of all the teachers I met and it also includes things of mine; for example, it mentions Estación Tapia: my first job was at Estación Tapia, which is where the teacher Perla from *Present, Señorita* works. So, my life as a human being and as a citizen coincides with the author. The autobiographical is always there. I grew up alongside my plays.

GCT: **When did you begin to write?**

DA: In 1965 I took part in a contest of the theater El Tinglado. I had never written a play. I was reading Tennessee Williams and my first play was very Tennessee Williams: the title was *En otro y último verano*.[4] And that play got a mention for the first prize. I had never written, but I had that amazing reading background that helped me.

GCT: **As you started writing, what other authors, theories, styles, and movements influenced your writing career?**

DA: [I was influenced] a lot [by] the "criollo"[5] theater, sainetes, Armando Discépolo (*Babilonia*[6] is a play that fascinates me), Federico García Lorca, and

---

4   TN: "In Another and Last Summer."
5   TN: In general, when the term "criollo" is used for artistic expression, it refers to local works that do not try to simply emulate European cultural manifestations but integrate aspects of the local culture and identity (in form and/or content).
6   TN: "Babylon."

Florencio Sánchez. My own way followed that direction. [Also, I was] influenced by Lorca, Williams, and others regarding the technical part of how to write a play and how the characters are developed. And then the contributions of film; for example, I like a lot Alfred Hitchcock and his search for the ideal woman in *Vertigo*. Film had an enormous influence on me, even in the way of working the scenes. I work the scenes very short and overlapped, where there are a lot of characters, as if it were the editing of a movie. My plays have a lot of visual elements and all that comes from film. The influence of film can also be seen in the presence of melodrama in my plays. I like melodrama a lot and there's a lot of that in my plays. My characters are always on the verge of melodrama.

GCT: **And on the verge of madness, too.**

DA: Yes, on the verge of madness. That's something that interests me a lot. It's something that mattered a lot to me and that I lived through.

GCT: **Because of your family, your history.**

DA: Yes, of course, because of my experiences, my family. For example, my grandmother died at a mental hospital. [They're] things that sometimes authors do not confess, but I do. Why not? If I put it in a play, why couldn't I say that it happened and, at the same time, that writing it helped me and saved me?

GCT: **We return to the therapeutic effect of writing.**

DA: Yes, we return to the same: the therapeutic, cathartic effect.

GCT: **I think about the theater as catharsis, not only of personal conflicts but also of collective conflicts (for example, as a way to exorcise the dictatorship effects). How did the dictatorship affect your plays? Some of your plays can be considered examples of socially engaged and politically engaged literature. What is for you a socially and politically engaged play?**

DA: A socially and politically engaged play is a play that is not a pamphlet, a play that reflects what actually happened to the individual (for example, what happened to me). I always say that during the dictatorship I had that "C" category, but I wasn't a hero. I was an average citizen, an ordinary citizen who suffered through that period. There were other people that were tortured or killed who were indeed heroes. Also those who had to leave the country. But I wrote about what happened to me, to that citizen who didn't want to leave or couldn't leave and had to live in the country during the dictatorship.

GCT: **Did you ever think about leaving the country?**

DA: Yes, I thought about leaving, but later it didn't crystallize.

GCT: **Why?**

DA: I was already mature; I had my roots here, my jobs here.

GCT: **So, in your plays you show the drama of the ordinary citizen (like you) during that period of the dictatorship.**

DA: Yes. For example, *Just Yesterday*, which you include in the book, tells how terrible it was for ordinary citizens to live under a dictatorship: not being able to express themselves, being afraid of going out into the street, the fear of being stopped and asked for identification documents. It's a play I recently read again and found a truly heartbreaking play, a lot more than I thought or remembered.

GCT: **In that and other plays you show family dynamics and conflicts during that time of the dictatorship.**

DA: Yes, the different stances that occurred in every family.

GCT: **Because no family was monolithic. Not everyone thought alike and all this caused conflicts, fights.**

DA: Yes, there were different opinions: the one who wanted to leave, the one who wanted to stay, the one who thought differently. In the play *Just Yesterday* it's said, "a war happened here" (265-266). There were no massacres but there was a war.

GCT: **This makes me think about the absurdity of dictatorship and how some of your engaged plays have a touch of the Theater of the Absurd, perhaps as a way to show the absurd aspects of reality.**

DA: Yes, on one hand I have plays like *Just Yesterday*, which is a very naturalistic play. And on the other hand, some of my engaged plays, such as *Sea Murmur*, get close to the absurd but keep a realistic theme. ([*Sea Murmur*] has some plot twists at the end but it's always tied to reality).

GCT: **As is reality itself, with at times absurd aspects that get inserted into reality… such as the absurdity of the dictatorship.**

DA: Yes, it is. There are absurd aspects of reality.... [He laughs and then pauses.] Anyway, I'm glad to have written all those things and different types of plays about all those subjects.

GCT: **I would like for you to explain what you think about this project, this book, grouping and studying your plays that deal with the subjects of dictatorship and migration.**

DA: I already have my fifty years as a writer. And, with this book of yours, it's the first time that researchers have paused to study my plays in a group. It's very important, because theater critics see the isolated plays, and directors too. You made me realize that I have a series of plays that are worthwhile to consider as a group. It's very important and worthy to group these plays and to include the analysis and opinions of different investigators from here and abroad. It's very important for me, the author, and as a Uruguayan playwright even more, because this is not something that is normally done.

GCT: **How has the reception of your work both in Uruguay and abroad evolved?**

DA: In my career, in Uruguay, I was generally lucky. I've had bad reviews, good reviews; I've won every possible prize there is, but I was always considered a minor author.

GCT: **What is the reason for that?**

DA: Because of the characteristics of my dramaturgy, because I deal with quotidian things, my work has been classified as localist. Now, lately, the critics' views have changed, but these views changed when my plays began to be valued abroad. *Pagar el pato*[7] opened in Buenos Aires in 2000 and later it was staged in Chicago. And it was then that the view of Uruguay's "intellectuals" started to change, that they started to appraise me in a different way. And from there a whole international career started. My plays began to be performed in New York, Madrid, Chicago, etc.

GCT: **The localism is rather in the language and the mention of places in Uruguay, right?**

DA: Yes, and that thing about being localist is very interesting. Even though I've

---

[7] TN: *Pagar el pato* is a Spanish idiom used when someone suffers the consequences of another person's actions, close in meaning to "taking the rap."

been criticized for it, the fact is that my plays are performed exactly as written in Buenos Aires, in Madrid, in Chicago, in Italy, in New York.

GCT: They reach people in different countries.

DA: Yes, they do. The thing is that they're universal plays in spite of the localism.

GCT: I see the localism in your plays in regard to the local color, the places, and the language, but not regarding the conflicts. The conflicts are universal.

DA: They're utterly universal conflicts, which could happen anywhere in the world. What matters is the interior conflict of these characters, what happens to them. The emotions, the feelings, love, hate are universal.

GCT: So, when you write, you don't write for a specific audience.

DA: Not anymore! I did before. When I started my career, I thought about what critics would like, for example. But afterwards, no! I forgot about the critics and everything and I began to write what I wanted to write. Because what is important is to be consistent with oneself, with one's dramaturgy and thoughts. It's important that there is consistency.

GCT: It's important to be authentic; otherwise, it's noticeable, isn't it?

DA: Yes, yes! It is. [Dino nods and they laugh.]

GCT: On the evolution of your dramaturgy, can you identify periods in your work?

DA: Yes, I think so. There are plays that can be grouped together, such as *Feliz día, papá, Extraños por la calle*,[8] *Sus ojos se cerraron*.[9] These are choral plays and were written one after the other, with a lot of characters, and with conflicts that crisscross. And, after my heart surgery in 1997, my writing changed and my style changed.

GCT: The heart surgery affected you a lot, didn't it?

DA: Yes, it did, because you acquire a notion of finiteness that you can die. Until that moment I was "immortal" and then I had a heart attack and my perspective

---

[8]   TN: "Strangers on the Street."
[9]   TN: "Their Eyes Shut Down."

changed. My first play after the heart attack was *Rifar el corazón*,[10] which is very unlike the previous ones.

GCT: In what way would you say that your writing changed after your surgery?

DA: I changed especially regarding the writing technique, trying to manage to write with fewer words but saying more. It was like a rebirth as a writer. Then there started to be different plays, different characters and conflicts. I think my best plays are in that post-surgery period, with plays like *Ave Mater* and *Lucas o El contrato*.[11] One grows with the plays. My plays followed my road as a person. The author always accompanied the man and the man the author.

GCT: Of all your plays, which was the hardest for you to write from an emotional point of view and which was the hardest to write from a technical point of view?

DA: *Rifar el corazón*, given the emotional circumstances, was the most difficult to write because I had the pressure of the surroundings. I had a block. Before the heart surgery, I was a smoker and I would smoke a lot while writing. So I was missing the cigarette while I worked. Besides, after the surgery, I was more concerned about living than about writing. I began to understand that writing plays wasn't the most important thing, that living was the most important. I also had the pressure of the social environment. After a year or two, people would ask me, "When are you going to write again?" "Why don't you write?" And that was worse. Then, at one point I resolved to overcome those circumstances and I made an outline and I started to write. The first page was horribly hard. That syndrome of the blank page… until one day I started making some scrawls and I finished the first act with a lot of effort. After that first act, I got going. That was the hardest play emotionally.

GCT: Technically, which was the hardest play?

DA: Technically, it probably was *Sus ojos se cerraron*, because it's set at a wake and next door there's a wedding. I had to make all the characters from the wedding get into the wake and stay there. It was a kind of sainete. So the hard part was to justify well that the wedding characters moved to the wake. And, aside from that, *Ave Mater* was also hard, because of the religion, the topic, and the structure, which followed Christ's stations. But in general I don't have a problem with

---

[10] TN: "Raffling the Heart."
[11] TN: "Lucas, or the Contract."

technique since plays come quite easily to me.

GCT: **Do you start with a character, a topic?**

DA: I start with an image, an image that later might reappear in the play or not appear, an image of something that surprises me on the street or at home or watching a movie.

GCT: **Afterwards, does that image start acquiring a life of its own?**

DA: Yes, it does, it starts acquiring a life of its own. And sometimes that image or that thing that happened to me doesn't appear in the play.

GCT: **Was the process of starting a play always like that?**

DA: Yes, it was always like that.

GCT: **What is your process of creating a play like and when do you feel that the play is finished?**

DA: I have somewhat of a routine. Generally, I write three drafts. In the first draft I write everything, on used sheets and using all the space. I still write by hand, in black pencil over white sheets. I write whatever comes out. Afterwards I move on to the second draft, where I start removing some things and leaving others. And the third draft is the definitive one, where the play is just like it's going to open. But it's always like that: first, writing whatever, gushing out, whatever comes, characters that talk and talk, getting it out; and afterwards comes the polishing.

GCT: **So first you free associate and then you start polishing. Have you directed your plays? Do you think that, when directing a play, the creative process continues in a way?**

DA: They're two different jobs. I've directed plays of mine, but only plays that have been premiered by others. I have never premiered a play of mine. But, in general, when I direct, I forget about the author and I cut a lot; I cut myself, too. Because they're two very different jobs: one thing is the written play and another is the play you're going to direct, the play you're going to stage. That's why, when people propose to direct plays of mine, I allow them to cut, to adapt, since, having directed, one knows there's a difference in the transfer from the paper to the stage.

GCT: **As author, is it difficult for you to separate yourself from your play and**

leave it in the hands of directors, authors, critics? What feelings get stirred up? Are the plays "intellectual children" and there comes a moment when they must be allowed to become independent?

DA: I don't have that problem. I'm like a bad father. [He laughs.] I let my plays leave, become independent. I even like to see them staged and to get surprised, sometimes for better and others for worse. But the important thing is that they get staged. When a director tells me about directing a play of mine, I trust they're going to do it well. If they request a play, it is because they want to do it well. And you learn something when you see the plays staged. And sometimes I get surprised when I listen to a line and I say, "But that was written by me?"

GCT: **It's like you rediscover your own plays…. Your plays generally have open endings: what is the function of the open endings in your plays?**

DA: Those open endings allow the spectator to complete them.

GCT: **You grant the spectator permission to participate in the creative process and to be able to create their version of the play's ending.**

DA: Yes, on one hand is that. And, on the other hand, it's also like saying there's always a tomorrow. I always think that in life the future is going to surprise you in one way or another. In our lives we have an open ending every day. We don't know what is going to happen tomorrow. The plays reflect that.

GCT: **What final comments do you have about the project of this book?**

DA: Well, the important thing is that all of you have taken these plays as a group to analyze, research, and study for a new market. It's important to have grouped them. I really had not felt I had so many plays about dictatorship and migration. Returning to what I said before, the importance of researchers studying these plays in a group and not in isolation. So, for the first time I am becoming aware that I have a private universe. That's what researchers are discovering.

GCT: **Discovering and making you rediscover your own world. Are you writing? What are your future plans?**

DA: Generally I write one play a year. And next, living. But the interesting thing is that I used to write more when I was working double shifts at two schools than now that I'm retired.

GCT: **What do you attribute that to?**

DA: Because writing was an outlet to escape from work. I remember that sometimes I would even sneak away during breaks in order to write. And I would also write after work. Now I wonder how I could have worked mornings, afternoons, and sometimes evenings, and written more than I do now that I have all the time in the world.

GCT: **It's said that the busier you are, the more you can achieve.** [They laugh.] **This has been a very interesting talk and I thank you very much for having received us at your home in order to do this interview.**

DA: I thank you and I look forward to the work and the book. Reading this book with so many different opinions is going to be like a premiere to me. It's wonderful! It's going to be very interesting for me and for all the readers.

GCT: **As always, a great pleasure and thank you so very much, dear friend Dino.**

DA: Yes, we have been friends for so many years. Thank you, Gabriela.[12]

---

[12] Interview translated by Álex Omar Bratkievich.

ABOUT THE CONTRIBUTORS

Dino Armas (Montevideo, Uruguay) was born in the neighborhood known as "Villa del Cerro,"[1] son of Matías Armas, *el Canario*[2]–boatman for the port, socialist, and atheist–and of Nicanda Lago, *la Gallega*[3]–housewife, believer, and reader of Corín Tellado's novels. He is the brother of Hilda Mercedes Armas, former director of the Escuela Especial para Discapacitados Visuales nº 198[4] and first male grandson of *Doña Mercedes*, famous healer in a unique neighborhood made up of workers and immigrants: Russians, Galicians, Italians, Armenians, and Lithuanians, among others.

El Cerro was also known as "Paralelo 48";[5] when there were strikes, the bridge over the Pantanoso stream would close and nobody could get into or out of the village. There, Cerrenses[6] had the meat plants to work, churches to get married, and a graveyard to be buried. In that neighborhood, Armas retired from teaching (as director at Escuela nº 271 Ana Frank[7]); in a perfect circle, the neighborhood that saw his birth also saw the end of his teaching career.

Likewise, his calling to the theater began in El Cerro when, as a teenager, he worked as prompter, stage designer, and actor for an amateur theater group directed by Francisco Gulli and Francisco Noble at the Rampla Juniors Fútbol

---

[1] Translator's Note: *El Cerro de Montevideo* (literally: "Montevideo's Hill") is a hill adjacent to the Bay of Montevideo. One of the neighborhoods located on it is called *Villa del Cerro* (literally: "the Hill's Village") or, simply, *el Cerro* ("the Hill").

[2] TN: Demonym used for people from the Canary Islands and, given the huge numbers of immigrants from the Canary Islands to Uruguay, also for people from the Uruguayan department of Canelones.

[3] TN: "the Galician woman."

[4] TN: "Special School for People with Visual Impairment No. 198."

[5] TN: "Parallel No. 48."

[6] TN: Demonym used for the people of the Cerro neighborhood.

[7] TN: "School No. 271 'Anne Frank'".

Club. Among the plays this pair of veteran sainete writers–students of the Podestá Brothers–would perform were *El conventillo de la Paloma*[8] and *El corralón de mis penas*[9] by Alberto Vacarezza,[10] and *Los mirasoles*[11] by Julio Sánchez Gardel.

In time, Armas created his own company, Grupo Teatral Cosmópolis, with a repertoire made up of sainetes, which supported national authors, staging plays by Florencio Sánchez, Ruben Deugenio, and our very own Armas. They also performed foreign texts, such as Patrick Hamilton's *Gas Light*. Grupo Teatral Cosmópolis had many members and performed alternately at the Nuestra Señora de Fátima Church and the Federación Autónoma de la Carne.[12]

The latter was fundamental to the personal and artistic formation of Armas thanks to its library, a library ahead of its time, where he could read Jean-Paul Sartre and Simone de Beauvoir, Albert Camus and Aldous Huxley, novels by Edgar Rice Burroughs and Emilio Salgari, and where he could alternate Federico García Lorca with Jean Anouilh, and Arthur Miller with Tennessee Williams. Cinema also contributed to his development as a playwright thanks to the continuous sessions offered daily at the Edén, Apolo, Cosmópolis, and Cerrense movie theaters.

The "downtown lights" attracted him when he took part in a contest organized by El Tinglado theater in 1965. And that young man from El Cerro, with his theater experience, the cultural baggage provided by the Federación's library, and his education from Liceo n° 11,[13] was nominated for first prize for his play *En otro y último verano*.[14] This play had a curious fate: under the title of *¿Conoce usted al Doctor Freud?*,[15] it was a finalist in the VII Concurso Tirso de Molina[16] (Spain) years later, and in 1981 it opened in Montevideo after winning the contest organized by the Sociedad Uruguaya de Actores[17] with the title of *Los soles amargos*.[18]

---

8   TN: "Paloma's Tenement."
9   TN: "The Yard of My Sorrows."
10   TN: Also spelled "Vaccarezza".
11   TN: "The Sunflowers."
12   TN: "Meat Autonomous Association."
13   TN: "High School No. 11."
14   TN: "On another and final summer."
15   TN: "Do you know Dr. Freud?"
16   TN: "7th Tirso de Molina Prize."
17   TN: "Uruguayan Actors Association."
18   TN: "The Bitter Suns."

In 1968, together with Carlos Aguilera and other enthusiastic young people, he founded Grupo 68, where he carried out roles as director, actor, and author, staging his own texts (such as *Viva Florencio*) and those of others (such as Bertolt Brecht's *Die Gewehre der Frau Carrar*,[19] Juan Carlos Patrón's *La novia de Gardel*,[20] Carlos Manuel Varela's *Happening* and *La enredadera*,[21] and Víctor Manuel Leites's *Crónicas de bien nacidos*[22]). Grupo 68 was a militant group which supported the mobilization of the sugar cane workers, as well as the newspaper *El Popular*, with concerts and performances at partisan establishments or in the street. Those concerts and performances were photographically documented by the government and caused Armas to be designated as a class C citizen according to the government's criterion of Democratic Commitment.[23]

In addition to his adult-themed plays, between 1966 and 1995 he wrote children's theater. Worth noting from that period are his adaptations as well as his original plays *La hormiguita viajera*,[24] *El Principito y la rosa*,[25] *Carlitos del mar*,[26] and *La murguita de la amistad*.[27] This interest in children's theater was linked to his teaching career, which began when he was still a student, at several rural schools in Canelones.

In his fifty-year career, Dino Armas has always been present in Uruguayan theaters as well as abroad, with more than sixty plays staged. The opening of *Pagar el pato*[28] at Buenos Aires's Actors Studio in 2003 introduced his career to an international audience. This play has opened, among other places, in Chicago, Washington, Miami, New York, Porto Alegre, São Paulo, Asunción, Santa Cruz de la Sierra, Córdoba, Mar del Plata, Tandil, Chivilcoy, Bragado, Ferrara, Bologna, and Madrid. Three of his plays—*Rifar el corazón*,[29] *¿Y si te canto canciones de amor?*,[30] and *Dos en la carretera*[31]—have toured in Spain. In November 2014, Armas was invited by the Asociación de Directores de Escena de España[32] (ADE),

---

19   TN: Known in English as "Señora Carrar's Rifles."
20   TN: "Gardel's Girlfriend."
21   TN: "The Vine."
22   TN: "Chronicles of Well-Bred People."
23   TN: Cfr. Chapter Six, "*Just Yesterday*: Life Histories Impacted by Dictatorship and Exile," p. #.
24   TN: "The Traveling Ant."
25   TN: "The Little Prince and the Rose."
26   TN: "Charlie from the Sea."
27   TN: "The Little Murga of Friendship."
28   TN: *Pagar el pato* is a Spanish idiom used when someone suffers the consequences of another person's actions, close in meaning to "taking the rap."
29   TN: "Raffling the Heart."
30   TN: "And If I Sing Love Songs to You?"
31   TN: "Two on the Road."
32   TN: "Spain Stage Directors Association."

along with the Centro Uruguayo de Madrid[33] (CUM), to the book presentation and dramatized reading of *Pagar el pato*. The same reading was repeated in Valencia with the support of Amnistía Internacional Valencia, which has shown *Pagar el pato* throughout the city's high schools.

He has received many awards, including the Candelabro de Oro[34] (awarded by the B'nai B'rith) and the Morosoli de Plata[35] (from Fundación Lolita Rubial) for his entire theater trajectory, and the Florencio Sánchez[36] prize (awarded by the Asociación de Críticos Teatrales del Uruguay)[37] for *Se ruega no enviar coronas*[38] and *Sus ojos se cerraron*,[39] in addition to countless nominations and special mentions. Several of his plays have been translated into English, Italian, and French. In March 2017 he presented his latest creation, *Julia, la pasionaria* [40] in Madrid, which premiered in Montevideo with the title of *Pasionarias* in August of the same year.

Gabriela Christie Toletti was born in Montevideo (Uruguay) as Gabriela Toletti Altieri. She is Liberal Arts chair and professor of Spanish at Tidewater Community College (Norfolk, Virginia, U.S.). She is also adjunct professor of literature and world cultural studies at Old Dominion University (Norfolk, Virginia, U.S.). Previously she taught Spanish and literature at Wingate University (Charlotte, North Carolina, U.S.), and English at the Alianza Cultural Uruguay-Estados Unidos[41] (Montevideo, Uruguay). She has specialized in the areas of Latin American literature, Hispanic theater, world cultural studies, psychology, pedagogy, academic program development, and Spanish and English teaching and translation. She graduated as Teacher of English as a Second Language from the Alianza Cultural Uruguay-Estados Unidos, as clinical psychologist from the University of the Republic (Montevideo, Uruguay), and with an MA and PhD in Latin American Literature from the State University of New York at Buffalo (Buffalo, New York, U.S.). She has been a speaker at literature conferences and has been interviewed for TV and radio on issues of Hispanic heritage. She

---

[33] TN: "Uruguayan Center in Madrid."
[34] TN: "Golden Candelabra."
[35] TN: "Silver Morosoli." Juan José Morosoli (1899-1959) was a Uruguayan writer.
[36] TN: Florencio Sánchez (1875-1910) was a Uruguayan playwright.
[37] TN: "Uruguayan Association of Theater Critics."
[38] TN: "Please Do Not Send Wreaths."
[39] TN: "Their Eyes Shut Down."
[40] TN: "La Pasionaria" was the pseudonym used by Dolores Ibárruri, a famous Spanish Republican heroine and Communist politician. Her first article was published on Passion Week 1918, hence, her chosen pseudonym.
[41] TN: "Cultural Alliance Uruguay-United States."

has written articles, has translated plays, and has been granted scholarships to carry out literary research. She has also dabbled in drawing. Her articles mainly address issues of migration, oppression, dictatorship, cultural identity, and group dynamics. "El reencuentro de una familia del Río de la Plata"[42] was included in a book on experiences of migration entitled *Transatlantische Auswanderergeschichten: Reflexionen und Reminiszenzen aus drei Generationen. Festschrift zu Ehren von Robert Schopflocher.*[43] She resides in Norfolk (Virginia, U.S.) with her husband Charles "Chuck" Cody Christie, Jr. and their pets.

Marcelo de León Montañés, native of Maldonado (Uruguay), is a historian and lawyer who graduated from University of the Republic (Montevideo, Uruguay). There, he studied history and began his teaching and research career. In the U.S., where he currently resides, he has worked as a history researcher, Spanish teacher, translator, and editor. He has extensive experience in research projects, both institutional (Schools of Law, Engineering, and Humanities and Education Science at University of the Republic, and Centro Latinoamericano de Economía Humana[44]–CLAEH, Montevideo, Uruguay) and independent. Related to migration, acculturation, or military dictatorships, noteworthy projects include: his participation in "Archivo de la Memoria Popular en el Uruguay"[45] (CLAEH); his presentation "El problema indígena";[46] the historical research for the novels *The Invisible Mountain, Perla*, and *The Gods of Tango*, by Carolina de Robertis; his article "El Castillo del Dr. Perujo"[47] and his book *El temerario y deslenguado Dr. Perujo.*[48] He has been a speaker on local history and oral history issues. He has also authored *Mentalidades y estratos sociales en las máximas de La Rochefoucauld,*[49] *La reflexión histórica en María A. Díaz de Guerra,*[50] and numerous history articles.

Aida Heredia (Santo Domingo, D.N., Dominican Republic) is a professor of Latin American literature, Caribbean literature, and Spanish at the Hispanic

---

42 TN: "The Reunion of a Family from the La Plata River."
43 TN: "*Transatlantic Stories of Emigration: Reflections and Reminiscences from three Generations. A Festschrift in Honor of Robert Schopflocher.*" This book compiled by Dr. Frederick Lubich and published by Königshausen & Neumann in 2014 is a commemorative compilation in honor of the Jewish-German and Argentine author Robert Schopflocher (1923-2016) who fled Nazi Germany in 1937 and started a new life in Argentina. The book includes essays in German, English, and Spanish.
44 TN: "Latin American Center for Human Economy."
45 TN: "Archive of Popular Memory in Uruguay."
46 TN: "The Indigenous Problem."
47 TN: "Dr. Perujo's Castle."
48 TN: "The Bold and Blunt Dr. Perujo."
49 TN: "Mentalities and Social Strata in La Rochefoucauld's Maximes."
50 TN: "Historical Reflection in María A. Díaz de Guerra."

Studies department of Connecticut College (New London, Connecticut, U.S.). Previously she was a professor of literature and Spanish at Howard University (Washington, D.C., U.S.). She received a PhD in Hispanic Literature and Caribbean Studies at State University of New York at Buffalo (Buffalo, New York, U.S.). Her research interests include the African diaspora to the Americas and the critical theory of the humanities. She has been a speaker at Hispanic literature conferences; she has written book chapters and has published, in academic journals, articles on national identity, memory, and religion as countercolonial practice. She has authored the books *De la recta a las cajas chinas: La poesía de José Kozer*[51] and *La representación del haitiano en las letras dominicanas.*[52] She has also received continuing education scholarships, including the program Fulbright-Hays Seminar Abroad: "Argentina and Uruguay 2006."

Álvaro Loureiro (Montevideo, Uruguay) is an actor, theater director, translator, script adapter, and English teacher. He was a teacher of film history at Escuela de Cine de Cinemateca Uruguaya[53] (Montevideo, Uruguay) and of musical comedy history at Escuela de Comedia Musical[54] (Montevideo, Uruguay). As a film and theater critic, he worked for–among others–the newspapers Últimas *Noticias* and *El País* (Montevideo, Uruguay), and currently writes for the weekly publication *Brecha* (Montevideo, Uruguay). Radio stations such as CX8, CX4, and CX26 have featured him as entertainment critic. He has been a speaker at theater festivals (e.g. in Caracas, Venezuela) and film festivals (e.g. Porto Alegre, Brazil). In 1988 he founded Compañía Teatral Aventura, where he leads the Theater Workshop and has directed more than fifty plays. In 2013 he was awarded the Victoria prize for his cultural contributions to the season. He was also awarded the Florencio prize as director for *Spencer P: Una historia de superhéroes*[55] in 2008 and *Piratas y el tesoro de la sirenita*[56] in 2009 (both plays also won Best Children's Production), and in 2011 he was nominated for *Dinosaurios: La extinción*[57] (the play was also nominated for Best Production). *Aventura extraterrestre,*[58] co-directed with Fabián Silva, was nominated to the Florencio as Best Children's Production in 2010. In 2012, *Los fantasmas de Scrooge*[59] was

---

[51] TN: "From the Straight Line to Chinese Boxes: The Poetry of José Kozer."
[52] TN: "The Depiction of Haitians in Dominican Literature."
[53] TN: "Film School at the Uruguayan Cinematheque."
[54] TN: "School of Musical Comedy."
[55] TN: "Spencer P: A superhero story."
[56] TN: "Pirates and the Little Mermaid's Treasure."
[57] TN: "Dinosaurs: The Extinction."
[58] TN: "Extra-Terrestrial Adventure."
[59] TN: "Scrooge's Ghosts."

nominated to the Children's Florencio in several categories, including Loureiro's direction.

Lourdes Martínez Puig (Colonia, Uruguay) is a teacher of literature and literature didactics at Centros Regionales de Profesores del Consejo de Formación en Educación[60] in Colonia and Maldonado (Uruguay). She has worked as director and literature teacher at Consejo de Educación Secundaria[61] (Montevideo, Uruguay). She graduated from Instituto de Profesores Artigas[62] (Montevideo, Uruguay), received an MA in Writing and Literacy from National University of La Plata (La Plata, Buenos Aires, Argentina), and completed postgraduate studies (Curriculum and Teaching Practices in Context; Social Sciences with a Mention in Constructivism and Education; Specialization in Reading, Writing, and Education) at the Latin American Social Sciences Institute (Montevideo, Uruguay). She has been a speaker at conferences in Cuba, Mexico, Argentina, and Uruguay. Her research on Dino Armas' dramaturgy include: the presentations "Investigación para la enseñanza de la literatura: *Los raros* de Dino Armas,"[63] "La enseñanza del género ensayo en la clase de Literatura: Un aporte desde el interaccionismo sociodiscursivo,"[64] "El abuso de poder y la reivindicación social en la obra *Pagar el pato* de Dino Armas: ¿Una historia de amor?";[65] the prologue "La voz de los marginales en Dino Armas"[66] (for the publication of *Pagar el pato*); her article "Temas y personajes femeninos protagonistas en las obras dramáticas de Dino Armas: Estudio comparativo entre *Queridos cuervos, Sus ojos se cerraron, Rifar el corazón y Pagar el pato*";[67] and the book *Temas y personajes principales en las obras* Rifar el corazón *y* Los raros *de Dino Armas.*[68]

María del Carmen Montañés Tejera (Maldonado, Uruguay) is a literature teacher and an amateur theater director, with more than sixty years of teaching experience. From the very beginning of her teaching career, she promoted an interest in theater and the performing arts as a vocation among her students. Together with fellow teacher Mirella Izquierdo, in 1982 she founded

---

[60] TN: "Regional Teacher Centers of the Board of Education Formation."
[61] TN: "Board of Secondary Education."
[62] TN: "Artigas Institute of High School Teachers."
[63] TN: "Research into Literature Teaching: Dino Armas' *Los raros* (literally: 'The Weird Ones')."
[64] TN: "Teaching Essays in Literature Classes: A Socio-Discursive Interactionism Approach."
[65] TN: "Abuse of Power and Social Vindication in Dino Armas' *Pagar el pato*: A Love Story?"
[66] TN: "The Voice of Marginalized Groups in Dino Armas."
[67] TN: "Themes and Female Protagonists in Dino Armas' Plays: A Comparative Study of *Queridos cuervos* (literally: 'Dear Ravens'), *Sus ojos se cerraron, Rifar el corazón,* and *Pagar el pato.*"
[68] TN: "Themes and Main Characters in Dino Armas' Plays *Rifar el corazón* and *Los raros.*"

and directed the students' theater group at Liceo Departamental de Maldonado[69] (Maldonado, Uruguay), which relied upon the directing guidelines provided by Gustavo A. Ruegger and the participation of Dino Armas, who wrote *Te quiero, che...*[70] especially for them. In 1984, she founded the students' group at Liceo Álvaro Figueredo[71] in Pan de Azúcar (Uruguay). In collaboration with her colleague, she has promoted the performing arts by organizing student tours to theater performances in Montevideo, participating in theater conferences, and staging volunteer performances at several inland Uruguayan localities (San Carlos, Solís de Mataojo, Minas, and Gregorio Aznárez, among others). Currently she is an honorary co-director of the theater group at the Universidad Abierta de Educación No Formal de Adultos[72] (UNI 3) in Maldonado (Uruguay). She has authored the article "Elodia Montañés Honoré, docente y poeta"[73] as well as several sainetes, including *Lisístrata en el Siglo XXI*,[74] *El encuentro de dos grandes en el Más Allá*,[75] and *Hay que casar a la Eulalia*.[76]

Susana **Mosciaro** (Lanús, Buenos Aires, Argentina) is an actress with an extensive artistic career. She has performed important roles in plays by Dino Armas and other playwrights. Her studies include acting courses with Lorenzo Quinteros, Walter Rosenzwit, Sergio Amigo, Dora Baret, and Matías Gandolfo; directing with José María Muscari; music in the theater with Jean-Jacques Lemêtre (from Théâtre du Soleil); and theater festival management and production. She has acted in plays by Dino Armas (*Sus ojos se cerraron* [Argentinean version], *Esos locos locos amores*,[77] and *Present, Señorita* [Argentinean adaptation]), as well as many others: *15-Minute Hamlet* by Tom Stoppard, *Queda poco que contar*[78] (based on four brief pieces by Samuel Beckett), *La Cantatrice Chauve*[79] by Eugène Ionesco, and *La muerte es una costumbre*[80] by Darío López. She directed *Historia del joven que se casó con mujer brava*[81] by Alejandro Casona (original title:

---

69   TN: "Departmental High School of Maldonado."
70   TN: "I Love You, Pal..."
71   TN: "Álvaro Figueredo High School."
72   TN: "Open University for the Informal Education of Adults."
73   TN: "Elodia Montañés Honoré, Teacher and Poet."
74   TN: "Lysistrata in the 21st Century."
75   TN: "The Meeting of Two Giants in the Great Beyond."
76   TN: "We Must Marry Eulalia."
77   TN: "Those Crazy Crazy Love Stories."
78   TN: "There's Little Left to Tell."
79   TN: Known in English as "The Bald Soprano" or "The Bald Prima Donna."
80   TN: "Death Is a Habit."
81   TN: "Story of the Young Man Who Married a Ferocious Woman."

Entremés del mancebo que casó con mujer brava),[82] *Cuando la suerte no es tal*[83] by Darío López (monologue), and *The Bear* by Anton Chekhov. She directed and staged ¿*Y si te canto canciones de amor?* by Dino Armas and *Separarse de uno mismo*[84] by Fernando Salvucci. She adapted, produced, directed, and starred in the one-woman tribute show to Niní Marshall *Anoche soñé con ella.*[85]

Dolores Rangel, native of Monterrey (Nuevo León, Mexico), is a professor of Spanish and Hispanic literature at Georgia Southern University (Statesboro, Georgia, U.S.). Previously she taught literature at the University of Texas at Brownsville (Brownsville, Texas, U.S.), at Queen's University (Kingston, Ontario, Canadá), and the Monterrey Institute of Technology (Monterrey, Nuevo León, Mexico). She received a BA in Spanish Literature from the Monterrey Institute of Technology, an MA in Spanish from New Mexico State University (Las Cruces, New Mexico, U.S.), and a PhD in Latin American Literature from the State University of New York at Buffalo (Buffalo, New York, U.S.). Her main research interest is contemporary Latin American literature. She has been a speaker at academic conferences, has written articles for literary journals, and has contributed to books with the chapters "Metafísica y estética en los ensayos de Borges"[86] and "Creación y locura en la visión apocalíptica de Dulcinea encantada."[87] She has also authored the book *Artemio de Valle-Arizpe y la visión del México colonial.*[88] Her publications deal mainly with issues of identity, exile, memory, and patriarchy.[89]

---

[82] TN: "Entremés of the Youngster Who Married a Ferocious Woman."
[83] TN: "When Luck Is No Longer Such."
[84] TN: "Separating From Oneself."
[85] TN: "Last Night I Dreamt About Her."
[86] TN: "Metaphysics and Aesthetics in Borges' Essays."
[87] TN: "Creation and Madness in the Apocalyptic Vision of Enchanted Dulcinea."
[88] TN: "Artemio de Valle Arizpe and the Vision of Colonial Mexico."
[89] Information about the contributors translated by Álex Omar Bratkievich.

Made in the USA
Middletown, DE
05 October 2021